"Karen Speerstra takes us on a journey of the mi
psychology, myth, archeology and architecture; th~~rough the~~ ~~~~~~ ~~~~
of time and culture. She finds Sophia wherever she turns, in us, in life, in
death, in the past, and in our hopes for the future. Hers is a tapestry of words
that would have made weavers of the ages proud."

> — Craig S. Barnes, author, *In Search of the Lost Feminine: Decoding the Myths
> That Radically Reshaped Civilization*

"May this book be wrapped in white light and fly through inner and outer
space into the hearts of all who are open. Allah knows, it is time for something
new on planet earth, which will not be born of an old way of thinking."

> — Barbara Cecil-Coffman, leader of international women's leadership
> programs (www.ciyowomensretreat.com)

"Karen Speerstra's Sophia is not an abstract idea or a metaphor. She is a living
spirit who, in the words of C. S. Lewis, 'invades' our earthly domain — in
the very best sense of that word. Weaving stories of her own experience with
historical threads reaching far and wide, Ms. Speerstra shows us how to access
this profoundly wise feminine spirit; or more accurately, she teaches us how to
open our hearts to Sophia's wondrous potential influence on our lives."

> — Carol Frenier, author, *Business and the Feminine Principle*

"Every day, I work with decent and powerful women and men who aspire to
bring good things into the world. They also long to be true to themselves.
There's no shortage of theories, methods and tools, yet so little wisdom. In
Sophia, Karen Speerstra reminds us that we are not alone. Like an experienced
travel guide, she elegantly describes ancient and reliable paths to reconnect
with the wisdom that's already inside each of us, and waiting for us at every
turn. The key, however, is to "stay awake." Reading this book woke me from
my own trance. As a result, I found myself much clearer about what really
matters, breathing more deeply, and centered in the wisdom that flows through
my heart. Read *Sophia*, and as Karen says, 'snuggle up, settle down and smile.'"

> — Mitch Saunders, founder & director, The CEO Studio

"*Wow!* Makes me want to hang up my other work and just read this all the day! Karen Speerstra's book is nothing less than an uncovering of the face of God. Intricate and at times poignant, *Sophia* turns complex and sophisticated theologies into tracings of experiences across cultures, faiths, and time. You will come away from this reading satisfied and also curious, with a new understanding of 'minding your Mother' and a desire to know and experience much more of *this* God."

— Susan Ohlidal, Canon for Ministry Development, The Episcopal Church in Vermont

"In mythology, folklore, and varied spiritual traditions, Sophia has been the one to lead us to wisdom. Called by different names and appearing in different dress, she beckons us to follow her and recognize ourselves in her reflection. Karen Speerstra's *Sophia* is a loving embrace of her essence, an invitation to make known the invisible, receptive, vital, and passionate energies that lie within each of us. Karen follows the golden thread and brings Sophia more clearly and urgently back into our collective Sophia-consciousness — timeless, and urgently needed in today's world. I highly recommend this book."

— Alan Briskin, Ph.D., co-author, *The Power of Collective Wisdom, Daily Miracles*; author, *The Stirring of Soul in the Workplace*

"Beginning with her introductory voice, the author offers a veritable cornucopia of insights into, and images of, the Eternal Feminine Wisdom-figure Sophia (of Proverbs fame) in a 9-fold 'nonagram' chapter arrangement. Speerstra has called up an amazing spectrum of relevant scientific and historical concepts that range from the Pythagorean triangle, Grimm's fairy tales, Harry Potter's adventures, to Greek/Babylonian mythology. Who knew to link Whale-songs and Cosmic Hen-nests in her chapter on creation? Her self-confrontation with her cancer diagnosis in Chapter 5 is astounding. I can see this used in book clubs as well as in spiritual direction sessions."

— Joanna B. Gillespie, historian, Women's Studies

"A big-hearted book, luminous in spirit and generous with its wisdom, like Sophia herself. Open it whenever your soul says 'Feed me.'"

— Sara Tucker, author, *Our House in Arusha*

"Speerstra's examples of the Sophia spirit in our world, and indeed across the ages from early human history, range from engaging tales from her own experience to profound stories that embody the strength of the feminine spirit borne in our hearts, in our relationships, and in our world. Her dialogue with us, the readers, is vibrant, alive, and illuminating as we seek our own way to Sophia wisdom. It's an elegant, wise and wonderful book."

— Julia Blackbourn, artist

"A delicious book! Karen Speerstra has brought Sophia to life. Sophia, breath, Shekinah, Spirit, poetry, beauty, wisdom, love, intuition, sensuality, creativity, female knowing and strength burst forth through Karen's elegant writing and knowledge. I felt as though I was in the presence of the Divine Feminine while reading this thoroughly researched and inspiring book."

— Cheryl Anne Gilman, author, *Doing Work You Love: Discovering Your Purpose, Realizing Your Dreams*

"Karen Speerstra shows us most compellingly that when we open our hearts, we can discover the wisdom of the Feminine to be all around us. Alas, the way we have been in the world has often confronted us with overwhelming problems and life can become an endless struggle. Karen reveals that the simplicity of Sophia's understanding presence is the antidote to all this, leading to the deepest sense of hope and healing. A totally refreshing exploration, and beautifully researched read."

— Michael Cecil, author, *Living at the Heart of Creation*

"I first learned of Sophia when I immersed myself in experiencing Judy Chicago's *The Dinner Party*, one artist's testimonial to the feminine. Speerstra's book, *Sophia*, certainly expands and enhances an exploration of wisdom and how it appears in our daily life and in the universe. Karen has once again written a book that takes her extensive and eclectic knowledge and reorganizes it around a central concept: this time, Sophia. But this book isn't just about knowledge, it's about reflecting and connecting that knowledge with the heart. And isn't that where it all begins ... and ends?"

— Genevieve Brandt Kirchman, trainer & mentor, Tribes Learning Communities

"*Sophia: The Feminine Face of God* reminds readers of the unconditional love and healing awaiting us. After being diagnosed with MS, I was comforted by this book and the knowledge that Sophia is with us always, waiting for us to integrate her into our lives and accept her gifts. By finding Sophia within ourselves, we are co-creators who have the opportunity to share her healing, love and abundance with ourselves and the world. A wonderful read. A wonderful message."

> — Ann Garrity, founder, www.organicdivas.com (online health website for women)

"Wrap yourself in Karen's magical Sophia-cloak and travel through space and time to the many hidden faces of the Divine Feminine. With her genius for treasure hunting, Karen has gathered jewels from every tradition and woven them together with rainbow threads from her own Sophia-inspired meditations. The result is not only a dazzling work of intellectual creativity, but a direct initiation into the cosmic Oneness underlying all divisions. Here is a spirituality that can reconnect us with the Wisdom needed to heal our wounded planet."

> — Sharon Bauer, psychotherapist & women's spirituality teacher

SOPHIA

The Feminine Face of God

Nine Heart Paths to Healing and Abundance

KAREN SPEERSTRA

Published by Michael Wiese Productions
3940 Laurel Canyon Blvd., # 1111
Studio City, CA 91604
tel. 818.379.8799
fax 818.986.3408
mw@mwp.com
www.mwp.com

Cover Design: Johnny Ink. www.johnnyink.com
Cover Painting: Pablo Amaringo (Courtesy of Cassidy Pope)
Interior Design: Gina Mansfield Design
Copy Editor: Marsha D. Phillips

Printed by McNaughton & Gunn, Inc., Saline, Michigan
Manufactured in the United States of America
Printed on Recycled Stock

Library of Congress Cataloging-in-Publication Data

Speerstra, Karen.
 Sophia : the feminine face of god : nine heart paths to healing and abun-
dance / Karen Speerstra.
     p. cm.
 Includes index.
 ISBN 978-1-61125-004-6
1. God (Christianity)--Wisdom. 2. Wisdom (Biblical personification) 3.
Femininity of God. 4. Feminist theology. 5. Spiritual healing. I. Title.
BT150.S64 2011
231'.6--dc23

                                        2011017593

Mixed Sources
Product group from well-managed
forests and other controlled sources
www.fsc.org Cert no. SW-COC-002283
© 1996 Forest Stewardship Council
FSC

To all my Sophia-friends

ACKNOWLEDGEMENTS

When someone you love as much as I love Sophia finds a home with a line of books called "Divine Arts" you just know it's right. Thank you, Michael, for believing in her — and me — enough to make it happen.

Early on, you said, *"I think the secret lies in conveying 'an experience of Sophia' in the reader that excites, calms and illuminates. The book is NOT ABOUT information about Sophia. Sure it covers that, but the book IS ABOUT us all having a direct experience of her. Your mission is to write so that that happens in the reader's heart. You do that and everything else will take care of itself!"* May it be so.

And thanks also to Geraldine, Manny, and Ken, who make Divine Arts and Michael Wiese Productions what it is. "Sophia" and I also appreciate the careful attention Gina and Marsha paid to "our book." I am deeply indebted to Pablo Amaringo, whose mystical painting brings "Mother" and the cover of this book alive.

Thank you, Joel, for rendering the beautiful crop circles that grace the openings of each of the nine chapters. Your artist talents are only surpassed by your fine editorial eye, keen ear and large heart.

Thank you, John, for your ongoing support — proofing and otherwise. Your Sophia love has kept me. Thank you Nathan, Traci and Josie for being my inspiration and my joy.

And a deep bow of gratitude goes to the numerous "Mystical Dancers" and other authors and mentors who have added to my understanding of who Sophia is and why this is the time for all of us to re-acknowledge her.

And finally, a very large thank you to the many Sophia-friends who appear throughout these pages. I write for you. I write because of you.

Hagia Sophia

There is in all visible things an invisible fecundity, a dimmed light, a meek namelessness, a hidden wholeness. This mysterious Unity and Integrity is Wisdom, the Mother of All, *Natura Naturans*. There is in all things an inexhaustible sweetness and purity, a silence that is a fount of action and joy. It rises up in wordless gentleness and flows out to me from the unseen roots of all created being, welcoming me tenderly, saluting me with indescribable humility. This is at once my own being, my own nature, and the Gift of my Creator's Thought and Art within me, speaking as Hagia Sophia, speaking as my sister, Wisdom. I am awakened, I am born again at the voice of this my Sister, sent to me from the depths of the divine fecundity.

~ Thomas Merton, *Emblems of a Season of Fury, p. 61*

CONTENTS

Illustration Credits for *Sophia — The Feminine Face of God*

Watercolor illustrations of Chapter Opener Crop Circles,
created by Joel Speerstra

Sophia Icon, author's, written by Katriina Fyrlund of Varberg, Sweden

Elise Boulding photo, courtesy Russell Boulding

"The Baptism of Christ" Piero della Francesca (c. 1420-1492),
used by permission, National Gallery, London/Art Resources,
NY Image Reference: ART374312

"Umilinya Mother of God,"
courtesy of the Museum of Russian Icons, Clinton, MA.

Yellow Moon's family tree by George Armstrong from *The Earthshapers*

All others public domain or by author

Introduction

. . . .

"The Divine Feminine (Sophia/Mother God) is returning to collective consciousness, all right. She's coming and it will happen whether we're ready or not."

~ Sue Monk Kidd, *The Dance of the Dissident Daughter*

Who IS this "Sophia/Mother-God," really?

Journal tracks led me back to the very week I met Sophia. It was October of 1989 — the same week I met Michael Wiese, founder of Divine Arts. Michael and I were attending a Las Vegas film convention. We were both publishing film books, so we decided to meet for dinner at Bally's to explore how we might partner to create something new. "I know we will," I later recorded in my journal on the plane heading back east. "It may not be what we met to discuss, but it will be something. And it will be fun!"

Little did I know.

Michael was making a dolphin film at the time and regaled me with his plans to suction a camera onto the cheek of a sperm whale in order to film a squid. This was so out of my normal realm that I sat there, fork in hand, speechless. My awestruck state continued as I waited in airports, reading the new book I'd popped into my briefcase before leaving Boston: *Wisdom's Feast: Sophia in Study and Celebration* by Susan Cady, Marian Ronan and Hal Taussig. I'd already read several "goddess" books, but nothing about Sophia. Who is/was she, really? The book began this way: "She is strong and proud. She is creator and designer of all things. She promises to teach us about herself and earth."

Sounded good to me, so I suctioned a metaphorical camera onto my cheek and swam around for over two decades attempting to learn more about who this divine feminine being might be and what she had to show me. I waded over Gnostic shoals, snorkeled over Rudolf Steiner reefs and delved into the outer banks shored up by feminist theologians. I floated past Russian Sophiologists; paddled around Jungian psychologists and Hebrew scholars. With my friend Sharon, steeped in women's rituals, I crawled ashore and drummed up the moon.

Finally, barnacled by more questions than answers, I knew I had to write about her.

She wouldn't leave me alone.

I was raised a Midwest Lutheran. Martin Luther even threw out Mary, so how was my little mental model supposed to integrate a female face on God HIMSELF? And how would I come to grips with what I'd been taught about "original sin"? Has Martin's dark view of human depravity shielded me all this time from her radiance? And how does Sophia relate to Christ? To Mary? To all the other divine feminine figures I had begun to know? And there are many. In *The Goddess Guide*, Brandi Auset lists over 400 names people have called Sophia over the ages and across cultures, which she claims is by no means a complete list. From *Abundantia*, the Roman goddess of prosperity, to *Zywie*, the Polish goddess of healing, this Divine Woman shows up in our lives in many ways — sometimes even clandestinely.

I attended a Gimbutas lecture and began learning the pictorial "script" she called *The Goddess Language*. It goes back thousands of years and is filled with birds and bones and life-giving bounty; meander lines and breasted mothers, spirals and horns, deer and bears and lions.

I had to figure out how to find Sophia. Or make the space for her to find me. One day I came to realize she's been here all along. Through all my questions she continues to hold my hand. She nudges. Cajoles. Entices. Winks. Learning more about her seemed of utmost importance. Why? Because, as the *Wisdom's Feast* authors point out, all of us are impoverished. Our culture and its male preferences for logic and abstraction over feeling and experience, for head over heart, has to be transformed or we're doomed.

When I left the corporate book publishing scene and moved to Vermont, I decided to name my little one-woman company, Sophia-Serve, hoping some of her wisdom might rub off on me. My masthead is a daily reminder that Sophia is front and center in my life. Most people look at the name and think it's some fancy internet server — and in a way, I suppose it is, for Sophia definitely serves!

Sophia is not a name many people, other than biblical scholars, recognize, and that's O.K. They sense her presence even if they don't know what to call her. She's the Divine Feminine who has been a part of our world from its very beginning. She's bigger and more inclusive than any of the names people have called her over time.

We might recognize Sophia as The Great Mother, the Provider, an archetype or great field of fertile energy. Gaia Earth. Our Matrix. Early people called her *Cybele*. Some Jews still call her *Shekinah*; pre-Islamic Arabians called her *Al-Lat*. Latte-milk. Abraham's mother and his wives baked her moon-cakes and climbed up mountains to visit her sacred groves.

I'm comfortable calling her *Sophia*. For some time I have substituted "she" for "he" in my liturgical practices and I feel I'm in good company since Sophia is firmly rooted in Gnostic, Hebrew, and Christian traditions. You might think I'm just retro-fitting my theology when I also call the Holy Spirit *Sophia*. According to the Biblical Book of Wisdom, "She spans the world in power from end to end, and gently orders all things." I view her as my mother, sister, mentor and friend. "Her radiance never sleeps."

Wisdom's Feast showed me how she's not just God's original playmate. She's not a weak-kneed namby-pamby, and certainly not a painted up "virgin" or some gorgeous statue. She can be proud, assertive, threatening and even angry at times (though not as angry as her male counterpart) if the biblical book of Proverbs can be believed: "You ignorant people, how much longer will you cling to your ignorance? ... Pay attention to my warning.... Listen, I have some serious things to tell you and from my lips come honest words.... Accept my discipline rather than silver, knowledge in preference to gold. For wisdom is more precious than pearls, and nothing else is so worthy of desire." Strong words.

Sophia has reason to be more than a little miffed. For the last several centuries, Sophia has been repressed, banished, outlawed, and forbidden. Her name has been scrubbed off scriptural parchments and deleted from computer screens. Her sacred groves have been cut down and burned. Her priestesses eliminated. In the wake of her departure, "Father-figure-gods" began to dominate all the major religions around the world. As a result, the hierarchies of pyramids (man at the top followed by women, children, animals, plants, minerals) prop up the framework of our churches, families, workplaces, government, military, and education. Our Mother seemed to have left us orphaned — but of course she didn't completely disappear. She stuck around in oral traditions. She stayed in folk songs and stories. Even though her dove-wings were clipped, she flew below the radar.

The early Egyptians knew Osiris, the male energy, the "All-Man" needed to be balanced by Isis, female energy, "All-Woman." They lived their polarities. When one gender becomes all-important, all-dominating, everything gets unhinged. Tipped. Off-kilter. When things become unbalanced, we all suffer and so does our soil, our waters, our air. Our planet. Our universe.

Many first peoples speak reverently of Mother and Grandmother. The Ecuadorian Indians call her Pachamama. To Western Indians, she's Buffalo Woman. Changing Woman. Or Grandmother Spider. Isis. Shakti. Kuan Yin. Mary. Call her anything you like, the Jungian author Marion Woodman says, but call her!

"God" and "Goddess" are rather puny words when you come right down to it. Overused. Misunderstood. Maligned. Off-putting. And just because old concepts of who gods and goddesses are, and what is and what is not idolatry, still exist, it doesn't mean they're always wise or even relevant to our time. Nor do we need to continue to bounce along in old "man-centered" rutted tire-tracks.

Teilhard de Chardin, a French Jesuit, paleontologist, biologist, and philosopher, described Sophia this way:

I am the beauty running through the world ... I am the essential Feminine. In the beginning I was no more than a mist, rising and falling ... I was the bond that held together the foundations of the universe ... I am the single radiance by which all is aroused and within which it is vibrant ... I open the door to the whole heart of creation ... Lying between God and the earth, as a zone of mutual attraction, I draw them both together in a passionate union ... I am the Eternal Feminine.

> ~ Pierre Teilhard de Chardin, *Writings in the Time of War*, "Hymn to the Eternal Feminine."

Who is Sophia?

She is *The Eternal, Essential Feminine.*

The key word here is "essential." We've overlooked her through numerous world and regional wars; we've hidden her away as our planet deteriorates and 200,000 people become homeless every day across our globe because of ecological disasters we've orchestrated — mainly through our greed. Our children don't have adequate food. Our women continue to be raped and murdered. What's wrong with this picture?

Our future depends on our "finding" her again. For that matter, so does our present. Alice O. Howell, the Jungian author, says Sophia is everywhere, and "Everywhere is here. Everywhen is now."

She Hides in Plain Sight

Sophia can be found in, but not confined to, the Bible and myths. With rare exceptions the church doesn't talk about her. So we look for other places to "read" her. She's in nature, sacred geometry, folk dances, symbols, fairy tales, and within our own bodies. This book is my humble attempt to show her in her various hiding places. When I contemplated writing about her, I thought, "Karen, how *can* you? You're not a "Sophiologist!" (Yes, that's what scholars of

Sophia call themselves.) But then, in the next breath, I thought: "How can I *not?*"

When I turned sixty, my family gave me the gift of materials with which to construct a huge Chartres-style labyrinth in our south meadow, including two tons of marble which my husband lovingly cut into small enough chunks so I could line all the paths. I planted thyme all around the perimeter — to remind myself I have plenty of "time." I liken our religious wanderings to walking a labyrinth. We carefully follow paths someone else has laid down, and when we reach the center — the inner core of our being — we may receive insights we didn't have before — insights even the path-makers may not have known. But the labyrinth-walker knows what she's experiencing. And it's real! She knows that after she's reached the center, only half the journey is complete. It's not enough to begin to know who Sophia is. Now we have the opportunity to integrate her into our lives. We accept her gifts. We share them with the world. The labyrinth walker retraces her steps, carrying out to the world what she's learned, then applies it.

Sophia's always been there, at the center, but she's becoming more evident now. She appears in the foreground where we spend all our waking hours. She offers her wisdom to our everyday world.

This book's three parts mirror a labyrinth path by going into the heart center, through relationships, and back out into the world. It's my feeble attempt to make her a bit more visible. Together, we'll crack her codes embedded in our hearts, our families and communities and in the wider world.

To begin to understand the magnitude of her matrix, the nine chapters in this book echo nine ways of "being" with Sophia, and therefore, with everyone and everything else. They are the nine aspects of Sophia's large heart, so to speak. Those of us who follow Paul's writings know that in his letter to the Galatians he mentioned her nine gifts — these gifts illuminate our nine chapters.

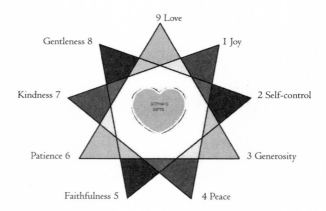

Nine Ways of *Bee-ing*

Nine means completion. It stands for wholeness. It's a strong number made up of three sets of threes. A trinity of trinities. Given that it's the last number before ten, it's a number filled with forward movement and positive direction, a metaphor for the goal of this book, and a goal for our time.

Edgar Cayce, the Sunday School teacher from Virginia, who back in the '30s and '40s spoke profoundly and prophetically about things that his waking mind could not begin to grasp, once said that nine is a sign of imminent change. Nine speaks to something poised to begin. A year ending in nine always launches us into a new decade. A year ending in 999 launches us into a new millennium.

Remember how we tiptoed into our brand-new millennium steeped in deep fear of how our computers might all malfunction at midnight on December 31, 1999? We called it Y2K, Year 2000, and many, including myself, I admit, thought we might be in for big trouble. Because programmers wanted to save space, they had not planned ahead to the time when computers would change to a year ending in zeros. Recognizing how vulnerable our interlaced computerized world is, from cars to traffic lights, airplanes, trains and satellites, computers very well could have crashed at that bewitching hour. In preparation, we encouraged each other to build communities of support just in case. We made sure we had water and food stashed away. Programmers worked through many nights to quickly build "patches" around the systems.

Thankfully, our computers held. In the process, we learned something about ourselves. At the time, I called it a dress rehearsal for a potential future. After 9/11, when terrorists became very real to us, we created different "patches." We started taking our shoes off in airports and installing scanners everywhere. Anything to make us feel safer. Then came an election year and people overwhelmingly voted for "change" because deep down we knew the way we were living just wasn't working for all of us on this planet.

Because Sophia is coded into everything around us, she also appears in the *Enneagram* — an ancient nine-fold template originated from Zoroastrians, who passed it along to Pythagoras, who eventually handed it to a wandering teacher, the Tiger of Turkestan, G.I. Gurdjieff, who brought it to us. Rather than use the Enneagram to categorize a particular personality type, I suggest integrating each type into our hearts as another facet of Sophia's nine-sided life-prism.

A nonagram is composed of three overlapping equilateral triangles and creates a symbol rich in "star" connotations. Nine has been, through time, linked to the feminine. As a Scandinavian, I'm naturally drawn to the nine Scandinavian moon maidens, the *maers*, or Marys, who marry the depths of the sea, the *mare*, with the stars. She, in her many names, lends us inspiration and powers of speech and poetry, teaches us about births and deaths, and enables us to give and receive from her abundance.

Sacred women or female spirits, in groups of nine, appear throughout religion, folklore and mythology, and so, this nine-pointed star is often called the "Star of the Muses." Most memorable may be the nine muses of classical Greece, but nine female helpers appear in Celtic traditions as well as many others. The muses were figures assigned to the Greek classes of arts. Since giving and receiving is indeed an art, it might be worth our time to consider what those Muses, as faces of Sophia, have to say to us now.

The nine chapters speak to how we're called right now to open our hearts to healing and abundance. We'll take a look at what I call *Sophianomics* — what our economy might look like if Sophia were more evident — and how ancient economies, based on her, functioned. Her dove manages to swoop over local economies, gift economies, and alternative exchanges that bring communities together to celebrate the wealth all people have to offer and contribute. Here, we'll ask ourselves what it means to experience a heart-based economy balanced with our rational heads. Indigenous people say it's time, now, for the condor (intuitive heart-based ways of knowing) to fly with the eagle (our rational head-based technology and science).

Each chapter will look at various ways she is embedded in our hearts, in our relationships and in our world. We'll find her hidden in symbols and immersed in fairy tales. She dances in sacred places and warms the hearts of those who meet her. She's evident in crop circles, in sacred geometry, and in the **Heartbeat Questions** that open each chapter. At the end of each chapter, we'll "hear" her actual voice.

Sophia invites us to come together to evolve and enrich our future. For men and women alike, she is our Essential Feminine, for right now. Not for yesterday. Not only for tomorrow. But for right now. Ready or not, here she comes.

part one

SOPHIA IN OUR HEARTS

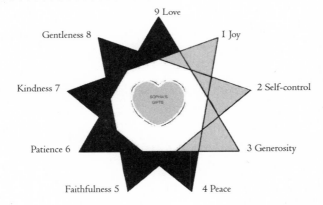

9 Love

Gentleness 8

1 Joy

Kindness 7

2 Self-control

SOPHIA'S
GIFTS

Patience 6

3 Generosity

Faithfulness 5

4 Peace

chapter one

SHE CALLS US TO CREATE

Crop Circle: Pewsey White Horse, July 17, 2002

· ·

*"Sophia is the One at the heart of creative acts. She was present at
the beginning and she is the ongoing process.... Her vision will
keep us moving."*

~ Susan Cady, et al., *Sophia*

MOUNTAIN JOURNAL ENTRY

Half a moon hangs in the lauds-sky. Balance. Symmetry. Perfection.
I have never traced the moon across the sky as I do here in Vermont.
Is it because I have the time/the inclination/the fuller views? Or is
the moon more compelling here? Even with my poor morning eyes,
I can see the hollows and ridges that cover her surface. The moon
shows me her skin.

The sky is brushed with pink; layers of blue-grey velvet hang
in the sky. Vermont's colors never cease to stir my soul. *Stirring my
soul* — what a strange phrase. It's as if Sophia's standing with a long
wooden spoon over the cauldron that is me. Froth up. Boil!

"You are embarking." Those are the words I hear this morning.
Getting on a boat? Starting an adventure? Throwing myself into a
future unknown?

Each of us can be a "Little Sophia." My fingers shake just
thinking about it.

HEARTBEAT QUESTIONS

What does it mean to be a child again?

How do I differentiate "happiness" from "joy"? What brings me true joy?

What "straw" in my life could become "gold"?

How might I play in new, creative ways?

CROP CIRCLES: SOPHIA'S CODED SURPRISES

In August of 1980, a mysterious design appeared in an English farmer's grain field. The farmer said it hadn't been there the day before. People who saw it realized that it wasn't a little fairy circle, but rather a huge geometric form sixty feet in diameter. Soon three more elusive pieces of grain-art appeared; people began calling them crop circles. Between 1980 and 1987, one hundred and twenty were recorded and then, in 1990, a peak year for crop circles, over 1,000 were reported. Every year since, in late summer, an average of fifty designs "crop up" in summer barley and wheat fields overnight. And they're not simple figures a few friends could do with some boards

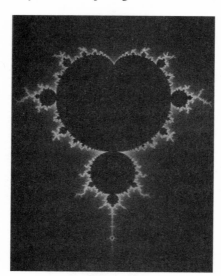

Mandelbrot set: a set of mathematical points forming a fractal named after Benoit Mandelbrot

and string overnight, as some have tried. They're becoming even more intricate and complicated as the grain seasons go by. And they often appear in a matter of seconds.

One branching 1991 design, the Mandelbrot set, was a replica of Benoit Mandelbrot's elegant computer-generated unfolding fractal view of infinity. Sophia winks. It appeared in a field near where he taught at Cambridge. Sophia loves to hide things in plain sight.

It looks like a giant heart to me. It's as if she is reminding us all things branch and grow out of her expansive heart that holds us fast.

"O resplendent jewel and unclouded brightness of the sunlight streaming through you — the world's first matrix ... that luminous matrix through which the same Word breathed forth all virtues, as in the primal matrix it brought forth all creatures."

~ Hildegard of Bingen, *Scivias*, III.13.1

Who creates these ephemeral matrices? Like dreams, or a brilliant sand-mandala, they appear and then fade away — but they continue to lurk in our peripheral vision, like grainy snapshots.

I've seen many crop circle fields, but never when the designs were intact. So, I haven't experienced what some people describe as real physical phenomena around crop circle sites, such as bright flashes and high pitched sounds that can interfere with electrical equipment, dizziness and headaches. I've only seen pictures of twisted stalks, but scientists have found alterations at the grain's cellular levels and testify to the fact that crop circle seeds germinate more vigorously. Some powerful energy is at work here.

I join the host of people who aren't as concerned about how grain circles are made, but rather wonder what their symbols mean. They are perfect circles, triangles, cubes. Pythagorean geometry. Many of the teasing designs appear around Stonehenge and Avebury, two places in England long known for *her* energy. Like music, this geometry is available to anyone. Steve Alexander, who has photographed many crop circles, calls them "temporary temples." I call them Sophia's Codes.

It's as if Sophia is saying: *Come into my earth-temple. But be quick about it. I won't leave these designs long. There's a broader-based reality than you currently recognize. Look for my mathematical messages and figure out what they mean. For you. It's not that hard. They may be your link to your stars — to your broader universe. They may be pictures of your DNA. Maybe my crop circles are simply combinations of light and sound — listen for the vibrations, their energy. Feel the music embedded in them. And play with them! For heavens sake, lighten up!*

"LET US PLAY!"

My husband John and I took a recent road trip from Vermont to Colorado because our three-year-old granddaughter, Josie, invited us to her birthday party, and we had a big doll house to deliver. Imagine eight three-year-olds all engaged in various activities on the back deck. Think about an ant hill. Think purposeful activity. Think intense focus. Think how tired and in need of naps we'd all be if we actually engaged with the world as they do.

I watched, wondering what these three-year-olds might teach me. I immediately noticed that they "owned" wherever they stood and whatever was in their hands at that moment. It was "theirs" and they intuited what they should do with it. They shared (mostly) and made things that were creative and very important — but only for that moment. Children know how to celebrate the temporary. We adults tend to cling and store and save. They teach us how to let go. They easily move on when a particular play ends — the play for which they've made all the rules themselves. No regrets. No clinging. They just move on to something more intriguing. When the bubbles you're blowing burst, you just pick up the play dough. If somebody else is using a sand toy, you select a different one. No stockpiling of resources. No pyramids of power. No greed. These little imagination-machines are pure. They engage in intense activity. Diane Ackerman describes this in her book, *Deep Play,* as "a state of unselfconscious engagement with our surroundings; an exalted zone of transcendence over time; a state of creative capacity."

I was discussing this creative capacity with Ria, an online So-phia-friend, who said, "Children don't go through their day think-ing, 'What am I going to do first?' They just follow their energy. Wherever it takes them. I surely think this is our way forward in the world, a world that gets more and more complex ... it gets to be too much for our minds to overview, as lots of things are related, but not in a linear way." Just follow the energy.

Gandhi called that untapped well of courageous creativity in each of us our "wild card." He said we don't know that deep well is there until we tap into it through our spirituality. Proverbs 8 tells us Sophia is there ... "ever at play by God's side, at play everywhere in God's domain...."

Whale Songs and Bricolage

The French have a brilliant word for play: *bricolage*. It means picking up and using whatever is at hand. Kids do it all the time. Kitchen pots turn into drums. Cardboard boxes become forts. Teddy bears and dolls morph into real people sitting around a tea table. Wooden blocks run as well as real cars and trucks. These objects have no payoff other than fun.

Children show us how to create whole new worlds from what's at our fingertips. *Bricolage* means to put together unlikely ideas just for the fun of seeing what happens. We bricolage fabric snippets into quilts, eggs and flour into cookies, words into books, images into reality, and finally the biggest bricolaging of all: ova and sperm become precious children. And when we're done playing for now, we bricolage life into death and back into life again.

James Watson, the DNA researcher in search of a model for life, said, "All we had to do was construct a set of molecule models and begin to play. With luck, the structure would become a helix." It did. Innovation and inventions usually stem from active play. Once someone looked hard and long at a flying bat, for instance, and invented radar. Blue mold floated through Alexander Fleming's open window and landed with a microscopic thud on his plate of bacteria: penicillin. The leaf of an ash tree inspired an airplane propeller and maple keys, helicopter blades. Sea nettles turned into parachutes. A wheat stalk became reinforced steel. Charles Goodyear dropped some raw rubber on a hot stove one day and gifted the world with vulcanized rubber. And, in 1904, a St. Louis World Fair vendor ran out of dishes for his ice cream, so he went next door and said, "Roll up some of those sugar waffles — quick. I need them for ice cream."

Play is filled with expectancy. It's similar, in many respects, to the state one arrives at in mediation. Susan Griffith says, "It is, on the one hand, very calm and very quiet, but on the other hand, abundant — a fountain of everything."

In *Life on the Mississippi*, Mark Twain wrote: "When I'm playful, I use the meridians of longitude and parallels of latitude for a seine, and drag the Atlantic Ocean for whales!"

A Boston-based naturalist once told me about a whale behavior never documented before. Over a dozen male whales surfaced from their winter feeding grounds in the Caribbean and gathered, heads up, in a circle. For a full sixteen minutes they engaged in what the befuddled observers could only call a "choir practice." This playful song-circle was intended, it seems, to bring boy-whales up to speed. Only the adult males sing, and usually only in winter. They all sing the same song, but every year they make up new phrases to add to it. In the summer, they break the song off, and when they return the following winter, they pick it right up where they left off, as if there had been no six-month intermission. Why? We're not sure, of course, but Patricia Pereira, the woman who single-handedly brought the wolves back to Yellowstone, offers some ideas. She has written (with extra-ordinary help) the *Arcturian Chronicles*, and in it says that whale songs reverberate through the deep, setting up vibrations in order to keep our planet whole. If that's true, we must fight to keep them alive. Gigantic crystalline pyramids are located deep within our oceans, and dolphins and whales sing to coordinate planetary information stored there. Perhaps our world is more wonderfully bricolaged than we might imagine. That verse in Genesis that says, "Let us make humans in our own image," might just as well read: "Let us sing and vibrate people and all things into being."

Ancient Hawaiians cherished a designated chant for every craft or art work that they created. Imagine doing bark woodblock printing as you sing the very same old songs your great-great-great grandmothers sang as they created these same designs. It's evidence that a cosmic larynx sings the old songs through us again and again.

I once heard the Sami Folk Minister of Culture in Stockholm describe the dark time when Lutheran missionaries lugged their

Bibles across plains of snow and ice to convert her people. When the missionaries, at last, reached her people, surrounded by their tinkle-belled reindeer, the stony-faced missionaries tried to impose and enforce many rules. For instance, they forbad the Sami to sing anything but Lutheran hymns. That futile gesture was about as effective as telling children, "You can't play any longer." Naturally, they kept on singing, albeit quietly.

The beautiful Sami-Sophia said, "May I sing you the song I composed for our daughter when she was born?" On a magical candlelit night I sat in a quiet dialogue circle, and her clear voice entered my chest and vibrated like a trapped bird. I could not understand her words with my head, but my mother-heart knew this song. Like the whales who add new phrases to their songs, she sings a new verse to her daughter on her birthday every year.

Edward Whitmont, in *Return of the Goddess*, described the best sort of play as performed "for its own sake, not for any purpose or achievement other than itself. Play is the self-discovery in the here and now ... light, yet potentially passionate. It is discovery, and it is enjoyment of one's own and of other's possibilities, capacities and limitations." When music and dance are banned, women are compromised. It's no coincidence that the Taliban in Afghanistan cracked down on women at the same time they banned music. They did make an exception for men's a capella singing, but no musical instruments were allowed.

THE ECSTASY OF IT ALL

When all my Berg aunts and uncles gathered on summer Sunday afternoons at our grandparents' farm near Sand Creek, Wisconsin, much to our parents' relief, we cousins would rush in to greet our grandparents, grab a cookie, and then slam the screen door behind us as we raced to the front lawn. Our favorite pastime was race-rolling across Grandpa's freshly cut grass. We could get about ten good roll-overs before we hit the garden. We did it again and again and again. *Ad nauseum*. When we grew tired of that, we held our arms out and twirled to see who could get the dizziest and had to fall down first. Without realizing it, we "would-be" dervish dancers were seeking ecstasy — *ek-stasis* or the state of standing outside one's self. Like Sufi dervishes, my cousins and I were, if only for a few minutes, egoless and beside ourselves with joy. Our little out of body experiences helped spin the universe. As the Sufi poet Rumi said: There are hundreds of ways to kneel and kiss the ground. We must have practiced at least ninety-nine of them on those hot summer afternoons.

Whenever we act out our most precious stories, we call it liturgy, the mass, or sacred ritual. Early Greeks tied on costumes, held up masks and play-acted "the other." Mayan athletes pulled on protective leather padding and gloves and played dangerous ball games in walled courts. Some Zuni men ran up to forty miles, kicking a "sacred stick." Mt. Everest climbers push themselves up 29,028 feet just to feel the *ek-stasis* of sticking their heads up into jet streams. Even through their oxygen-deprived brains they realize that only nine out of ten of them will make it safely back down to Base Camp at 17,800 feet. Still, they continue to climb. The sinewy-muscled sherpas who accompany them up *Jomolungma*, or Goddess, Mother of the World, know that climbing is sacred play. Before they ascend, they hang images of winged horses (*lung ta*), wind horse prayer flags, and burn juniper incense to ensure their safety. *Om mani padme hum.*

The Creation Spirituality theologian, Matthew Fox, said that the work of the future will be art work, heart work, and ritual. Through ritual, which is simply devoted play, energy comes alive and can be passed along. Bernard of Clairvaux, the man who founded the Cistercian order of white-clad monks, described the monastic life as "a good sort of playing which is ridiculous to men, a very beautiful sight to the angels ... a joyous game." Many still play this joyous prayer-game and their tonal intervals set up sympathetic vibrations across our planet and out into the cosmos.

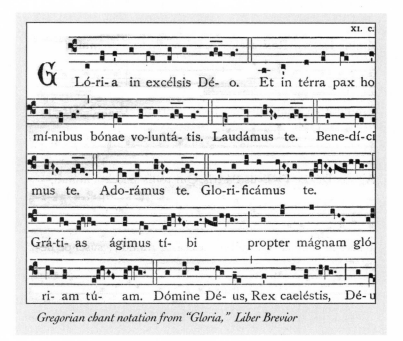

Gregorian chant notation from "Gloria," Liber Brevior

Gregorian chants penned onto parchment with little square notes showed early monks when to breathe and which pitch to use. Then around 1000 C.E. the notes split into two chant melodies. One group of singers held on to the lower drone notes while the rest soared above. Gregory, the pope who started this form of chanting, is said to have received it from a dove sitting on his shoulder, singing into his ear. (Sophia obviously loves plainsong, but then, I believe she loves all music. Perhaps opera most of all, since women singers, Diva, means "divine.") Gregory started a school for chant, the Scola Cantorum in Rome, and monks spent up to ten years there learning how to sing the Bible in pure vowel sounds. Vowel sounds can, according to music therapists, stimulate the brain's frontal lobes, the area linked to higher thought.

You'll find no soloists among monks; Gregorian chant can't be sung alone. And like whales, some Tibetan monks are able to sing two or three pitches at once and send low overtones booming through the cosmos, just as my vowel-singing cousins did when we sang "Old MacDonald," as loudly as we could, just to see who could hold notes the longest: E, I, E, I, OOOOOOO....

Joseph Chilton Pearce says, in *The Magical Child*, that when we play, we bend the world to our desire. Sacred play is remembering *how*, and then *daring* to bend the world. Like jazz, it's improvisation. It's painting, without a preconceived design. It's dialoguing while sitting in circles, not knowing beforehand what words or ideas will surface. It's engaging the uncertainty principle. It's living in the country of possibilities.

But it's not easy. There's something engrained in each of us that says:

I want to paint but I don't want to get my brush dirty.

I want to write but I don't want anyone to read or criticize what I've written.

I want to play the piano but I don't want to practice.

Sophia invites us to become "real players" who don't just sit on the sidelines, but who inhabit space. Even when it's risky. Life isn't really about playing it safe. Children instinctively know that. They leap without caring where or how they will land. They say, "Let's pretend like...," without knowing the script, because there is no script. Real players leap full throttle into every creative adventure. It's good to remember Mary Oliver's poetic advice: "I don't want to end up simply having visited this world."

A SOPHIA PAINTING CIRCLE

Creativity is womb-work. Before anything can be created, it first has to float in the salty amniotic waters of the unconscious. We are perpetually pregnant. When the time is right, we can no more hold back our creative moments than we can prevent a child from forcefully moving down the birth canal to announce: "Surprise! I'm here!"

Cambridge Sophia Painting Circle: left to right: Sharon, Karen, Lillian, Christina, May and Jean

Shortly after moving to Cambridge, I joined a collaborative painting group with five other women. We often painted on one large canvas spread across our living room floor. We'd pause to view our work from our upper balcony and to wonder what we were really doing.

How could five strong women wielding paint-laden brushes actually paint *together* onto one canvas? We did it because Lillian, one of several professional artists among us, taught us the value of underpainting. Sophia was prompting us: *Paint away. It's like life. You can't make a mistake and nothing ever totally disappears.* Earlier brushstrokes always formed the foundation for something newer and even more wonderful than what was laid down before. So we swallowed our egos and valued the *next* lines, the *next* colors regardless of who brought them to the canvas. Christina described our process in this portion of her poem, "Underpainting":

Chiaroscuro is like that ... one's eye travels to bright detail, the poignant black quietly there to illuminate in contrast.... "Ah," she said, "these too I must truly see." ..."Let me absorb the Light and use it to examine these dark corners...."

The poem ends with these words: *"in those darkest places —
illumination of the complexity of the whole."*

We lived complexity and chaos as we knelt and swirled color
onto our oversized canvas "prayer rugs." No longer splintered parts,
we began to see how each of us was crucial to the whole even though
we didn't know how at the time. On our painting evenings, our
world collapsed into the middle of our canvas. We became part of
a whirling centrifuge, a spinning universe, and our brushes brought
order out of chaos. We painted from our centers.

Before we started, we placed various objects that meant something to us on our white canvas "altar" and then meditated, usually
to the music of the 11th century Rhineland mystic, Hildegard of
Bingen. Her words inspired us: *"I dwell in the dew and in the air and in
all greenness...." "Thus every creature is linked to another. And every essence is
constrained by another...." "Everything that is in the heavens, on the earth, and
under the earth, is penetrated with connectedness, is penetrated with relatedness."*
Sometimes we painted her words right onto the canvas, and the objects we shared often showed up later in our brushstrokes.

We gave our jazz-paintings various names: "At What Point Does
the Larva Become a Butterfly," "Brigit's Fire," and "In the Face of
Injustice, Creation is Not Silent." One night we were so anguished
by the First Gulf War we wanted to show the explosive hatred it
had unleashed. Our "War and Peace" canvas clanged alarms of red
and orange. Sharon, Christine and May pounded and scratched the
surface with angry fingernails. Another Kim Phuc from the Vietnam
War, all afire, fled in vain; her burning flesh mirrored burning cities and keening women with fists raised to the sky. Working on the
"peace" part of the canvas, Lillian's brush swept tears into a dove —
a weeping aurora borealis; I painted a woman's face in a bright rose
sky suspended above the destruction and mayhem. Jean's shell-spiral
showed the turns of our collective life-times. Beginning in helpless-
ness and despair, we finished with a sense that somehow this very
canvas might make a difference within the interrelated wholeness of
things. Or, at least, a difference in how we each dealt with war.

One night Lillian appeared at our door late because she had been visiting her dying brother in the hospital. Her first words were not, "Hi, sorry I'm late," but "We have to paint Jacob's ladder! For Edward." Within minutes our canvas became a ladder and angels danced up and down that evening as we thought about Lillian and her brother. With each brushstroke, we sent healing prayers his way. Sophia must have carried the essence of our prayer-painting from the canvas in our townhouse, across the city to Edward's hospital room, because he recovered. In some mysterious fashion none of us could explain, certain living paintings later became empty chrysalises. The enlivening energy each of us felt, as we created the canvas, dissipated as the paint dried. When I look at photos of that canvas now, I no longer see the angels, but, instead, an amorphous pastel mist. I swear, they *did clearly climb* up and down that canvas as we painted them.

After spending a whole retreat day together playing "The Transformation Game," which was developed at Findhorn, Scotland, we painted what we experienced. Women, like old dryads, sprouted from a huge central tree. It became our world tree, filled with life and possibility. Eden's tree, laden with apples. Angelic beings peeking around every branch.

Once I took a mandala canvas to Cape Cod to share with Matthew Fox as a thank you for his having shared Hildegard's Four Paths of Creation Spirituality with us in *Iluminations of Hildegard of Bingen*. "Let's hang it right up there," he said, "so everyone here can see it." I explained to Fox that our artists' circle co-created that particular painting at Eastertide. In one evening.

Using the empty canvas as an altar, we invoked all our grandmothers as well as Earth, Air, Fire and Water. In the center, Lillian placed a round loaf of her Polish Easter bread with a red egg at the center. We had no idea what this canvas might become, but we had been learning about Hildegard's four ways of being, so we started by imagining the canvas in quadrants. At one point, after we'd devoured Lillian's bread, it reappeared at the center. But it was no longer bread.

After we brushed the crumbs away, a red Maypole with streaming ribbons divided our "Floor Plan for the Garden of Eden." Watching precious images vanish under a sister's paintbrush, we created crisis and breakthrough in terms of trusting one another and trusting the process. We became more and more willing to sacrifice what we had once held so precious. With minor exceptions such as, "Where did my basket of violets go???" we instinctively knew that the process was the important thing — not the end result. That night, by painting all four quadrants at once, without conscious direction, we illustrated four ways to recognize how Sophia grows and transforms us, inside-out.

Like all expectant women sitting around fires, around birthings, around quilts, we knew when it was time to begin. That's when our brushes quartered our canvas.

Via Negativa: Winter. Here we spread purplish, black nothingness — silence, emptiness, pain and suffering. We dared the dark. We painted our points of pain. Sadness crept over the center spot where Lillian's red egg's ova of hope earlier lay. Now everything nested in the grey space we called our wintery *negativa*. Slow brushes stroked this quadrant with uncertainty.

Via Positiva: Spring. The way of awe and wonder. We rejoiced in the mystery of nature; of all beings. Crops of crocuses, underpaintings of lavender-lush baskets of violets sprang up across this quadrant. Suddenly, Lillian's lion roared past us and leaped across the divide into the grayness of the *negativa*. With paws outstretched to the dark. Waiting to pounce.

Via Creativa: Summer. Here the pace quickened and we painted generativity and beauty, trusting our imaginations to birth the entire universe. Summer lemon dreams, warm-wombed, thrusting, daring brushstrokes burst wildly from this hot quadrant.

Via Transfromativa: Autumn. This quadrant remained invisible for some time. How do you paint justice? How do you portray change? Compassion? Then turquoise and purple peacocks began to swirl around an old woman. Out of deep, dark colors, she came to remind us of our elder-wisdom firmly held in her autumnal grasp.

Her crone-face watched us circle, moving from autumn to spring again, feeling the thaw deep within our fingers as they wrapped themselves around brushes of all sizes.

As we painted that night, we caught a fleeting glimpse of what Lillian called her Aslan lion image: the "Wild Pronoun." Shoes off, we dipped our toes into deserts, oceans, savannahs of our common being, and we followed the brush strokes that marked, inch by inch, the footprints of our spiral dance. We followed her flute music.

From a common palette we painted to stretch our spirits. Our collaborative paintings were eventually shown in a Harvard Square gallery so we could let others know that Sophia is alive in each of us. We unrolled our canvases, like Torahs, so all could read mysteries waiting to be fleshed into shape and color.

JOY: "I LIVE IN YOUR HEART"

Our painting sisterhood deepened. Together, we rejoiced. *Re-Joy-ced.* According to Paul's letter to the Galatians: "joy" is one of her nine sweet gifts. I like what Timothy Keller says in *Counterfeit Gods*: "Rejoicing is a way of praising God until the heart is sweetened and rested, and until it relaxes its grip on anything else it thinks that it needs."

By painting together, we learned to relax our grip — not only on our brushes, but on each other, and on ourselves.

The Aboriginal Australians understood what it meant "to relax its grip." They were painting on rocks and wood 30,000 years before our ancestors stenciled their hands onto cave walls in Lascaux and around Southern France. Those early Australians created lovely pottery and exported it. But at some point they decided it wasn't healthy to be so bound up in material things, so they never made pots again. Deep within their "dreamtime," the time when the world came into being, they remember how the rocks and mountains, caves and water, plants and animals, first appeared. They honor these ancestors by singing back portions of the songlines to connect landforms to their kinship systems.

Tolstoi likened the secret of everlasting happiness to keeping a green bough in your heart. If you keep it green, the "singing bird" will come. Happiness, however, lies on the surface of things and easily slips off. Joy lives in a deeper place, and is a mightier thing. C.S. Lewis called it the serious business of heaven.

Since this is Sophia's book, I asked her questions from time to time. Early on, I asked that common question we all use for conversation starters, "Where do you live?" I think she smiled. *Mary hailed from Judea. Ix Chel hung out at Cozumel. Isis came from Egypt. Artemis from Delos, Demeter from Eleusis. I've been here all along; I live in your heart.*

We try to make Lady Wisdom-Hagia Sophia so terribly theological, so sophisticated and cosmologically complicated, but it all comes down to five little words: *I live in your heart.* That's where the cosmic hen nests. She covers us with her warm feathers, and broods and fans us until we hatch into little chicks, little chunks of her great wisdom and love.

SHE TURNS US AROUND

As I set out to write about Sophia in the world, our families, our hearts, I confess, I can easily sink into "overwhelm." My gut cramps. People of my Scandinavian heritage are subject to self-doubts. (Just listen to Garrison Keillor some time if you don't believe me.) We say, "I'm not worthy of this." When we live in our heads — where our interior editors and judges hang out — we so easily rationalize things away. What if I offend people? What if no one "gets" it? What if I do Sophia a dis-service somehow, rather than serve her with this offering?

But when we live more in our hearts, we intuit what to do next without having to figure it all out beforehand. When I live in my head, I'm conflicted and guarded; when I live in my heart, I'm open, I'm free.

As I was thinking about my head-heart dichotomy, she seemed to say: *"Don't be concerned. You will learn by what you have turned and by what you have left unturned."*

I can breathe again. I think, perhaps I really *can* turn this pile of words into something useful. So I looked at what I had already researched and what I had yet to "turn." It's our human nature to turn. We turn around. We turn things over, upside down. We turn ideas into actions. And we do this best when we take the quiet time to turn within. We turn things into other things because she calls us to create. Creating is part of our spiritual intelligence. Our heritage. So I turn to the task of helping to reveal Sophia.

Like you, I've been turning things all my life. I turned my Wisconsin high school diploma into a college degree — the first in my extended family. For a while at Wisconsin State College Eau Claire I literally turned clay into wet wobbly pots and I turned lines of script into passable theater. At some point I decided I'd seriously pursue English rather than dabble in art. After a few years of teaching high school English, I decided to try my hand at morphing words into money. I had a Sophia-friend named Carol at the time who encouraged me and pointed me to a possible magazine which, as it turned out, published my first article. What a rush of joy I had as I held my published work in my hands. My own byline! It was published in *One* magazine and launched me into decades of wondering how we could be one, yet separate and free. It also propelled me into a freelance writing career. At some point I admitted "I am a writer. I am an author." I turned on my IBM Selectric and cranked out articles and poetry, newspaper columns and books. Our young sons learned it wasn't always a good thing to interrupt mommy when she was bent over that rattling machine. Once four-year-old Nate came in, plunked down a little jar and said, "Here's a snail! Write about it!" Later, as an editor, I turned other people's passions into books.

In Vermont, I continue to turn. Soil into gardens, vegetables into hearty soups, ideas into books.

And now, Sophia says, "Turn *me* onto your pages," so I try to notice how she appears — not just in words and books and art, but in our hearts, in our deeper knowing.

My Sophia-friend, Betty, tells of how, when she was about three, "a lady" appeared to her. Betty had followed an older girl over to some swirling water — "Let's play," her friend called. As they neared the water, Betty heard "a lady" who said, "Get out of the ditch and go home." Her friend wanted her to stay and play, but Betty said, "No, the lady told me to go home." She learned years later from her father how fortunate they had been. The city trucks had been at the construction site for a couple of weeks laying culverts in the ditches to connect them to the city sewer lines. "If we had gone further, the speed of the water flow would have pulled us into the culverts and we'd likely have drowned."

As she did for Betty, Sophia "guards us from evil and protects us from danger." Luther's small catechism explains the Holy Spirit: "She delights in us and seeks to keep us safe."

Sophia appears to us as "a lady" from time to time. Sometimes she appears to be Mary who speaks to children, as she did on the mountain in 1981 near the little village of Med-

jugorje in Bosnia-Herzegovina. Her initial messages of love and peace were given to six children: Ivan, Jakov, Marija, Mirjana, Vicka, and Ivanka who are now adults. People call them visionaries because she continues to speak to them. "I have come," she said, "to tell the world that God exists. God is the fullness of life, and to enjoy this fullness and peace, you must return to God."

In 1858, she appeared to a fourteen-year-old girl, Bernadette Soubiroux, in Lourdes, a small market town in south-western France. Bernadette said she saw a young beautiful lady in the hollow of a rock — not just once, but eighteen times. A spring gushed forth and a grotto was built to honor her healing presence. Two hundred

Our Lady of Guadalupe

million people have visited the sanctuary since the Lady was first encountered there.

In 1531, a beautiful brown-skinned woman appeared to Juan Diego. He thought she was Tonantzin, an Azetc female divine presence. This logic made sense to him because his village of Tepeyac, just north of Mexico City, was her old pilgrimage location. She appeared in a rainbow mist, spoke his Nahuatl name (*Cuauhtlatohuac* — He Who Speaks like an Eagle) and wore the colors of Aztec royalty. The lady told him she was the mother of the god of great truth and creator of the universe, the ever-virgin — *Totl*. When Juan told the Franciscan bishop about what he'd seen and heard, the bishop instructed him to go back up the mountain to find out if it might be the Virgin Mary and to bring back a sign.

It was the morning of December 8th — the day set aside to honor the immaculate conception of the Virgin Mary.... When Juan climbed back up to his little village of Tepeyac, what did he find? A rose garden. Roses are symbols for Mary, but they are also the Aztec symbol for truth. He picked a bunch and brought them back to the doubting bishop who was mystified, not only by the roses, but also by a mysterious image of a woman that had appeared on Juan's tunic. It has since been embroidered over and the *tilma* is on display just north of Mexico City. Surrounded by sunlight, she stands on the moon, and at her belly is an Aztec symbol for "the heart of the universe." Her hands are raised to her chest in the old Nahuatl gesture of offering and a black maternity band around her waist signifies her pregnancy. People asked Juan what she said her name was. He said, "She called herself *Tlecuauhtlacupeuh*," which apparently sounded like *Guadalupe* which, ironically enough, was Corez' original home in Spain before he came to ravage Juan's land. It means "sacred place of light."

Throughout these chapters, we'll see how Sophia has appeared to various people throughout recorded history. I'm calling these segments "Sophia's Mystical Dancers" because I imagine people linking hands and moving to her music, starting in this chapter with Augustine.

A SANCTUARY FOR CREATIVITY

Sophia loves to gather musicians to her, as well as martyrs and strong wise women. Her wisdom makes all things joyous and fruitful. She offers us a sanctuary for creativity, and beauty. She's a mystery, a bridge, a Mistress of Paradox, for she's found in chaos and in order. She gravitates to verbs ... to singing, moving, dancing, creating, building, loving.

The people living on Crete honored her presence in all women and in her many images and symbols of cyclical life. Then the Greeks began recording their view of the world, and when "ladies" appeared they called them goddesses. Interestingly enough, there were nine muses, nine daughters of the Greek character Zeus and Mnemosyne, the goddess of memory. Each goddess carried within them everything that happened since the beginning of time. They helped people remember so they could tell and retell stories. They encourage us to sing and dance and joyfully remember how to create. Writers and other creative people invoke them..."Come help me. Don't leave me, muse." If these archetypal women could speak to us today, they might say:

Calliope: Use your own beautiful voice; you are so eloquent.
Terpsichore: What are you waiting for? It's time to dance!
Melpomene: Yes, tragedy happens, but not forever.
Urania: Get out your telescopes and look to the stars!
Polyhymnia: Raise your voice in sacred song.
Erato: What are *you* passionate about?
Thalia: Let your writing flourish — poetry, song, comedy — it's
    all there for you.
Euterpe: Bring out your flutes and recorders!
Clio: Tell your stories.

Once upon a time, at the very beginning, Proverbs tells us, Sophia joined a masculine presence — but not as an administrative assistant or junior partner: "*Ages ago I was set up, at the first, before the beginning of the earth. When there were no depths I was brought forth, when there were no springs abounding with water. Before the mountains were shaped, before the hills I was brought forth — when he had not yet made earth and fields, or the world's first bits of soil. When he established the heavens, I was there, when he drew a circle on the face of the deep, when he made firm the skies above, when he established the fountains of the deep, when he assigned to the sea its limit, so that the waters might not transgress his command, when he marked out the foundations of the earth, then I was beside him, like a master worker; and I was daily his delight, rejoicing before him always, rejoicing in his inhabited world and delighting in the human race."*

She's like a mother hen warming and delighting in her eggs. Or a Mother Goose.

MOTHER GOOSE AND BABA YAGA

Every Saturday morning, I balanced my beige melamine Motorola on my eight-year-old lap while my inner world magically connected to the world beyond the farm where I lived.

I plunked "Froggie with its magic twinger" along with Buster Brown and his Dog Tige. I shivered to hear Ramar of the Jungle's elephant! I flew with Sky King and the Royal Mounties and I traveled with Uncle Ted to the land of "Let's Pretend."

My mother usually gave me a few slices of sausage and some crackers. I stacked them up on top of the radio in spite of the fact that seeping plastic into food now seems like a very dangerous habit. Good thing I did it only on Saturday mornings. I savored every sound and saved every crumb.

Although I didn't know Sophia's name back then, I recognized her in my mother and I deduced that there had to be kind mothers to balance all those "evil step-mothers." Stories informed me of hidden powers, love that comes in unexpected ways, strength in adversity, treasures waiting to be found, heroic quests to be endured, families to be reunited, loves to be cherished.

We each carry storylines deep inside. We yearn for "home." As my friends Penny and Joe who work with addictions and recovery say, each one of us has a God-sized hole in our hearts, and we long to fill that vacancy. If we don't allow Christ-Sophia to fill it, we stuff other things in and can easily become addicted to those other things. All the while, Sophia waits patiently, offering us her "crackers and sausages."

Eventually we come to the understanding, as St. Francis put it, that our heart-hole can only be filled by what we give, for "by giving, I receive." We are able to give when we finally realize that we swim in abundance, not scarcity. We are able to give when we finally realize that we swim in abundance, not scarcity. Buying and keeping *things* will never bring happiness.

"Human beings, vegetables, or cosmic dust — we all dance to a mysterious tune, intoned in the distance by an invisible piper." Albert Einstein said that, but I wish he'd have added, "Sophia's that piper!" She encourages us, in muse-voices, to create.

Baba Yaga, that wrinkled old Eastern European woman (usually with a rather large nose with a hairy wart on it), appears when we least expect her. Sometimes she arrives on her broom — the one she uses to sweep the heavens and our souls.

Baba Yaga often offers blessings or grants wishes if you give her an onion. Some say she lives in a hut at the edge of the forest. Ask the Russian Vasalisa about her doll or Hansel and Gretel about their walk in the woods — but she isn't always scary. In many stories she's an old figure who protects the forests. Baba Yaga appears in all colors. People in the west turned her into the "Green Man," (and then put his picture on vegetable labels as the Jolly Green Giant). We might do well to invite the "Green Woman" to protect what's left of our old growth forests.

Indian traditions call her Kali — a black figure who gathers skulls. The Sioux call her White Buffalo Woman, the one who gave them their sacred pipe and showed them how to use it. The Maya call her Lady of the Rainbow.

Our Sophia Wisdom can be darkly veiled by all that we fear — the Baba Yaga within. We fear aging. We fear loss. Let's face it, when men fear women's power, what they may be fearing most is Baba Yaga because, deep down, they fear their own deaths. Baba Yaga comes and says, "So what? Let my broom sweep away your illusions. I come in three forms: mother, virgin, crone. Get used to all three of me!" Baba Yaga embodies all medicine women, all the midwives birthing people into this world, and all the hospice workers birthing people out of this world. She's the "hag," the "holy one," Hagia Sophia. Fairy tales fill our heart-holes and storytellers shower us with tales in which she hides, waiting for us to take notice.

SONGS FROM THE SACRED GROVE

My Sophia-sister told me to go *be* with the trees, so one weekend I hopped in the car and headed west. I'd arranged to spend two nights with some monks. Surely they'd be able to reduce my stress.

There was only one other woman guest. She talked. A lot. I went to my room and read. One night, instead of a quiet eucharist, I found myself on a sagging sofa sharing a bowl of popcorn with a brother on each side of me. We watched an old Alfred Hitchcock movie on their outdated television screen. In the words of William Sloan Coffin, we were living "the ordinary life extraordinarily well." It was good popcorn.

After lunch one day I wandered over to a grove of cedar sisters — at least twelve of them. So lush. So vocal. So abundant. I stretched out under them and from a nearby maple, four leaves landed onto my chest. Each with imperfections. Black dots. Broken tips. The only perfect, unchanging things are plastic.

As I wandered the monastery grounds, I thought: trees are the most patient things around. They never rush the seasons, yet they never refuse to give up their leaves or their seeds — sometimes even their very trunks, when the time is right. They know about cycles.

Leaning back into an oak, I sensed its strength. The leaves all sang together yet there was strength in each being slightly different. I shut my eyes and saw a dancing orange web, orbs, cosmic circles — all connected. Like Monet's poppies they danced before my closed lids, hot in the sun. Two little acorns, green with brown curly hair caps — monks' tonsures — perched at my feet, waiting to become big oaks. No hurry.

One huge Grandmother Pine seemed to call me over. I leaned against her scraggly bark. Looking up at her, I thought: "Well, she's not afraid of having a few barren branches." And from all the fuzzy saplings around me, it was obvious she ran some sort of day care center for baby pine trees. I picked up a cone and marveled at how she keeps all those seeds safe until it's time to send them out into the world.

Across the top of my fresh journal page I wrote: "Songs from the Sacred Grove," subtitled, "Tree Truths."

Be still and know.
Stand tall.
You have all you need, just as we do.
This is a world of light and shadow; embrace it all.
Use your diverse *green* gifts.
Lichen grows where it likes. Let it.
You're ready to stand tall and strong.
The people who need you will find you, just as you
    found this grove.
Nurture the saplings.
Don't cling; we don't.
Be your purpose.
Remember what makes you happy.
A tornado could come any time. We're ready.
Don't fear imperfections. Take a good look at our leaves.
Use your greenness and your energy.
Be still at your core, but move from your limbs.
There's not just one way of "doing it."
Grip the earth, but let your body dance!
Remember, you're fed from the lower depths.
Celebrate your freedom and individuality, but remember
    you're rooted with others.
Trust your seeds to sprout; they're not under your control,
    so just let them go.

Catch the breezes and make music.

Don't infringe on others' space.

Bend, but don't snap. And if something brittle does snap,
    just let it go.

You have strong bark enclosing your tender parts, too.

Don't leak your sap. Value all your energy.

Raise above all the minor irritations.

Don't carry excess baggage.

Let your scars show. It's who you are.

Love your greening — then when it's time, rejoice in joining
    the forest floor.

On Sunday morning, well-rested, I headed for my car to return to Boston, thinking: "What has become of me? I speak leaf-talk." Crazier still, the trees answer.

Once Upon a Time:
Rumplestiltskin

I'm not sure how I got into that room full of dusty straw. One minute I was baking bread for my father's dinner and the next thing I knew I was sitting in the dark, sneezing. If my dad didn't boast so much I'd still be home brewing beer and mending his socks. My mother died several years ago. But, before she died, she said, "Esmerelda, you'll never catch a man if you don't know how to sew and spin, so watch carefully."

She taught me to spin wool, but I certainly have no experience spinning straw! This all happened because my boastful father claimed that I, "his very talented miller's daughter," could spin straw into gold. An enviable craft, indeed. I wish I'd known it. Now I'm in big trouble. The king still doesn't know that I've deceived him, and the little man who helped me is coming to take my baby. I know, it sounds preposterous. But here's what happened.

About a year ago the king said if I didn't spin a whole room full of straw into gold before the next morning, he'd kill me! From the way he slammed the door behind him, I knew he meant it. Click. I was locked in. I coughed from the dusty straw and cried so hard I thought I'd never stop.

As I sat there with my tears falling into the straw, a little man suddenly appeared. "Who are *you?*" I asked. He didn't answer me; he just leaned against my spinning wheel, looking strangely pleased with himself. "I'll spin this into gold for you if you give me your necklace." Agreed. Whir. Whir. Whir. Soon the room was filled with gold and the straw was gone, and so was the little man and my mother's necklace.

Then I heard the key in the lock and the king stood there looking mighty pleased. I gathered my things thinking I'd be going back to the mill when he said, "Oh, no. Not so fast. I have another room." He led me down the hallway to a bigger room piled to the ceiling with straw. A servant pushed the spinning wheel into the room behind me and I heard the king say, "She's quite the spinner, this girl. A real asset." Before he locked the door, he looked at me over his shoulder and ordered, "All gold by tomorrow morning or you know what."

Again the funny little man came and spun gold from straw — but only after making me promise something I never should have promised: If I become Queen, I must give him my first born child. "That will never happen," I think. "Sure!" I said, thinking: I just need the gold or I'll never live long enough to marry anybody! Straw miraculously became more gold and he disappeared as fast as he'd come.

Now, here I sit in the dark, the queen of all the land, knowing that tonight the little man will come for my child.

Living in the palace has been quite pleasant, actually, when I'm not engaged in such deadly games. My father visits often. He loves his grandson. One day as I am sitting rocking my baby, the little straw-spinner shows up again and demands his payment. I plead and wail. "All right," he says, "I'll release you from your promise, but only if you can guess my real name. You have three days." Giggling into his hand, he disappears.

I've been calling out names until I'm hoarse. I've scoured the palace library and now I'm on the last page of the last book of the last census. I'll never find it.

Someone knocks. Oh, it's the woodsman's son. I say: "What is it? I'm very tired. And my head hurts."

"Queen Esmerelda, I'm sorry to bother you, but I think you might want to know this. I was walking in the forest and heard a strange song coming from a little hut off the beaten path. So I crept over and watched a little man dancing and singing: 'Today I brew, to-morrow I bake. After that the child I'll take. I'm the winner of the game. Rumpelstiltskin is my name.' That's what he said. It seemed important."

Important, indeed! "Good work, lad. Here, take this pouch of coins." What a silly name. It means "little rattling pole." Ah, and now here comes the little rattler himself. He moves toward the bassinet, his long twitching fingers reaching for my baby. "RUMPELSTILTSKIN!" I say in my most queenly voice.

"The devil must have told you that!" screams the little man and he stamps his foot so hard into the ground that his whole leg goes in. Then he pulls so hard to get his leg out that he splits himself in two and disappears!

My husband is so pleased with the birth of his son, he never again asks me to spin straw into gold. And that is a very good thing.

Spinning Stories

What do we make of *Rumplestiltskin*? All of the characters seem to lack intelligence and morals; the father is a braggart, the daughter is naïve and needy. Maybe she felt she didn't have a choice, but why did she marry the king? She must have known what sort of man he was. Esmerelda makes ill-advised choices. She also makes stupid promises and then breaks them through duplicity. The king — well, we know how immoral he is. And the little spinning guy ... first he takes her necklace, then he wants her baby. But like all little elemental people, he does know about metals.

If we take the view that each of us is a character is this story, as we may also be each of our dream characters, Sophia seems to be warning us against giving away our necklace (our throat chakra — our speech center), and that we *need* far less than we think we need. The Jungian analyst, Louise Von Franz, says that dwarfs and trolls and "the hidden folk" can be tricky. They can draw humans into nature and turn them into stone. In other words, she says, our emotional selves can be deadened.

Each of us holds muse-like power; the old Hermetic principle of "as above, so below" takes on a fresh meaning in this tale. All the company of heaven is reflected in us, and what we are is reflected in them. It's not just "higher beings" that can create. It's not just Rumpelstiltskins who can spin straw into gold. As the 17th century mystic, Jacob Boehme, said, we each hold the "gold in the stone." Each of us has transformative, creative power. We, too, are storytellers and magicians capable of spinning despair into hope, doubt into faith, darkness into light, sadness into joy and fear into love.

Sophia exists out of time. She created; she creates; she will create. The Hopi people don't worry about time or space. They experience only "the manifest, the manifesting and the unmanifested." They aren't concerned with *where* or *when*. A lot can be learned from their view of the world. We are more anchored, however, in all our "befores" and we worry about the "afters." I'm calling these little glimpses into Sophia's tales "Once Upon a Time" stories because they include her time past, the present time and the time to come — the after time. Breton storytellers begin their stories with, "Once upon a time there was no time. It was then that...." and the story unfolds from there. I retell these nine tales in the spirit of the Swahili storyteller who said: If the story is beautiful, its beauty belongs to us all. If the story is not, the fault is mine alone who tells it — or in my case, who rewrote it.

My friend Bill White is a Lutheran pastor and master story-teller. In one of his books, *Stories for the Gathering*, he says, "Since traditional stories have already gone through numerous adaptations we can be free to tell them in new ways." I'm retelling these "Once Upon a Time" stories in first-person. It's in keeping with how each of us has to tell our Sophia-stories ... through our own "I's." As vice-regents of Sophia, *we* are the ones accountable. *We* tell the stories. *We* participate in how everything evolves. But we are not without resources. There's another old Hermetic principle that says, "As in the past, so in the future." Earlier eras are mirrored in our later ones. We learn from them but are not bound by them. For instance, we borrowed the early views of Babylonian heavens and turned astrology into astro-physics. We built chemistry from alchemy. What comes next? Let's hope we can spin unconditional love out of unreasonable fear.

NINE ENNEAGRAM NUMBERS AND ANGELS

The number 9, mathematicians say, is incorruptible. It is the only number that when multiplied by any other number reproduces itself. Take 9 x 6, for instance. You get 54. Five plus four equals nine. Get it? Try it. It always works.

Nine is a holy number — a trinity of threes and threes are important because they remind us that we no longer have to live in a world of opposites; we no longer, as the Egyptians once believed, live only with dyads. We've become more harmonious than that. We know how to reconcile opposites, even if we don't always practice it. We can bring the third element of anything in to become more balanced, more whole. I think of threes as a combination of body/ mind/spirit-soul. Father, Son, Sophia. Mother, Virgin, Crone. Mother, Father, Child.

During ancient Christian Eucharistic liturgies, the bread was broken into nine pieces and placed on the altar. Seven pieces represented a part of our earthly journey we each take from embodiment to resurrection, and the final two launch us into "glory" and "kingdom." Thus, in eating and drinking Christ's body and blood, we are strengthened for our earthly work and are given the means to go on to the mystical regions we can now only dream of.

Nine great Egyptian gods sat in council called the *ennead*. Out of Nu, the primal nothingness (or Sophia), came Atum who created Shu and Tefnut. From their union came Geb and Nut followed by Osiris and Isis, then Set and Nephthys. In sacred geometry, the enneagram forms a nine-pointed geometric figure that has been traced back to Pythagoras who lived from 580 to 500 B.C.E. It shows diversity and unity. People who work with enneagrams view this structure as representing nine personalities that form our human development. Three are head-centered, three heart-centered and three belly or gut-centered.

Pythagoras had a following of disciples, including Aristotle, who later wrote down his teachings. Aristotle once had a vision of a lady who came to him and instructed what rituals to perform under various constellations. I suspect it was Sophia, but he may have given her another Greek name.

Pythagoras passed his insights on to the Desert Christians and the Sufis. George Gurdjieff, an Armenian-Greek spiritual teacher, was the first to make the enneagram widely known. He claimed the nine-pointed figure is more ancient than the Pythagorean pentagram. He called it the gateway between the seen and the unseen, a condensed map of the cosmos. What each of the numbers means and how they interact with each other can be learned from enneagram personality systems. Each of our chapters has a corresponding enneagram number and a brief explanation of what it might mean.

Nine also plays a role in how 6th century philosophers described angels. But what I didn't learn in my 1950s Lutheran confirmation classes — I guess angels weren't very important to my more literal Norwegian pastors — is that, according to Rudolf Steiner, these angelic groups aren't static. It may take a while, but they eventually transform into other higher beings. Even we humans are not destined to be humans forever. We aspire to become angels. Angels seek to become archangels and so on it goes. It's all part of what Rudolf Steiner calls the living "supersensible" cyclical world, a world we can know only if we stop depending on our usual senses.

Sometimes I mentally place angels onto our nine-pointed star. Forming one triangle are the angelic beings closest to God. They're the ones with six wings, four heads, and many eyes: the *Seraphim, Cherubim* and *Thrones.* I'm not sure what the Thrones do, but I have no doubt that one day we'll find out. Seraphim are spirits of love and they work in our ether body. That's the misty body that exists closest to our physical self. Sometimes we call it our aura. Hebrew scholars tell us the word *seraphim* means "those who kindle or make hot." *Cherubim* denotes an abundance of knowledge or an outpouring of wisdom. Sounds a lot like Sophia, and I have no doubt they assist her.

Next comes this trio: the *Dominions, Virtues* and *Powers.* In Greek, they're called *Exusiai, Dynamis* and *Kyriotes.* Dominions were around at the beginning of earth. Together, they assume interplanetary priestly duties of a very lofty nature, and since most of their work takes place after our death, it's understandable that we're not really sure what it is that they do.

And finally there are the *Principalities (Archai* in Greek), *Archangels* and *Angels.* Cherubs, those chubby little winged baby-like beings, as Renaissance painters imagined them, must fall under the "angel" category. Principalities are sometimes called "authorities." They are like folk-angels assigned to various geographical areas. If only Google-Earth had a program for zooming in on them, we'd know more. Some "angel experts" claim we usually have only three or four angels around us during ordinary times. But in times of great trouble, angelic clouds hover around us like a flock of butterflies. There must have been a huge cloud of them on 9/11. Frederick Buechner says, "Angels are powerful spirits whom God sends into the world to wish us well. Since we don't expect to see them, we don't."

While not exactly in the angel-realm, there are all the earth elemental beings hidden in rocks and stones. They're very clever and playful and are hitched to the angelic realms by cosmic strings. They can, at least according to Steiner, lead us right to the Seraphim, the Cherubim and Thrones. The beings that hang out around plants can lead us to the Virtues and Powers. When we see spiritual beings close to animals, they can lead us to the Principalities, Archangels and Angels.

Thousands of books have been written about angels and I confess I've read many of them. The main thing I've learned is that we better not limit them.

According to Rudolf Steiner, Angels, Archangels and the Principalities surround children and work on their souls and spirits. Angels work through the air, and Archangels are more effective through fluids — such as our lymph and circulatory systems. By the time we hit puberty around age fourteen, the second group of angels join in: the Dominions, Virtues and Powers. Then, at about age thirty-five, the Seraphim, Cherubim and Thrones move in and they pretty much stick with us our whole lives.

Enneagram Number I

Enneagram personality type models, like Myers Briggs and others, help us figure out which type or number we "are." At one time, I determined I might be a "nine," but now I believe I'm all of them. Just as you are. Some archetypes may be closer to the surface than others, but just as we learn to integrate all the astrological signs, we also hold all the enneagram numbers inside us.

Number Ones are "Reformers." They have a sense of a "higher good." Ones hold a sense of duty, responsibility and a sense of justice and fairness. They are idealistic and often in self-denial. They tend to procrastinate and usually have trouble receiving. They feel they earn love by being perfect. This can cause all sorts of problems, including being angry and critical. Ones like to feel in control, but may have boundary issues. Anger is a familiar emotion; integrity, a key value. Ones tend to address reality through symbols. They lovingly respond to others' needs, but it's sometimes hard to give up their psychic or physical space. They tend to forget the past and often seem more able to envision the future because, for Ones, the present can be blurred and unclear.

SOPHIA'S MYSTICAL DANCER:
St. Augustine, Bishop of Hippo (354-430)

Aurelius Augustinus Hipponensis lived in the Roman province of what is now Algeria. Strongly influenced by his Christian mother, Monica, he studied at Carthage, in Rome, and later in Milan where he became steeped in rhetoric and philosophy: Philos-*Sophia*. He once prayed, "Grant me chastity, but not yet." He had many mistresses but loved one woman all his life and together they had a son, Adeodatus. He later called her "The One."

As a young man, he heard a playful voice saying: "Take up and read," and so he picked up an autobiography of St. Anthony of the Desert which led to a profound conversion experience. By that time, many writings had already been destroyed by various bishops. For instance, Aurelius was four years old when most of Sappho's work was burned, but St. Anthony's work remained. He read it and was convinced he, too, needed to write. Eventually he wrote 350 sermons along with *Confessions* and *Of the City of God*, which represent only a fraction of his hundred or so books. He wrote at length about Sophia and her wisdom, *Sapientia*. Wisdom is the highest of the seven life stages, he said. He defined the godly threesome this way: "The Knower (the Father); The Known (the Son) and the Bliss of Knowing (the Holy Spirit).

It's obvious Sophia loved him in spite of his teachings of original sin and "just wars," as well as for all the harm he and the later church fathers caused women. Women were, he preached, simply soil for man's seed. He justified killing your enemies to ward off evil. As a result, he turned this new Jesus-religion into one that *men* could accept. Furthermore, he influenced one religion yet to come: Islam. Muhammad's Allah is built on Augustine's teachings of Yahweh, as a god who loses his temper, bears grudges and inflicts violent punishment. Muhammad, like Constantine, brought religion at the tip of a sword.

Augustine thought there were two Sophias, two wisdoms: one uncreated and one created. He called the uncreated one the Logos and associates her with Christ, but calls her Our Mother from Above, God's Logos, God's City and dwelling in heaven, our Heavenly Jerusalem. The Lord's Prayer in Aramaic begins: *Abwoon d'bwashmaya*: "O Birther! Father-Mother of the Cosmos." The other Sophia was the "Created Sophia." He describes her as having a rational and intellectual mind and relates her to both this world and the world to come. She is Eternal, Unchangeable, Unchanging. She is both illuminating light and the illuminated. He taught that time exists only in our minds; she is eternal because there is no time before her. She exists outside time.

As the designated Church Father, Augustine fought many theological battles. The Celt, Pelagius, for example, taught that God was in nature and in all people. Augustine got him banished and excommunicated. Augustine insured that there would be many future arguments about Sophia's role as Logos and what part she plays in the Trinity.

Chartres Cathedral, Chartres, France

SOPHIA'S SPECIAL GEO-SPOT: CHARTRES

"Viewed geomantically, the cathedral stands on a power point.... The whole countryside is nourished by the pure and subtle lie-powers which distribute themselves over the surrounding area from this spot.... The physical cathedral ... represents the power of earth growing towards the spiritual dimension of the Whole. Through the architectural magic of Gothic forms which conjure the impression of weight-less space, the world of earth is lifted towards the world of light."
~ *Marko Pogacnik,* Christ Power and the Earth Goddess

Once the area around Chartres Cathedral was dense, dark forest. Then, as the old story goes, a magnificent magical white horse galloped through the valley, swishing her long tail, clearing most of the trees. The valley was called *La Beauce*: the female face of God.

Seven deep streams criss-cross through granite near a well that goes down perhaps thirty-three meters. A standing "Mother" stone marked this exact spot when the Druids built a university here. They called themselves *Guardians of the Stone at Carnute-Is. Chartres.*

The Romans recognized the strong power this place held. Marching all turtle-shielded across Gaul, they burned the Druids' sacred oaks but left the pearwood statue they found at the well, adding this inscription to the bottom of the statue: "*Virgin Pariturae*, the Virgin who is to give birth to a child." In their *future*.

Later, Romans threw Christians into the well that provided water for the city whenever it was under siege. Vikings came in 858 C.E. and threw the ashes of their victims into it. Then about fifty years later, Rollo, a Viking Jarl, came to Chartres, but before he could kill anyone, he saw Our Lady's tunic flying over the city. He was converted, married the princess Gisele, and having found a good thing, settled down.

Over the years, some of the people who drank from her well were miraculously healed and the area around it became a hospital. Once, a choir boy fell in and was saved. Fulbert, the bishop who built the first cathedral atop this ancient well, was cured of Saint Anthony's Fire (ergotism) by its waters. Around 1655, the "pagan" well was covered, only to be excavated in the early 1900s.

Christians built five churches on this sacred spot. Fires destroyed all but the last. The one we see today still holds remnants of earlier Romanesque walls, as well as some windows and statues that survived the horrific 1194 fire. The fire nearly destroyed either her tunic or her veil. This undyed cloth has been carbon-dated to the first century. People say it once wrapped Jesus and has protected this building during subsequent wars. French queens kept it near them during the births of their babies and now it's locked in a casket of cedar wood covered with gold and gemstones.

Chartres is the first church in France to be dedicated to Mary. One hundred and eighty-six stained windows grace the walls, some with rare sapphire and lapis-lazuli alchemical blue glass, held by iron lacework. Twenty of them portray Our Lady. The one on the north wall called *Notre Dame de la Belle-Verriére* — The Blue Virgin — positions her against a ruby background surrounded by angels. The bird above her head is Sophia's dove. When her hymn "O Gloriosa" is sung, it's as if all the vowels float up to rest at her feet. Once she spoke to Marco Pogacnik, a man from Slovenia who runs the Hagia Chora School for Geomancy in Germany. He was standing by the old altar under this "blue" window, according to his account in *Christ Power and the Earth Goddess*, when Sophia told him: "The cathedral is so constructed that it enables the Second Coming of Christ to occur at every moment — not as a future event, but now and always, when the principle of the eternal Soul joins with the principle of the eternal Earth."

The window nearest the labyrinth tells the story of Mary Magdalene in twenty-two panels. Like all the windows, this one called "the grail window" can be read from the bottom up in five ways: the actual story; the artful beauty; the symbolism; the iconography and teachings about Christ, Mary and other biblical figures; and finally, the windows can be a path to a deep spiritual initiation and experience of the Divine.

Nine master builders directed the rebuilding of Chartres after the fire. Over those thirty or so years, each made his own imprint, yet the unity of this magnificent cathedral is exquisite. Nine teams worked on the construction, many entailing up to 300 people all creating this stunning building in perfect proportion and scale.

Architects planned that the Chartres cathedral would have nine towers. Only two were finished. From the shorter Lunar Tower, Our Lady rests her feet on the moon; from the other, the Sun Tower, rays of light create her dress. The archangel Michael's golden wings follow the direction of the sun from his perch on its copper clock. Bernard of Chartres was only one of many famous teachers who influenced scholars with Sophia's seven-fold wisdom: grammar, rhetoric, logic, arithmetic, geometry, music and astronomy. He once said, "We are like dwarves seated on the shoulders of giants. If we see more and further than they it is not due to our own clear eyes or tall bodies, but their bigness."

Everything about this building is symbolic. Cathedral stones, for example, were set in mortar of lime (symbolic of fervent love), sand (earthly toil) and water (the Spirit who unites the first two.) People can enter through nine doorways. Nine bays are held by nine arches. Blue-black marble edges the labyrinth people walk, turning at the double axes or the labyrs or crescent moon shapes, in order to reach the center.

Stone figures stand and perch everywhere — 1840 figures outside with over 2000 more inside. The last flying buttress was erected in 1222, only twenty-eight years after the big fire. This building feat is simply amazing given the fact that twenty other major cathedrals were built in France around the same time.

Chartres can be read like a book — a limestone and granite book layered with rich Sophia-meanings.

Sophia invites us to be co-creators with her. In the few written accounts we have of her teachings, we realize that she doesn't shy away from her own gifts. She claims them and proclaims them. And she encourages us to do the same. *Use your talents and your gifts without binding them up in your egos, for they belong to all.*

Every creative act is cushioned by faith: faith in your ability to pull it off; faith in those around you to be compassionate and accepting; and faith that in the universe, the muses, and the divine source will uphold you long enough to accomplish what you set out to do. Faith that if you enrich and support your environment, it will enrich and support you. Faith that your friends will stand by you, and those who are not your friends won't harm you.

All beginnings hold immense promise even if they are filled with fear and pain. Every birth is bloody and usually something gets pulled and ripped before the new life bursts into being. Each of us is a midwife to our own birthing/creative process. A Vermont midwife once told me that midwives honor the spirit of the birth. In other words, they let the baby decide when it is ready to meet the light. We approach each creative act wearing our midwife aprons, honoring the spirit of its birth. And, like anyone giving birth, we must be prepared for all that birthing brings.

FROM SOPHIA'S NOTEBOOK

Joyful — full of joy. To be full of something, the vessel must first empty itself.

Empty yourself of yourself. I will paint you onto my canvas; you will shimmer and hold. You will rejoice in the dazzle of your colors in galleries to come. I will place you in my potpourri of petals to fragrance the stars. Your spiciness lingers on meteor breath. Your dusty aroma dances to Pleiades' beat and brushes Sirius' hair.

We stand by you, always. Your passion will lead you. Begin and it will come.

chapter two

SHE ENERGIZES US

Crop Circle: Stantonbury Hill, Somerset, July 7, 2007

. . . .

*"In the cells and in the soul of every woman this ancient knowing is
waiting to be awakened, so that once again the sacred feminine can
make her contribution, can help the world come alive with love and joy."*

~ Llewellyn Vaughan-Lee, *The Return of the
Feminine and the World Soul*

MOUNTAIN JOURNAL ENTRY

I try to remember New England back at its beginnings. Everything
is awash in glaciers and runoffs. Humpback whales cavort in the
waves. Seals and other wrinkled sea creatures I cannot clearly identify swim next to oversized salmon and trout.

Then, perhaps a mere million years ago.... The earth heaves and
rises in places, pushed by glaciers and bent ice. Four times the ice creeps
south, slowly, slowly. In my mind, I see land masses along the Atlantic
coast rising and falling as if inhaling and exhaling. Popplestones pile
up. Cubes of granite tossed like forgotten giant children's blocks litter
Maine's coastline. Musk ox run with the moose. *Then* and *Now* fold
together like the neat table napkin resting by my breakfast plate. I
shake out the folds and catch a glimpse of Lake Champlain — 700
feet higher than it is now. My toes tingle from standing in glacial water.
Next, I see bogs and marshes come alive, spewing forth life. Kettles
and basins. Places appear such as Lake Winnipesaukee — Algonquian
for "a pouring-out place where the fish live."

I leave these icy patterns of the past and glance around my present. I see patterns all around me. Laced. Entwined. Like rhythms, measures of music that match my heartbeat — my beating pattern — over years. Patterns pull and are predictable — to a degree. But then they can surprise me with a fugue-twist.

Patterns can be bold — written larger than only one segment of it would be by itself. They pull me into new ways of seeing. And hearing. When patterns are totally unpredictable I get scared. I tap my fingernails and wiggle my feet. Some patterns energize me, but not the ones that repeat — endlessly. So I guess the trick is to keep the patterns alive so they don't take on boring, dead edges. So the pieces don't fall off and get lost. Lines keep intersecting, but at more interesting places.

Patterns twist, and therefore can bend my thoughts and emotions as well. I see predictable patterns and I begin to believe that's really the way things are. But Sophia lies below the patterns. That's why people fear her chaos. But she holds larger patterns than we can know. Winking. Grinning. She's the coyote, the trickster, the Loki, the Hermes, the part of the bigger pattern that says, *Watch out! It may not really be like this. It may be totally unlike this. So let your senses wake up to all the possibilities. Come alive enough to sense some of my subtle pattern-shifts.* Patterns can morph before my very eyes. In a twinkling, as the Bible says. What then?

I write:

> A strange attractor, unaccountable factor
> flies into what only yesterday was a system
> surely defined.
> Loose canon. Different drum. Thrum. Thrum.
> Parchment wings fan hexagonal cells but
> still honey leaks. Strange attractors wait
> beyond the hive to upset time and rhyme.
> We're on our way to a new alignment.

HEARTBEAT QUESTIONS

What's putting me to sleep — and keeping me drowsy?

What energizes me? How do I sense energy?

How have I used my intuition today?

Can I see a pattern emerging around my spiritual life?

How does boredom, or even acedia, appear in my life?

What's the most courageous thing I've ever done?

CAN YOU HEAR ME NOW?

We often end the reading of our biblical lessons in our little Episcopal church with these words: "Hear what the Spirit is saying to God's People." I tell myself, "Wake up, Karen, and listen to what Sophia is saying!"

But hearing voices in our heads is tricky business. Sometimes the voices tell you things it's best you didn't follow. "The dark voices" pretend to be "the light voices." "Jesus" may encourage you to go to war or beat your wife and kids into submission, for instance. Voices have to be tested to determine their end-results. Take my husband's cousin, the one whose voices told her to throw herself under a train. She lived, but she lost part of her leg.

Aren't people who hear voices apt to have a brain tumor, Parkinson's, epilepsy, Alzheimer's, migraines, hyperthyroidism, schizophrenia? Or a drug or drinking problem? Not necessarily. Have you checked out the Bible lately? Lots of chit-chat with God going on there. Surely they weren't all old, crazy or drunk.

It's a fact that auditory hallucinations do increase among the elderly, but I figure that's just because they're closer to actually being with the spirits or other-dimensional beings interested in talking to them. I love the story of the ninety-five year old woman who decided to start learning Aramaic. That's a challenging language to learn at any age. When asked why she was doing this, she replied, "So I can talk to Jesus in his own language."

Language doesn't seem to be a barrier when it comes to hearing Sophia. When Socrates heard a wise woman's voice, he considered it a spiritual gift and was glad to have the intelligent company. Hildegard of Bingen writes many times: "I heard a voice saying...." And her voice usually told her "Write this." Joan of Arc heard St. Margaret and the Archangel Michael, along with a whole angelic council speaking to her.

"Wiser" folk throughout history have said, "Don't listen to unverifiable voices!" They usually killed people who did, as was the case for poor Mary Dyer, a Quaker who was hanged in the Boston Commons in 1660 by the very people who fled England because of religious intolerance. I visit her statue every time I'm near the statehouse and imagine that her mentor, Anne Hutchinson, would have been strung up, too, had the Indians not gotten to her first. Anne and Mary believed, as I do, that Sophia, the Holy Spirit, lives within each of us. The three of us believe inner light is more important than church hierarchies. Will I also be put to death? Will I have a statue? Will it matter?

When Theodosius, around 385 C.E., forbad the Delphic oracles to speak, one of the last priestesses said, "The voice of the water has faded away."

Teresa of Avila called the voices she heard "speech without sound." She began to hear inner voices and see visions and have what she called "revelations" right after her father died around 1555. Then, in 1558, she had her first "rapture" and heard Christ. She began writing *The Interior Castle* in 1577, and completed it in six months.

Every writer hopes for that sort of help, a "take over" when we sit, staring at the keyboard and no words come. Writing would be so much easier if a muse perched on our shoulder and literally told us what to write. Alas, most of us have to write on our own, but are we so sure what "on our own" means? I've come to the conclusion it doesn't matter where the words come from, or how they come. They're coming through me, so I can call them mine. Her voice, my intuitive voice — what's the difference? We're all one.

Sometimes in a very relaxed state, I sit at my computer and I shut my eyes, holding a particular question and then I write whatever comes. I don't stop to correct typos or edit — I just write. I'm in the zone. Her zone. I don't hear literal voices as much as *ideas of words* that I then put onto the screen. This goes on until I get too tired to hit the keys any longer — about fifteen or twenty minutes. Typing-mediumship is draining!

In my more playful moments, I call it my "Sophia-Writing." Some insights may be worth sharing with you — most, not. It's like what Julia Cameron describes in her writing books as opening the spigot and letting the faucet drain-drip until words worthy of your efforts begin to arrive. I'm smiling as the movie *Four Weddings and a Funeral* comes to mind. Do you remember when Rowan Atkinson ("Mr. Bean"), who plays the loopy priest, pronounces the bride and groom to be now married "in the name of the Father and the Son and the Holy Spigot"? Sophia *loves* that kind of word play. Imagine what gushes forth from the Holy Spigot! She is the water that flows over Niagara Falls to the tune of 600,000 gallons a second and she is the drip drip drip from the garden hose.

One morning I was wondering about how ideas come about, so I wrote this with closed eyes:

"You've been taught that thought creates reality for some time now. But when are you going to really 'get' that that's true? Thought creates. A lot of thought creates a lot. Stingy thoughts create stingy results. Abundant thoughts flow like waterfalls, leading to streams with rippling and far-reaching effects. You're here. Right now. That's all that really matters. Make the most of it."

As you can see, she brings me up short at times. Some people (perhaps more men than women) fear her dark energy. Psychologists might say that's because they fear the "Great Mother" — she's like the dragon mother — the deep, deep powers of the unconscious. Hers is a primal place — like the dark, moist recesses of the jungle. Take another look at this book's marvelous and complex cover image by Pablo Amaringo, who painted the visionary scenes he experienced as a result of drinking the ayahuasca-Mother Plant for a number of years. He died in 2009, but his vibrant energy still permeates his work. In this particular piece, the Mother figure surrounded by jaguars (the ones who see things as they are) dreams creation. She sends her electric energy into all corners of her domain as she calmly holds it and continues to birth ongoing possibilities. Everything is blessed by her rainbow of love. A copy of the original painting appears in Don José Campos' *The Shaman Ayahuasca: Journeys to Sacred Realms*. For 70,000 years, this plant teacher has offered physical, psychological and emotional healing.

When someone has not had a loving mother, it's harder for that person to identify with Sophia and with the world. Deborah Tannen said the parent of a child has the power not only to create the world the child lives in, but the ability to dictate how that world is to be interpreted. Some people have the misfortune of having a mother whose behavior is not only frightening and chaotic, but dreadfully harmful. We may never be able to forgive parents who have deeply scarred us, but we can rest assured that those scars have made us stronger and Sophia offers that gentle soothing hand we so longed for. Many myths grow up around our own mothers and around the Great Mother. Our task is to see with jaguar eyes and sort out what's real — for us. Sometimes the "voice" I get at my computer helps me. *"Just be open. Don't come with any pre-conceived ideas, but rather let your body 'hear' what it needs to hear."*

I ask Sophia: "How may I serve you?" She answers: *"You already are ... by being every minute 'me' in the world. See with new eyes; hear with new ears; walk with new feet and let your hands be my hands.... Nothing is accidental. It's not exactly planned out, but the possibilities are always ripe and yours for the taking. Like picking apples — red, ripe apples. They just fall off into your waiting hands, but you have to be near the tree."*

Linda Trichter Metalf and Tobin Simon call this process of tapping into the unconscious a "Proprioceptive Method for Finding Your Authentic Voice." I have followed their suggestions in *Writing the Mind Alive*. They recommend that you come up with your own repetitive comfortable ritual. Candle. Music. And then just write what you hear for about twenty minutes. Really listen to what you write and then ask the *Proprioceptive Questions*: What did you think, but did not write down? How do you feel? What larger story is what you wrote part of? And, the seed-thought for future writing is: What other ideas surfaced that you didn't write down? Date it and put it in a folder. When I re-read these pages I'm usually amazed at what came out of my spigot. I'm guessing you'll be amazed at what will come out of yours as well. Some of these spigot-drops appear at the end of chapters in "From Sophia's Notebook."

Gregg Braden, in *The Divine Matrix: Bridging Time, Space, Miracles and Belief*, says the simplest way of beginning to understand our Divine Matrix-Sophia is to think of her as three basic things:

1. The container for the universe to exist within. In other words, she's the Big Cauldron. The Cornucopia. The Womb. The Well;

2. The bridge between our inner and outer worlds. We can think of her as being in nature and in us at the same time; and

3. She's the mirror that reflects our everyday thoughts, feelings, emotions and beliefs. She's everywhere at once. And her energy-field is available to everyone.

I was first introduced to "the field" by Lynne McTaggart in her book, appropriately enough called *The Field*. She said, "There is no 'me' and 'not-me' to our bodies in relation to the universe, but one underlying field." This field of consciousness is a little like unset Jello. It's our attention that sets it up. By focusing on it, I can make it cherry red or lime green. Maybe even lemon yellow.

Author's Copper Goddess, after a 4,000 B.C.E. terra-cotta female figure combined with typical chevrons and zig-zags similar to those found in Albania c. 5,000 B.C.E.

Physicists call it "quantum entanglement." Einstein called these quantum effects "spooky action at a distance." Spooky, I guess, because one action affects another. And another. And you can't predict where this is all going. McTaggart thinks old paradigms such as "the world is a machine" and "things are separate" should have been put to rest long ago. We are, however, as she so eloquently put it, reluctant apostles. But maybe we are now — finally — "getting" what Edgar Mitchell realized as he looked through the window of Apollo 14: *We are one.* He felt an "ecstasy of unity" similar to what most mystics experience. McTaggart notes: "Edgar Mitchell's lightning-bolt experience left hairline cracks in a great number of his belief systems." We are no longer mired in a 400-year-old world-view. We're really beings of light and energy. We've gotten, as McTaggart puts it, "a telegram from Gaia."

ENERGY GRIDS

I've dowsed inside the big stone ring in Avebury in England and felt the tug over a spot where deep under the earth several lines crisscross. I hadn't planned to, and I certainly hadn't brought my own dowsing rods with me from home. But when the young man who drove the van on the day tour from Oxford pulled them out from under his front seat and said, "Anyone care to try these?" I wasn't shy. "Are we looking for ley lines?" I asked.

Ley lines come from an ancient English word that means "an old straight path." They can vary in length, from six miles up to thousands. He smiled and handed the rods to me. I'd read that these underground paths come together at Avebury. They're dubbed the Mary and the Michael lines: female/male energy that meanders across the British Isles like pulsing, undulating eels. The electromagnetic spectrum is stronger in some places than in others. And stronger in some people than in others, I thought as I walked around for a bit, not sure where my feet were taking me.

Suddenly the rods lurched together. I wasn't close to a standing stone. Or other people. I didn't see it at first, but then our van-driver came over to me and pointed to a little grass-covered marker. "There used to be an obelisk here to mark the spot. It's where they cross."

Joel and I decided to figure out where the center of our Vermont "Chartres" labyrinth should be by holding out our dowsing rods and walking across our meadow. I held one pair; our friend Laura the other. We stopped at exactly the same place when our rods twitched. Surely this had to be the center. Energy runs deep there, below the wildflowers and rock ledges. So, like the early Druid-inspired monastic companions who knew where to center cathedrals, Joel and I trusted the process and planted a stick. Then we tied a string to the stick and stretched it out to form the radius of our circle. Around we went. We limed the edges of our forty-two foot in diameter circle. It is now ringed with thyme.

If you've been to Sedona, Arizona, you may have marveled at all the strong energy vortices — places where polarized energy surfaces like mini-volcanoes. Sophia creates these ground-gripping grids, which can't be seen with our regular eyes, but are felt, like some cosmic super-glue that attaches the atoms of our own bodies onto, quite literally, all that exists. People tend to build special buildings on these pulsing, intersecting webs of energy. We visit them because it feels good to be there.

If we believe we are star-seeds and galaxy go-betweens, then everything that exists bonds us to our Divine Matrix's love-energy. All energy has already been created — it just gets moved around. Plants hold it and we eat the plants or eat the animals that eat the plants. We're not just place-holders, we're energy-holders. Maybe our primary task is to receive and send energy, but with static-free "radio" hearts that don't set up interferences.

You know how it feels to enter a room and sense the energy swirling there. Some people sap yours because they think you've got more than they do. They want yours because they think there's only a limited supply. Other rooms are filled with wonderful, life-sustaining energy and no darkness lurks in the corners. Energy there is on an even give-and-take balance beam.

My Sophia-friend Julia once felt powerful negative energy in an old prison in England. "I got terribly dizzy and suddenly felt like throwing up, so I got out. Fast!" My husband certainly knows what she means. He felt that kind of extreme negative energy when he visited Birkenwald (known as Auschwitz II) in the "Birch woods" of East Germany forty years after Himmler ended the Nazi extermination camps. Upwards to two million people had been sealed into gas chambers there, as German soldiers dropped Zyklon B pellets into the air vents. It took ten to twenty minutes to suffocate innocent men, women and children. The death-factory's wooden buildings are gone now but the brick guard houses and smoke stacks still remain along with the "Arbeit Macht Frei" sign on the gate. "I felt like someone punched me in the solar plexus," John said.

The more you practice sensing energy, the easier it becomes. When we moved into our Vermont house, we did a house blessing and walked around, feeling into the corners and "clearing" places that felt "bad." Or "sad." Often people entering our house for the first time, say, "Oh, this feels good." We're not feng shui professionals by any means, but we do recognize how energy sometimes gets hung up, and we know how to move it around.

There is an old Sufi story about a little stream that got mired in a sandbar. With a quivering, tense voice, the little stream wondered how it would ever get across this cumbersome sand. No matter how much the stream shivered and stressed and cried, it couldn't move. "Why can't I keep flowing?" Then it heard a voice, most likely Sophia's, saying, "You'll live longer if you give up your energy to the invisible wind, little stream. Let me help you change your form." Before the little stream knew it, it had given itself up to the wind and the wind transformed it into a cloud and then into rain. That's how it crossed the sandbar. She is breath, our wind, our oxygen. She moves us. Hers is the first, essential breath our baby lungs inhaled.

The Dalai Lama once said, "When you inhale, you breathe in all the sufferings of beings and dissolve them into yourself, and when you exhale, you breathe out your own happiness and

[send] happiness to others." So, we continue to breathe. On average, 23,000 times daily. The Hebrew word for breath, *ru'ah*, means both spirit and air, and, wonder of wonders, it's feminine. Who knew?

CHAKRAS: ENERGY POINTS

My energy was at a very low ebb during the first Gulf War as I watched us destroy sacred Iraqi sites. This was about the time Afghanistan Buddhist statues crumbled at the hands of the Taliban. *What makes some ancient artifacts last and others disappear?* our son Joel and I asked ourselves. We began collecting images and thinking about what they might be telling us. This evolved into *Hunab Ku: 77 Sacred Symbols for Balancing Body and Spirit.* The oldest image in the book is of an eighteen-inch-tall earth mother figure from Laussel in Dordogne, France. Conception takes place on the fourteenth day after a woman begins menstruating and this heavily breasted woman holds up a lunar crescent-bison horn with thirteen notches on it. Her limestone body has epitomized fertility since 20,000 B.C.E.

"Venus of Laussel," a limestone relief, c. 25,000 B.C.E., in Laussel, Dordogne, France

Hunab Ku, named after a yin-yang-like Mayan symbol for the One Divine, is organized by seven chakra colors beginning at our base with red, and ending at the tops of our heads — our crown chakra — in violet. This rainbow-map is one way of understanding the energy that constantly flows through us — unless, of course, like the little stream in the Sufi story, it's blocked. Various cultures give it different names: *prana, chi, qi, n/um.* Balancing this energy is something that can happen during meditation, by physical exercises, or with the help of experienced energy-workers. The chakra therapist and author, Anodea Judith, in her book, *Wheels of Life*, inspired us. She tells how the book came to her during a meditation when she didn't even know what the word *chakra* meant. It was birthed eleven years later. Chakras, she says, "are centers of activity for the reception, assimilation, and transmission of life energies."

Physicists tell us that atoms — regardless of where they appear — are about 99.9% empty space. But what they don't tell us is that She fills that empty space with her energy. Her powerful energy lights up our bodies in fields that surround us as auras of color. Like threads of fire, auras weave in and out filling us with healing, courage and new ways of seeing.

Doing the Heart Math

Right now your heart is pumping three to four ounces of blood sixty to ninety times a minute. It repeats this action a hundred thousand times a day — that's 40 million times a year without ever resting!

The Lakota Sioux says there are, in all things, an imagined heart. They call it *Wakan* — Holy. Black Elk said that the "eye of the heart sees everything ... if the heart is not pure, the Great Spirit cannot be seen." *Ah ba* means "heart-soul" in Hebrew. The Maya use this word for love: *Lak'ech*, which translated literally, means "I am another you. My heart is your heart."

In only six seconds after your father's sperm pierced your mother's ova, your heart — or the cells that will form your complete heart — started to beat. Our hearts know things it takes our heads much longer to comprehend. And, as the environmental activist, Joanna Macy, said: "The heart that breaks open can contain the whole universe."

Scientists can now measure electromagnetic fields. The field around the heart vibrates at a rate of about 5,000 times more powerfully than the field around our brain. And what's more, it radiates out from us to up to ten feet away.

Love is palpable. Doc Childre, the founder of Heartmath, discovered that the heart can transform stress, better regulate emotional responses, and harness the power of heart/brain communication. Heartmath now trains healthcare professionals and others to do just that.

Since the 19th century, we have come to understand that although energy can be transformed and moved around, it can't be created or destroyed. Energy just exists. Tibetan monks can wrap themselves in wet sheets and sit in the snow and their yogic energy creates heat — enough to keep them alive and to dry their sheets. They call it *tumo*. The !Kung people of the Kalahari bring *n/um* to the surface through dancing and trance.

VIBRATIONS AND ELECTRICITY

What is this universal energy current we call life? Anger and fear pump out a certain kind of "electricity" and we can feel it seeping over us from our television and computer screens and out through our radios, but it's not as strong as love-energy.

Dr. David Hawkins and I grew up in Wisconsin around the same time. He was a paper boy. One winter, on his route, he nearly froze to death. As a result of that experience, his fear of death was replaced by what he calls *Presence* — a silent state filled with peace. In his book, *Power vs. Force*, Hawkins explains that when you're in Presence, you know there is no loss, grief or desire, and nothing needs to be done because everything is already perfect and complete: "*The individual human mind is like a computer terminal connected to a giant database: human consciousness. The database is the realm of genius — the unlimited information contained in this database is available to everyone — anyone in a few seconds at any time in any place.*" This is the source of our true power. Hawkins treated about one thousand patients a year and came to the conclusion that most pain and suffering comes from our own egos — it springs from what we *think* we are. He describes the *Presence* as infinitely gentle, yet powerful. Once, when a person came to him, he asked, "What do you want me to do with her, God?" and the reply came: "Just love her." He came to the conclusion that every act we take to support life, supports *all* of life, including our own.

Our vibrational energy levels differ, he discovered, according to our various emotional attributes. He devised a fascinating way of measuring them. Fear, for instance, rates at 200, love at 500 and peace at 600. His research points to the possibility that even one person vibrating at a level of 700 (not many humans are at this level) can raise the consciousness of millions — sort of a tidal wave effect that can shift the awareness. Our military has conducted experiments around emotional stimulation and learned how to measure electrical changes in our DNA. They concluded that living cells communicate through energy that exists everywhere all the time. Sophia seems to be nodding her head. The Maya have a saying — roughly translated: I am you and you are me. What I do to you, I do to myself. Electricians might call it connectivity.

My husband and I visited Niagara Falls recently and we had time to walk around Goat Island — that bit of land that separates the two major falls. I paused at Nikola Tesla's tall bronze statue. He was an electrical wizard. The placement of his statue so near New York's largest electrical generating power stations struck me as very ironic because Tesla's dream was to transmit electricity through the ground and make it free and available to all. He erected a tower shaped like a letter "T" in Colorado Springs, Colorado, which he claimed could channel energy across the entire world-grid. But Thomas Edison changed all that and that's why you get an electric bill each month.

Tesla's idea came to him when he was walking with a friend. He was reciting a poem by Goethe. Suddenly he got a vision of a magnetic field rotating within another field all energized by alternating currents in varying phases. Not being an electrical engineer, I find all this extremely baffling. But not as baffling as the space-time experiments he also came up with. He warned that we shouldn't fool around with something we don't know how to control. Naturally the military longed to have sneaky, creepy weapons, so they enlisted him to conduct what is known as the USS Eldridge Philadelphia Experiment. It dealt with links between gravity and electromagnetism. I don't have the time, space, inclination or expertise to go into what all that was about, but it's fascinating, and Jules Verne would have been proud.

In 1919, twenty-four years before Tesla died, he said, "War cannot be avoided until the physical cause for its recurrence is removed." Besides free electricity for everyone, he had a global vision of everyone sharing resources. "What we now want is closer contact and better understanding between individuals and communities all over the earth, and the elimination of ego and pride which is always prone to plunge the world into primeval barbarism and strife. Peace can only come as a natural consequence of universal enlightenment." As a Serbian, he would have been saddened to have lived to see the wars and ethnic "cleansing" of the 1990s that affected his people — and all of us — so profoundly.

INTUITION: SEEING WITH "ALL OUR EYES"

Back when I was leading a Boston-based publishing group, I decided to host several half-day retreats for all the managers in the company. I called the event: "Unleashing Our Creativity." "But I'm not creative!" was the common response. "Well, we want you there, anyway," was my usual comeback. In the middle of the table, I had a brandy snifter containing jelly beans, which I had carefully counted out. As an opener, I asked them how many there were. Our more literal bean-counters began to count a square inch and multiply. One of my male colleagues who was most vociferous about *not* being creative immediately wrote down 120. The right answer. That launched a discussion of intuition, our immediate *knowing*, and how we use it in our work. We have to learn to trust it.

Laura, of our labyrinth dowsing fame, agreed to join us to talk about her work as a Boston sculptor and installation artist. "See with your peripheral vision," she said, with her arms outstretched, snapping her fingers way off to the side. "See with all your eyes."

We discovered that we are all in the process of process. We all learn by *doing* even when we don't know the outcome. Women can learn a lot from men about this. I'm like most women who want to read the manuals first in order to get it right; men and boys dive right in and learn by trying different things to see what works. They innately understand systems. It's a male-trait to want to breakdown everything to better understand it — even creativity. Just give us a list, men say, and we'll do it. Women better understand that many things, including creativity can't be programmed or controlled. Creativity isn't an end result. It's path-work, not "to the finish line" work.

My entire family once studied art with a woman named Loretta Grellner. She had been a faculty member of Chicago's Art Institute and was now a friend who lived just across the river. Sometimes I piled others' children into the car (or in a boat when our Mississippi River bridge closed for repairs), we climbed up Loretta's stairs, sipped her tea, and drew the same apples, the same geraniums, the same pot, again and again. "Work with familiar objects," she said. "It will make you see them as never before." We'd sometimes want to hold up our charcoal drawing and ask, "Is this good?" but we knew she'd say. "The work is what it is." Now and then she'd take a charcoaled dusty thumb and smudge something around on our paper and it would totally transform our drawing. It became "art" to us. When I look back on those playful drawing days, I think, "Loretta was Sophia. Sophia takes her smudged thumb to our life-canvases and then stands back and says, 'There. It is what it is.'"

During our half-day creativity sessions, my publishing colleagues and I asked ourselves what encourages creativity within our departments — from the warehouse to the board room. We came up with five ways to continue to "see."

1. We need a safe environment in which it's always OK to be vulnerable.
2. We must be able to ask any question and trust people's answers.
3. We honor diversity; people think and see differently, and that's all right.

4. We are enlivened by other people's energy.

5. We must have flexibility within reason.

While I didn't call her Sophia, nevertheless our conversation revolved around doing what my female colleagues recognized as "intuitive Mother work." We have opportunities to tap into her energy every time we pick up the phone, turn on the computer, pause at the coffee machine. Every time we talk to a client or vendor, every time we have lunch with a colleague or sit in a meeting, we can quietly breathe for a few seconds and try to "estimate the jelly beans." We ended our time together by encouraging each other to always try to see another point-of-view and draw wisdom from all our "eyes."

Creativity, we learned, isn't so much about devising something totally new, but turning up what's already there. Our left and right feet wore identical shoes until a black shoemaker looked down one day and said, "Look at this. Our feet aren't shaped the same way! I'll shape them to fit." Sophia is all about being curious. She loves to ask, "Why?"

To work more creatively, my colleagues and I decided we needed to reassess our resources. (We can't do this in a linear fashion, but must loop back to see what's spiraling in any given situation.) Above all, we decided, creativity means holding the expectation that something positive will happen.

I don't know who got more out of those sessions, the women or the men. Most women have always known that process is more important than the end result, so a great deal of what we talked about was second nature to them. Women have always valued relationships over spreadsheets. We can (usually) see bigger pictures, and we know how to use our diffuse awareness. We claim intuition as our birthright.

One of our authors is now very present in our Vermont Sophia Circle. In *Business and the Feminine Principle: The Untapped Resource*, Carol Frenier talks about our feminine wisdom and how it not only affirms life, but can quickly respond to the moment. Women are more accepting of life's cycles — from birth to death. As a result, we're more at ease with the "unknowing" and even the "dark."

A Sufi prayer I've repeated from time to time comes from the Qu'ran: "Lord, increase me in knowledge; Lord, increase me in bewilderment."

Corporations, like stock markets, don't like bewilderment. However, the feminine voice says, above all the computer noise and brokerage calls: If we learn to value feelings, honor our feminine depths and live with constructive doubt, we'll all be better off in the long run. Carol ends her brilliant, positive little book with this: "To tap into this energy, we have to know who we are, and that takes painstaking inner work. We also have to know who we are not, and that takes a willingness to value and collaborate with the 'other'.... I refuse to consider our difficulties with relationship as a natural and inevitable human shortcoming. That attitude seems to me to be a failure on our part to imagine what is possible."

IMAGINE WHAT'S POSSIBLE

He met me at the door with a sad expression on his face. "I can't find my wedding ring."

An intuitive flash prompted me to place my briefcase in my husband's hands, go down to the laundry, reach under the dryer. There it was. I came back smiling and said, "With this ring, I thee wed — again." Intuition can't be second-guessed and needs to be trusted and quickly acted upon. Intuition is only one of Sophia's inner tools that we all have. But like muscles, if we don't use them, they atrophy and disappear.

I link intuition and imagination with spirituality. Not everyone would, I realize, but I've learned from reading Rudolph Steiner that if we were to spend just ten minutes each day meditating, we'd strengthen both. We would be inspired to address our waking, active world in quite different ways. We can't program our insights, but we can make a quiet space for them to come in. A quiet place for spiritual truths to intuitively gather.

In her book, *God In All the Worlds*, Lucinda Vardey wrote: "Spiritual truth requires deep commitment to the divine in ourselves and others and can lead to transcended states of awareness, of consciousness that unites the mind, the heart and the soul. Spirituality is about being open to different realities of existence, about being guided by our intuition which is nothing less than the truth within us."

My mother was good at being open and helping people see what might be possible. I remember coming home from college once and finding a young woman whom I didn't know sitting at our kitchen table. I respected their privacy and made myself scarce, but I could still hear snatches of the conversation. The woman's husband, a stalwart in our church, was beating her. I heard that much. My mother wasn't a social worker or a psychologist — just a very good listener. Sometimes when someone else *knows*, you are made stronger. I hope the young woman escaped that horrible relationship. I hope she could imagine another life for herself.

Imagining what was possible in my little world of publishing led me to publish a variety of books on transforming business. I signed more women authors than any other publishing house during the 1990s, and, as far as I know, the first black business author, Barry Carter, who wrote *Infinite Wealth*, a book about abundance and scarcity. Women wrote on topics such as synchronicity, working from our core, relying on our inner knowledge, intuitive imagery, and our hidden intelligence: intuition. Sandra Weintraub, for instance, pointed to the Naskapi Indians of Labrador who are directed each day by their dreams. In her book, *The Hidden Intelligence: Innovation Through Intuition*, she described how they know where to hunt and when a winter storm is approaching. She talks about our "deep minds" and the creative leaps numerous companies have had: from Guttenberg combining a metal punch used for imprinting coins with a wine press to create moveable type, to the analyst who uses popular movies and sports attendance as stock market indicators. Sandra's convinced that seeing symbols and patterns and being able to interpret them sparks corporate creativity. That's what wisdom does, after all. It sees patterns.

Sophia walks us through old laws, through "established" facts, and then shows us possible patterns embedded in deep time — not on glossy surfaces. In *The Guttenberg Elegies*, Sven Birkerts says, "The old growth forest of philosophy has been logged and the owl of Minerva has fled. Wisdom can only survive in a cultural ideal where there is a possibility of vertical consciousness. Wisdom has nothing to do with the gathering or organization of facts ... to see through data, one must have something to see through to." By *vertical*, of course, Birkerts doesn't merely mean the opposite of *horizontal*....

"Do you celebrate Christmas?" I heard a colleague ask another. "No, we do a clumsy Hanukah." His family, it seems, are not "vertical" Jews. I admit, I'm a skimmer of many surfaces. I have knowledge about a half inch deep in many, many areas — Jewish theology being one of them — I wouldn't even be able to organize a clumsy festival.

Sophia encourages us to be deep sea divers, not floaters. Birkerts says, "Immersed in a ballet performance, planted in front of a painting, we shatter the horizontal plane. Not without some expense of energy, however.... We cannot be put off by fatigue or any incentive-withering sense of obligation."

Birkerts sounds like an borderline introvert-extrovert (like me) as he gives some thoughts about our soul-growth. "Soul waxes in private, wanes in public. We feel it, or feel through it, when we are in sacred spaces, when we love, when we respond to natural or artistic beauty.... Except in situations we deem communal when we have communion with other souls, soul is private."

Hundreds of Facebook friends or busy crowds won't "save" us. Nor will technology. Joseph Campbell said: "Our computers, our tools, our machines are not enough. We have to rely on our intuition, our true being."

Determination to explain more about "true being" prompted another of my authors, Michael Munn, to bring forth practical exercises for accessing these new dimensions in *Beyond Business as Usual*. Some are quite shamanic. Much of his inspiration came from dreamwork and the Q'ero people, Peruvian descendants of the Incas. They say we are at a crucial time in our world's history. The world is on the brink of extinction. They call it *pachakuti*, "the turning over of the world." By hiding in high mountain valleys, they escaped the Spaniards' killing machines and continued to practice their ancient traditions. Michael was one of the people "charged" by them to bring a message to the northern people. Others include Lynne and Bill Twist with their all-volunteer Pachamama movement, and Pablo Amaringo who has received visionary teachings several generations down from the ancient Incans.

The Q'ero use no money; they farm and raise llamas. They walk a lot. It takes them two whole days to even reach Cuzco. Because these messages are so important, I know Michael well enough to know he would want me to pass them along. He calls the section in the book where these words appear, "The Crack in the World."

The Q'ero believe we're lost in a world of logic and materiality, a soulless world. For them, everything is alive. Spirit is everywhere. They speak to the mountains, rivers, clouds and stars. They hear nature speaking. They want to help us regain our senses, to hear and see.

The Q'ero say that the north's eagle and the south's condor fly together in the pachakuti. The condor is the Q'ero's teaching, a re-perception of reality. The eagle represents Northerners, like myself, who carry the message. Their holiest mountain, Ausangate, spoke to them. Its message was, "Go north. Share your ways." They say, "When the mountain asks, you have to go." They did not want to leave their mountains, but they cared about us. They came to San Francisco, Chicago, New York, and other places. . . .

The Qu'ero see all things, rivers, clouds, mountains, people, as physical or material. They also see an egg of luminous fibers around people. They see dark spots in our fibers. We are unaware of these because we are lost in materiality and logic. They use ceremonies to connect us to luminous fibers, along which knowledge travels. They cleanse the dark spots. By traveling these inner dimensions, we survive the pachakuti to create a golden age as a new species, Homo Luminous.

Michael says the Q'ero people believe most of us are asleep. They want us to wake up.

I spent one spring Saturday with the Pachamama Alliance people at the Green Mountain Monastery near Greensboro, Vermont. *Pachamama* means Our Mother — not just of the earth, but of the entire universe. During a break, I walked through the woods, past enormous Vermont boulders to Thomas Berry's grave. It had been raining earlier so my feet, cushioned by the moss and wet leaves, made not a sound. I could hear a faint wind chime as the path opened out to a field. A mowed path led me over to a newly planted tree holding the little music-maker that called me. Next to a huge rock I saw a recent grave and a framed picture of a white-haired grandfatherly man. I spent a few quiet moments with this theologian whom ecologists, and many of us, revere.

In an essay called "The Viable Human," he once wrote: "To be viable, the human community must move from its present anthropocentric norm to a geocentric norm of reality and value ... the universe reflects on and celebrates itself in conscious self-awareness, and finds a unique fulfillment."

Can we, together, imagine a different outcome for our planet? We've changed the game many times in the past — we can do it again. (Remember when we thought people were property and women couldn't vote? Remember the Berlin wall?) But we need to take off our dark glasses and come to grips with what's happening to *Pachamama*. And we need to do it quickly. Imagine what we *could* do together.

Enneagram Number 2

Number Twos are helpers; they are warm and really do care. They have lots of energy, they revel in the social aspects of life and are generous and protective. At times, they're prone to flattery, enjoy recognition, and like everyone, they really want to be loved unconditionally. They often use their helpful nature to ensure love. They value integrity in themselves and in others. Anger is a familiar emotion because they can feel resentment about being taken advantage of.

I'M BORED!

Do you remember that Charlie Brown sequence when Lucy says, "Somebody's boring me." And in the next frame she says, "I think it's me." John Ciardi says: "Boredom is what happens when we lose contact with the universe." It's the opposite of desire and the antithesis of verve. And we do it to ourselves.

Children are easily bored if they spend a lot of time watching screens. Rather than real active living, they turn into passive observers. The storyline of the game or movie can't be changed, so why should they imagine anything? Everything has already been decided by the animator or filmmaker. To stave off boredom, parents are asked to come up with newer, more expensive, more complicated, and supposedly more engaging games. No matter how interactive these toys might be, children are still not creating their own games. Watching or pressing buttons does not invent sacred play spaces. I am saddened to realize that, on average, six-month-old American children already watch television several hours a day. At age two, nearly 30% of our children have their own TV sets in their bedrooms. Some more underprivileged children spend, on average, 30 hours a week in front of the baby-sitter tube. Entropy and boredom become their playmates. Entropy is the opposite of complexity — the opposite of exhilaration. It's when order dissolves into randomness. And anger. It's the feeling you get when you slip into a trance. Your body tightens up; you're arthritic; *you don't want to move.* After watching television for even just a couple of hours, I know how my own body feels. Lethargic. Tranced. I just click the remote without really thinking. No wonder it's called the plug-in-drug. Our lives can easily dissolve into entropy.

Entropy was discovered by Ludwig Boltzmann, a physicist in turn-of-the-century Vienna. He figured out how to measure disorder in physical systems. It's the opposite of creativity; the opposite of Sophia. Where orderly natural patterns form (think snowflakes), entropy decreases. A thing degrades unless positive loving energy is lavished on it at vulnerable moments — such as what my mother was providing the young abused woman slouched at her kitchen table.

Physicists tell us that disintegration is the law of the universe. That's why things fall into black holes. But entropy isn't the only law operating out there and in here. Creation and growth are every bit as present. They put disintegration, decay and death into balance. Sophia reminds us to embrace it all.

ACEDIA

That's a strange vowel-filled word, *acedia*. The more I read about early monks, the more I learn about this emotional ailment they called the "Noonday Demon." At noon, especially if it's hot, my energy is sapped. My brain stalls and I'm apt to fall into a "Whatever! Who cares?" attitude. Why make the bed when you will just mess it up again anyway? Why clean up the dishes? Why put on clean clothes or take a shower? Acedia makes you feel as if you'd had it with life. You move from laziness to sluggishness to neglect. It's not exactly sloth since that's more related to one's spiritual emptiness, but very similar. It's related in some ways to depression in that it's when you feel absolutely nothing is pleasurable. The opposite of depression isn't happiness. It's vitality and energy.

In *Acedia & Me*, Kathleen Norris calls it a paralysis of the soul. John of the Cross called it a spiritual dryness. Chaucer described it in, "The Parson's Tale," as a dull coldness that freezes the heart.

The early 20th century German philosopher (philo-sophia — lover of Sophia), Rudolph Steiner, said that if you grow up without fairy tales, it will later lead to boredom, to world-weariness. He believed fairy tales even have the capacity to prevent illness. Perhaps that's the appeal of animated films. They satisfy our soul-hunger. Something deep within us desires to turn straw into gold, to slip our foot into a glass slipper, to escape from a prison tower or a glass coffin. Our common folk memories seep up through the mundane and help us recognize who we once were — and who we might be again.

ONCE UPON A TIME:
Snow White

In the middle of winter, when snowflakes fell like feathers, my mother sat sewing by the window. She pricked her finger and three drops fell onto the snow. She prayed, "If only I had a child as white as snow, as red as blood and as black as the wood in this window frame."

She died the day I was born, but not before she named me, her tiny black-haired girl-baby, Snow White. The kingdom mourned the loss of their queen. I lost a mother.

When my father decided to remarry, I tried to like my step-mother. She was beautiful, but she spent hours before her magic mirror asking, "Mirror, mirror on the wall. Who in this realm is fairest of all?" The mirror always agreed that it was her, until one day it added, "...but Snow White is a thousand times more fair."

This news upset her so much she turned yellow and green with envy and paid a hunter to take me into the woods to kill me. "Bring back her lungs and liver as proof you've done it!" Luckily for me, he couldn't kill me. He killed a boar, instead, for its innards. "The queen will never know the difference. Now go!"

I wandered in the woods for days. Finally, I spotted a little cottage. The door was unlocked, so I went in. Everything was tiny and neat — with seven of everything. I was so hungry, but I only tasted some vegetables and bread from each of the tiny plates, and drank a drop of wine from each of the goblets. I was exhausted, but six of the beds were too short. Stretching out on the seventh, I said my prayers and went to sleep. Then ... many voices! "Who's this in our house?" When I opened my eyes, seven little men dressed like miners stood around the bed. "We don't know who you are, but if you'd like to stay here, you can. But you'll have to help us keep the place neat and clean and — do you cook?" Of course!

Things went on quite happily until the dwarves got wind of the queen's mirror message that I was still living. "Don't let anyone in!" they cautioned me as they left to work in the mines.

One day an old peddler woman came to the door. I asked her what she was selling. "Laces to make you small and beautiful." Laces! I let her into the parlor. She laced me up so I could barely breathe. The dwarves found me lying there on the floor and revived me. "Don't let anyone in!" they cautioned me.

Another day I heard a peddler. Combs for my hair! I reached for one and couldn't wait to use it. I woke up when the dwarves removed my step-mother's poisoned comb still tangled in my hair. "We said, don't let anyone in!"

When a wizened old hag appeared selling apples, I thought: Now, I'm no fool. "Old woman," I told her, "I'm not going to eat any-thing you wouldn't eat yourself." So the old woman cut an apple in two — one part red, one part white. "You eat the red part, I'll eat the white," she croaked. I only remember my head hitting the floor. My little friends tried to revive me, but couldn't. Nor were they will-ing to bury me in the ground. Instead, they built a glass coffin, wrote my name in gold letters, and put me at the top of a mountain. One dwarf always stood watch by my side, along with an owl, a raven and a dove.

I don't know how much time passed, but one day a prince came riding along, saw me under the glass, and offered to buy me. The dwarves told him I was not for sale. But he was smitten, so he asked the dwarves if he could have me as a gift. They agreed. His servants stumbled as they carried me down the mountain and the jostling dislodged the poisoned apple from my throat!

I lifted the lid and sat up. He kissed me completely awake. My prince asked me to marry him and I said "Yes!" A cooing dove accompanied us down the rest of the mountain. When my beloved heard my story, he said, "Let's invite your step-mother to our wedding. Let's make her wear red-hot iron slippers. Let's force her to dance until she dies."

A "CHARMING" STORY?

The villain of the story got what was coming to her, the dwarves lost their housekeeper, and Snow White woke up after a deadly sleep and married Prince Charming. But is this just some little tale decrying vanity? Or a morality story warning against clever manipulation? Is that all there is to the story? Might the red, white and black be a hidden symbol of the ancient goddess whose colors were known to be those three? In *Sacred Geography*, Michael Pogacnik says her "white" phase — wholeness, all-connectedness — represents her holistic, Virgin Oneness. The crescent moon. Red is for her creative aspect: learning, expanding consciousness. The full moon. Black is the crisis, decomposition phase — death and resurrection. We move from the old to the new. The moon is dark. She is all three.

Like Snow White, Sophia was banned from patriarchal culture. She can't be bought. She can only, like grace, be freely given. It takes strong men who recognize her to "kiss her" and help bring her back.

Sophia may be cautioning us that we Snow Whites need not fall for every beauty aid or latest fashion that comes along because we're beautiful enough — inside. She may be saying, "You won't find joy and happiness in material goods of any kind. In fact, they'll eventually 'kill' you if that's all you're relying on." And it is the kiss, a Divine kiss, that awakens men and women alike from acedia and boredom. While Snow White is sleeping, who watches over her? Birds — a dove, an owl, a raven, all symbols of Sophia. And the little elemental people who connect us all to the earth remind us that earthly gifts are not for sale, but yours for the asking.

There are seven dwarves. That's not an accidental number. In fact, seven is a balanced, complete number which combines the "male" four and the "female" three. Totality. That's why Jesus taught his disciples to forgive people seven times seventy. The Lord's Prayer contains seven petitions. We have seven notes in an octave, seven days in our week. Babylonian epics tell of seven creation winds, seven doors to the underworld, seven zones in the upper sky world. Hildegard painted Sophia standing on a seven-pillared temple. The seven dwarves represent wisdom. In trying to keep her safe, they caution Snow White again and again and never give up on her — even after she "dies."

Lady Wisdom watches and keeps us safe until we're ready to wake up, she lifts the lid and raises us out of our glass coffins. She empowers us to take responsibility for our physical, emotional and spiritual lives. And once we're awake, as Rumi cautioned: "Don't go back to sleep/People are going back and forth/Across the threshold/Where the two worlds meet/The door is round and open/ Don't go back to sleep."

WAKING UP TO SELF-CONTROL
By waking up, we can practice self-control, another of Sophia's nine gifts. We can exercise choice and choose between despair or hope, depression or joy, denial or acceptance, being greedy or giving, being alone or with others, to close down or open up.

The inscription found at Delphi was "Know thyself." Without self-knowledge, we are not likely to "know" anyone else. Or the world. Without self-knowledge, we will be asleep in the self-control department. By listening to our heart-intelligence, and to our bodies, we can learn new ways to respond to outside stimuli.

My son, who teaches keyboard music, recognizes the value of the Alexander technique for his students. Practicing it helps them learn new ways to hold and use their backs, shoulders, arms, legs and wrists. These "self-control" techniques were devised by a nineteenth-century Australian who had lost his voice as a young actor and decided to figure out why. F. M. Alexander stood in front of a mirror and watched how he moved and breathed. He didn't ask, "Mirror, mirror on the wall, who's the fairest," but: "How can I be more healthy?" He learned his "self" so well he could reinvent habitual actions, and his voice came back when he learned the mechanics of how our bodies work.

Our selves contain engrained ways of responding to the world, emotionally, physically, mentally and spiritually. We can wake these areas up and learn healthier ways of being. We can find our voices. The ancient concept for knowing yourself was called *sophrosyne* — Sophia-knowledge of what is important and why. Sophia frees us by helping us better know and control our *selves*.

SOPHIA'S MYSTICAL DANCER:
BOETHIUS (480-524)

There once was a Roman senator named Anicius Manlius Torquatus Severinus Boethius. Most people just call him Boethius. He lived from 480 C.E. to his agonizing death in 524 C.E., which was supervised by Emperor Theodoric. Ropes bound his head until his eyes burst, and then he was beaten and finally axed to death. It can be dangerous to be a philosopher, a Sophia-lover. He was a Christian, influenced, no doubt, by Augustine. He knew Greek, so he translated Plato and Aristotle into Latin. Prior to his death, as he waited in his cell, Sophia — Lady Philosophia he called her — appeared to him in a vision that lasted a couple of days. After their conversation, he wrote his famous *On the Consolation of Philosophy*. Her eyes, he said, "shown as with fire and in power of insight surpassed the eyes of men, whose color was full of life, whose strength was yet intact though she was so full of years that none would ever think that she was subject to such age as ours."

Botheus wasn't so sure of her height — at times it seemed that she was of normal human height and then at other times her crown seemed to touch the heavens. Her clothes were made of delicate, fine thread which she said she had made herself, embroidered with the first two letters of the Greek alphabet which Boethius took to symbolize the two divisions of philosophy: practical and theoretical. Sophia loves both/and. Her robe was torn by, as she explained, the dissent of philosophers.

He asked her where she'd been all this time and she responded: *"Should I desert you, my nursling? . . . When I saw you in grief and in tears I knew thereby that you were unhappy and in exile."*

Sophia goes on to assure Boethius that she was waiting for his silent attention before speaking to him: *"I was waiting for that frame of mind in you, or more truly, I brought it about in you."*

Boethius wrote to clarify his understanding of the soul's divine origins, which is in constant contact with divine elements on which all knowledge depends. Sophia explains that she will lead him to true happiness, but it may be difficult since his mind has been so clouded with false images. Eventually their conversation turned to a discussion about evil and she asked Boethius if he thought God could do evil. Of course not, he replied. Then, she said, *"Evil is nothing, since God who can do all things, cannot do evil."* And since Boethius was about to die, their conversation turned to thoughts of eternity. *"Eternity,"* she said, *"is simultaneous and complete possession of infinite life. This will appear more clearly if we compare it with temporal things. All that lives, under the conditions of time moves through the present from the past to the future; there is nothing set in time which can at one moment grasp the whole space of its lifetime. It cannot yet comprehend tomorrow; yesterday it has already lost. And in this life of to-day your life is no more than a changing, passing moment. And as Aristotle said of the universe, so it is of all that is subject to time; though it never began to be, nor will ever cease, and its life is co-extensive with the infinity of time, yet it is not such as can be held to be eternal . . . it has not yet experienced the future."*

King Alfred was quite taken with Boethius' little book and translated it into Old English. Later, picking up her royal pen, Queen Elizabeth I made her own translation. In its various versions, it influenced many, including Chaucer as well as Julian of Norwich. And it eventually circled back to Italy.

Dante, with no philosophical or university training, drew heavily from a copy he found just before he wrote his *Divine Comedy*. He had a vision at Easter in 1300 C.E. and he spent the rest of his life writing about what he saw: the whole "Throne of God" and countless beings ever-opening like a galactic "snow-white rose." Sophia.

We know, from documented 13th century Italian histories, that Beatrice, the woman who inspired his poetry, was a real woman as well as his own "Sophia." Both/And. They met as children at a May feast — he was nine and she was eight. She was wearing a red dress. He was so overcome by her that he trembled. She became the love of his entire life.

Sophia's Special Geo-Spot: Cozumel

Her little reef-ringed Island of the Sparrows bobs off the coast of Mexico's Yucatan Penninsula. If you leave San Miguel and its 70,000 weekly tourists, black coral shops and restaurants behind, and travel across the island, you'll perhaps stop at some tequila shops as we did, and eventually come to the ruins of a small Mayan village. It's dedicated to Ix Chel (ee-shell). Lady Rainbow. She's the Moon Lady who regulates fertility cycles, so women longing to become pregnant seek her blessing. Women come here to be with her. I was long past my child-bearing time, but that's why I came, too. I wanted to feel her energy deeply, intimately, womanly.

Ix Chel, Lady Rainbow, from "Mayan Village," Roatan

Ix Chel, who is also venerated on another nearby island, Isla de las Mujeres, weaves cosmic tapestries and is the creative influence for weavers, artists and crafts people. She wears a serpent headdress (her wisdom) and from her "earth gourd," her "womb jar," she pours birthing waters onto the earth. Stepped pyramids are her mountains; marigolds her flowers.

Ix Chel is a strong take-charge woman, keeper of dead souls and a symbol of how people can transform their lives. Ill-tempered, jealous Sun, the old story goes, noticed her fine weaving and wanted Ix Chel for his bride. He beat her because she was spending too much time with the Clouds and Venus. So she left him, but not before bearing four sons: the Jaguars who hold up the four corners of the sky. Ix Chel found refuge with the Vultures and hid in the night sky. As if she hadn't enough trouble, her grandfather struck her dead with a lightning bolt and the dragonflies grieved her absence. After thirteen days, however, she returned.

Now, Sun roams the sky trying to find her, but she only comes out in the night sky when he sleeps. Sometimes she disappears for days, but she is too beautiful to hide forever, so she always returns in splendid moon-lit glory.

Sophia created our energy and maintains it. She encourages us to use it. She's like an alarm clock, saying: *Time to get up!*

FROM SOPHIA'S NOTEBOOK

You've been sleeping for far too long.

Don't be fooled by all the things around you filled with poison.

Come into my dazzling light, instead of nodding off in gloomy darkness.

You are already radiant.

I hold you in my hand and stroke your loveliness.

You are woman. You are one with me. You are breathless energy bound for a time when your lungs will be beaten out of more malleable stuff.

chapter three

SHE PROVIDES

Crop Circle: Grey Wethers, Wiltshire, July 14, 2009

. . . .

"She is the tree of life for those who hold her fast, those who cling to her live happy lives."

~ Proverbs 3:18

MOUNTAIN JOURNAL ENTRY

Like bars of Bach, soul songs pull me along to secret rhythms beating deep. They pinch me on my arm to see if I'm awake. I sing them as I walk my woodland paths where leaf notes and root lines trace autumn measures. Deer stop to mouth fallen apples, pock-marked and wormy, but surely sweet to those wild tongues.

I often visit an outcropping, higher than my head, formed by greenish layered rock. Just into the woods near Apple Creek, an old jade-green rock, rounded by centuries, pokes up like a wizened turtle snout. The rock's surfaces on either side flail out like gigantic flippers. I call her Mother Turtle Rock. I showed this outcropping to my tracker friend Bob one day and he said, "Well, Karen, what you have here is sedimentary rock and all these upright layers were formed when all this was once lying horizontal at the bottom of the ocean." I knew Mother Turtle was old, but I hadn't thought of how she once lay, flippers and all, bent under tons of water. Her head rises above me now, and even though our elevation here on Kelsey Mountain can hardly claim mountain status at a mere 1800 feet, she's much higher than she once was. By 11,000 B.C.E. most of Vermont was ice-free, so, I decide, Turtle Rock has been here to witness it all.

We sit, Old Mother Turtle and I, surrounded by hills and trees. I tell her the story of the Native American woman trying to describe how the earth was formed. "The earth is Mother Turtle. It is her back that holds up the earth." "But what is below her?" the obtuse questioner asked. "Nothing. It's turtle all the way down." You go all the way down, Mother, just like the ancient Homeric Hymn says, "The Mother of us all, the oldest of all, hard, splendid as rock."

The Abenaki, the Dawn People, may have once walked the very woodland paths I now walk. They hunted and fished for leaping salmon in our own little valley, where the Second Branch of the White River flows into the other three, forming one of Vermont's major waterways.

Apple trees were born in western Himalayan mountains. If you cut an apple open sideways, you'll always find a seed-star. What star dropped these apple seeds, I cannot say, but I have heard these gently rounded mountains and the foothills where I live are older than any other range on the planet, except perhaps for some mountains in Africa. All I know is that these apple trees, so burly-barked and craggy-branched, blush my cheeks and spice the very air I breathe. I wander over to Apple Creek, a mere trickle now. Apple juice on the moss.

One of the Gnostic gospels says Seth (the son who came after his brother Cain, who killed his other brother, Abel) followed what was left of his family out of Eden's garden. But before he left, he turned one last time to see the tree of life entwined with the tree called Knowledge. All wrapped into one. Forever. As he stepped past the flaming angels, he heard a song — it's that one I hear sometimes when I walk through the trellis to enter the woods. Like Seth, I carry with me three seeds from that wrapped tree. "Plant them," the angel said. "They will grow into what humans will one day become." Even within me, a five-pointed seed-star gleams.

HEARTBEAT QUESTIONS

What makes me think I don't have "enough?"

How much *is* enough?

How much do I need to be happy? Do things *truly* make me happy?

Do people in malls look happy? Is shopping the *answer?*

If I give, do I have more or less left?

How do I know who to give to?

When did I give someone a "true" gift? When did I receive one?

ABUNDANCE AND SCARCITY

For years, I've had a recurring dream. I call it *my abundance dream.* I own a "dream house" with the most amazing rooms, all wonderfully furnished. I go through all the rooms I normally live in and then I discover additional rooms, usually one flight down, or attached to the back, that I have not yet explored. I see furniture I didn't know I had and think: "Where will I put that? How should I arrange this?" I think: "Wow! All this belongs to me!" Beyond the furnished rooms I come to storeroom after storeroom filled with shelves and library-type wooden ladders, so I can climb up and reach any shelf, look in any box, explore any treasure. I feverishly start, but then I realize I can return any time I choose, so I descend the ladder. There's absolutely no rush. My dream heartbeat slows as I realize I don't need to see everything right now. Nor do I need to stuff it into my bag to take back with me. I know I'll return. And finally, after what seems like hours of dreaming and miles of rooms, I come to the familiar warehouse leading to "outside." More treasures continually cross this loading dock into "my space." My heart expands to include all this "soul stuff."

One of my earliest memories is of sitting on the floor playing with a spool of thread. Like a kitten mesmerized by anything that rolls, I followed it until it disappeared under a wooden rocking chair. I remember my baby fingers were very small in contrast to the wooden runners which went up and down and could hurt me if I wasn't careful. I also remember my mother saying, "Karen. Give me that thread. It's rationed, you know." *Rationed.* A word not yet in my baby vocabulary but one that stuck, nevertheless. I knew it had something to do with the booklet of coupons my mother kept in her purse. And the way she sometimes scowled in the grocery store.

I grew up in a time of war and scarcity-thinking. Ball jar lids and precious wooden spools of thread were objects of great worth. Long after World War II, we still harbor the urge to hoard, to block things from moving around, to stockpile them for some other time. I knew *hoarding* was a bad word. Hoarders forget that everything is energy and the more we embrace it, the more we'll have. It's a matter of opening our hearts. The more we give, the more we receive. That sounds like a simple platitude, but it holds *her* wisdom fast.

Ninety-seven percent of the world's wealth is now owned by 3% of us. Even the 3% think they never have "enough." We look around, wrapped in our sense of lack, and wonder who's got more of the goodies. Who's keeping them from me? And how can I get them?

A BLACK-AND-WHITE MONKEY

I was no more than five when my parents and I took my grandmother Julia up to Superior, Wisconsin to visit Aunt Ida — the sister closest to grandma. We went "up" because it was up as far as you could go without slipping into Lake Superior or wandering off into the bogs of Canada. Julia and Ida were close — they'd even shared a wedding. From postcards back to her family, I learned my grandmother coped with depression by leaving the farm and going "up" to visit Ida (and who wouldn't be depressed with two sets of twins, five children in diapers at the same time — eleven in all). Perhaps it was the lake air that raised her spirits and helped to clear her mind. At any rate, while "up there" we visited a gift shop one day where I spotted a little black-and-white ceramic monkey in a glass case.

I have no idea why I wanted it, but I kept begging until my grandmother finally said to my dad, "Oh, she wants that so badly. Why don't you get it for her." The little tag on monkey's bottom said 98¢ — almost a dollar — for a useless monkey. I can still see my father reluctantly unfolding his wallet. I clutched my monkey in my fist all the way home. For years it sat on my bedroom shelf, a lonely reminder of a silly, foolish request. I didn't even like it. It was ugly. Still I kept it because it was the "monkey of great price."

I've come to believe my grandmother, wise Sophia-woman that she was, wanted me to always be reminded of what I *thought* I needed and what I *really* needed. It became the monkey on my back. The monkey made a monkey out of me. Every time I looked at it, I remembered how my father really didn't have an extra dollar at the time, and how to keep the peace with his mother-in-law, he caved. The flush of triumph I felt as I walked out of that Superior store lasted about five minutes.

LOST AND FOUND

Thanks to Netflix, my husband and I watched all seasons of *Lost* in record time. Like many aspects of pop culture, we missed it the first time around, although I remember people talking about it and thinking: What's this silly series? A cross between voting people off an island and Tom Hanks making friends with a volley ball? On the contrary. We loved it. The characters in *Lost* became old friends. One night Hurley (the big guy) tells Jack (the doctor) that he's not going to protect and ration out the cache of food they've just discovered. Instead, every one of their group gets invited to a feast. It's a loving, beautiful scene. Rather than living under the scarcity meme, they opted for abundance. It was a wonderful new twist on *Babette's Feast*, the 1987 Danish movie about a French woman harboring a past as a gourmet cook. As you may recall, she wins the lottery and spends it all on an amazing dinner which she lovingly prepares for the whole village. Babette is Sophia-in-the-kitchen, lavishing mouth-watering dishes on pinch-lipped Scandinavians used to living on mushy bread and dried fish. And it's all for free. Both Hurley and Babette echo Jesus' words: "I came that they may have life and have it abundantly." Sophia says, "Expect it."

Eileen Cady, one of the founders of the garden-community in Findhorn, Scotland, where oversized vegetables grew with the help of nature spirits, described expectancy like this: "Expect your every need to be met, expect the answer to every problem, expect abundance on every level, expect to grow spiritually." We can all become pregnant with possibilities; we're all "expecting."

Abundance is a communal act, educator Parker Palmer once wrote. It's "the joint creation of an incredibly complex ecology in which each part functions on behalf of the whole and, in return, is sustained by the whole. Community not only creates abundance — community is abundance. If we could learn that equation from the world of nature, the human world might be transformed."

STICKY REMINDERS

One of the best things — well three of the best things — about living in Cambridge, Massachusetts for about a dozen years was that (I) I could walk to Harvard Square in fifteen minutes — twenty on those days when I paused in front of certain store windows. Once I got there (2 and 3), I could visit my favorite bookstore and cross the street to Brigham's afterwards. Both are now gone — but I haven't forgotten them.

Brigham's was the closest thing 1990s Harvard Square had to an old fashioned ice cream parlor — the kind that served milkshakes in metal containers. And they used real, tall sundae glasses accompanied by long spoons so you could reach every crevice. I always suspected they made their own hot fudge.

It was the only kind of sundae I ever ordered. It came perched on a little plate. That was because the fudge ran over and dribbled off every glass curlicue. And it seeped way, way down inside the multiple scoops of hard vanilla ice cream so you never had to worry about running out of hot fudge before the ice cream disappeared. Brigham people didn't gussy it up with a lot of whipped cream or a cherry — just pure ice cream and a volcano of fudge, sweet chocolaty-lava puddling up on the plate. It seemed extravagant at the time and I loved every spoonful. It became my metaphor for abundance. "Scarcity" wasn't an item on Brigham's menu.

Chocolate, like red wine, is a heart soother "experts" say. My family jokes about these "experts." Who says this? "TOP DOCTORS!" *They* say chocolate chases away depression — something we women have known for centuries. Especially dark chocolate. Godiva, Ghiradelli. These are psycho-active words. Thank you, MezoAmerica. Thank you cacao beans, so precious you once masqueraded as Mayan and Aztec currency!

Swinging my carry bag with a couple of new books, I walked home at a more leisurely pace. I had accomplished my biblio-choco-mission. As I walked, I sometimes became a teenager again working at Stan's Roller Rink. Wearing pink pom-pommed skates, I'd leave the rink, float down a ramp into the soda fountain area, do a quick turn-around and dish up sundaes for people. Stan's cold Hershey's chocolate syrup came out of a pump. Three long squirts per sundae. That was it. Ding. Put the money in the till, then off I went to change the records, pump gas out front, or flirt with the boys.

The film, *Chocolat*, taught us that outlawing immorality never works; Brigham's taught me the same about calories. Avoiding those hot fudge sundaes never worked. I reveled in their sticky abundance — this soothed my heart.

SOPHIANOMICS AND YIN-YANG CURRENCIES

Bernard Lietaer is an economist by trade, but a philosopher at heart. He has spent a lifetime thinking about money and working on various currency systems, including five years in the Central Bank in Belgium devising the euro. He points out that many kinds of currency has existed throughout history. In America, today, we use various complementary forms of money: frequent flier miles, credit card bonuses, internet "cash," barter transactions, local community "chips" or currencies, corporate "script" issued and used only by particular corporations — with more to be devised — and that's good because we need all the forms possible to achieve sustainable abundance.

The English poet, Ezra Pound, may have been right when he said money is just a ticket. It has no real worth. It doesn't create anything. In my family we often talk about money being an "illusion" and I suspect it's true. Even with cut-backs, we always seem to have enough. It was white-knuckle time, though, when we had two sons in private colleges, a house mortgage with interest that went through the roof, and one of us looking for work. We still somehow managed. We created the illusion that we were rich — and we were. Rich in so many ways that had absolutely nothing to do with greenbacks. Money's not a thing; money is important only by what it can do. And, of course, money's good only when people agree on what it's worth. I remember how amazed my dad was the first time he saw money coming out of a wall at the ATM. Now we don't even fold it. We just trust that our electronic money moves, in the blink of an eyelash, around the world to the destination we have in mind. We *believe* it exists.

The Inca valued gold, not for what it could buy, but for its beauty. Their economy depended, instead, on people-power. Everyone contributed (by giving one tenth of their time) to building roads and following a central infrastructure plan.

Like energy, if we don't spread money around, it stagnates and we've already seen what happens when that sort of economic constipation happens. Like the rich fool in the Bible, we tear down our storehouses to build bigger barns. Then the winds come and blow the barns down.

I had squirreled two hundred dollars in the back of my desk for "some time of need." That time never came because when Aaron broke into our townhouse one day in Cambridge he found it. Making off with what he could carry, he planned to fence everything for drug money. But as it so happened, our neighborhood detective knew Aaron was out of jail again and he just happened see him as he left our house. Aaron dropped the bag, ran, and the police nabbed him at his girlfriend's house the next day. We got everything back, including the wedding gift from my husband — a precious cameo he'd bought on Capri for a woman he would one day marry, but hadn't even met yet. Of course my two hundred dollar bills were gone. But then they were just an illusion anyway.

Bali is an interesting country with a dual currency: one, like our green currency, is backed and managed by a national bank; the other, like the ancient Incas, is a community currency. They call it *Naravan banjar* and it dates back to 914 C.E. when people mostly lived in rural communities. It's the equivalent of three hours of work. A special wooden gong once summoned people when some sort of collective work was necessary. It might be for a school project. Or a road problem. Today the groups vary in size, from fifty to five hundred families, and are most likely organized online, not by a gong.

In our little seven-family mountain community in Vermont, we use the telephone. If a tree blows down in our road, a neighborhood crew assembles to deal with it within minutes. It's not a formalized system like Bali's, but it works. It's a smaller version of Amish barn-raising.

In assessing these two kinds of Bali currencies, people tend to call the established money system, Yang (masculine) and the community system, Yin (feminine). Both are needed to create a sustainable balance.

Yes! Magazine, in 1997, featured an interview in which Lietaer said to the editor, Sarah van Gelder: "Money is like an iron ring we've put through our noses. We've forgotten that we designed it, and it's now leading us around. I think it's time to figure out where we want to go — in my opinion toward sustainability and community — and then design a money system that gets us there." In a subsequent interview, he pointed out that "95% of all currency transactions in the world are motivated by speculation, and less than 5% are for trades of goods and services. This has been systematically possible only since 1972 when President Nixon created the floating currency non-system we now have."

There is a community in southwestern France, where every two weeks people come together to exchange. It's like a big party. Lietaer explained: "People come to trade not only cheeses, fruits, and cakes as in the normal market days, but also hours of plumbing, haircuts, sailing or English lessons. Only local currencies accepted!"

When people create their own system of exchange, like time dollars or community food exchanges, there is no scarcity. After all, *community* comes from the Latin word *munus* or gift.

When the Great Mother archetype, the one that says, "My fertile womb is open and ready to birth anything for anyone," is perceived as barren, hidden or suppressed, as it certainly has been since the Greeks put a premium on patriarchal property and women were no longer valued, we feel weighed down by fear and greed. As a result we're afraid of "running out." This big archetype is a Jungian concept, but one that Lietaer also espouses. Whenever an archetype like the Great Mother (and I'm not saying that Sophia is simply an archetype) is wounded, the civilization must either mutate or die. She's waking up now. Do we change to accommodate her, or do we continue to disintegrate?

It's perhaps no big surprise that Adam Smith, a Victorian Scotsman, came up with an economic model that viewed scarcity as the norm. He probably didn't even sweeten his oatmeal. Thanks to him, our current economic model is anchored in allocating scarce goods that only encourages personal and corporate greed.

We have been living for a long time under the belief that we need to create scarcity in order to create value. For far too long, we've pictured teeny slivers of pie, and if someone else gets a piece, we think ours would have to be smaller. Instead, we can opt for a larger pie all together. Whatever we *think*, we can create. Wherever we place our attention, that's what our energy goes. If we think there's not enough, there likely won't be. If we think more in terms of largesse, that's what we'll have. Anne Sexton described it as a well: "Then the well spoke to me. It said, abundance is scooped from abundance yet abundance remains."

Lynne Twist, who has worked for years with the Hunger Project, says in *The Soul of Money*, that scarcity is the great lie and sufficiency the surprising truth. You can reclaim the power of what is already there. "When you let go of trying to get more of what you don't really need, it frees up oceans of energy to make a difference with what you have. When you make a difference with what you have, it expands."

ENOUGH IS ENOUGH

My Sophia-friend, Renee, went to Bali and met the former Indonesian Minister of Culture and Tourism, I Gede Ardika, who told her about an old *ketupat* vendor in Denpasar. *Ketupat* is a popular rice delicacy wrapped in coconut leaves, boiled in hot water and served with meat, or vegetables, or chili, and the old woman was an expert at it. The vendor usually opened her little shop at six in the morning and closed it around 9:30. She did a brisk weekend business.

Ardika, having studied economics at the university, knew that as long as demand increases, supply must be adjusted to meet the demand to make a profit. So one day he said, "Madam, why don't you make more *ketupat* on Saturday and Sunday to serve your clients? It means you can increase the money you will take home and you will soon be a rich lady."

"Thank you for your kind advice," the vendor said. "The money I make is sufficient for me. I don't want to work harder because I have so much else in my life. I don't need more money."

What a wise woman, Ardika thought. She has been practicing this local wisdom for a very long time and is the richest person I have ever met. She knows when enough is enough.

In Bali, time isn't money; time is relationship, and, as Renee says: "Since building relationship generally takes time, efficiency and maximum profit are not necessarily the highest aspirations for the Balinese."

A similar story appeared in my e-inbox recently. A Caribbean fisherman smiled as the tourist — no doubt a corporate manager seeking a trophy fish for his office — kept asking him why he only worked half days. "Why would I want to work longer hours?" the fisherman asked. "Well, you're such a good fishing guide that you could make so much more money." "Why would I want to do that?" "So you could buy a bigger boat." "Why would I want a bigger boat?" "So you could take more guys like me out to catch more fish." "Why would I want to do that?" The now quite sunburned northerner said, "So you could become rich and retire and spend leisure time with your family on a beautiful island like this." The fisherman said, "I already do."

DO YOU BARTER?

Maybe Aaron, the Cambridge thief, and I could have struck up some sort of a barter arrangement if I had gotten to know him beyond the fingerprints he'd left. Perhaps there was something Aaron needed (beyond the drugs) that I could have provided. I'll never know.

At various craft shows where I sell my recycled wool hats, people will often say, "Do you barter?" Of course. I love bartering. I've bartered piano lessons for eggs and cheese; hats for Christmas gifts. Everyone wins. Bartering doesn't work for everything, however, so as Bernard Lietaer points out, we need both yin and yang currencies; both hard currencies and the social capital. We've tipped so far into the hard currency model, however, that we've lost sight of what Sophia's been trying to tell us about the Yin way of operating. Matthew Fox put it this way: "A machine cosmology gives rise to unemployment and scarcity, where a cosmology of connection would encourage economics of abundance." When "first people" cultures move away from their Yin standards to adopt Yang currencies, their way of life is invariably diminished, if not totally destroyed.

There are now, according to Lietaer, more than 4,000 communities around the world that have started their own complementary currencies. In Curitiba, the capital city of half a million people in the State of Paran in Brazil, pre-sorted garbage is exchanged for tokens. The tokens can be used on local buses or exchanged for food. Most of the people live in *favelas*, helter-skelter tin-roofed shacks. Their neighborhoods stand no chance of garbage trucks coming in.

So the mayor, Jaime Lerner, creatively came up with a solution. Why not give people chits for pre-sorting recyclables and organic compost materials farmers could use. In Curitiba, Yin currency makes people healthier, farmers more productive; it pays for public transportation and has created a self-reliant clean city. Yang currencies tend to foster competition; Yin currencies foster cooperation. Coins *and* community. But which coins? Could it be possible to come up with a world-wide currency? Lietaer thinks so. He calls this complementary currency, which could run alongside the country's currency, the *Terra*. It's based on a standardized unit — a bushel — of a dozen or so standard commonly traded commodities such as wheat or rice. It would be the first time since the gold-standard that an international monetary system could stabilize our fragile and volatile boom/bust global economies.

Many communities now have LETS, Local Exchange Trading Systems, that promote local shopping and self-reliance. ShareExchange, in Santa Rosa, California, claims their only currency is trust. Many communities are experimenting with creative ways to prolong their elders' quality of life, as opposed to just stretching out their days with drugs or invasive procedures. In Japan, for instance, they have a Yin currency for elder care that they call *fureai kippu* or "caring relationship tickets." At the time Bernard Lietaer described it in an interview with Ravi Dykema (in the July-August 2003 *Nexus Colorado's Holistic Journal*), there were three or four hundred such plans operating in Japan: "Here's how they work: let's say that on my street lives an elderly gentleman who is handicapped and cannot go shopping for himself. I do the shopping for him. I help him with food preparation. I help him with the ritual bath, which is very important in Japan. For this help, I get credits. I put those credits in a savings account, and when I'm sick, I can have other people provide such services for me. Or I can electronically send my credits to my mother, who lives on the other side of the country, and somebody takes care of her.... Youngsters who are taking care of the elderly in Japan can use their credits in partial payment for tuition at the university, so they solve two problems at the same time." It's like a super-caring-multi-leveled potlatch.

A POTLATCH WHOSE TIME HAS COME

My early Scandinavian relatives had what they called giving circles. "Things" kept going around. They were similar in some ways to designated areas at our recycling stations. Ours has a sign: "Please take or leave what you want — but don't take the table."

Wealth in Pacific Northwest cultures was transferred most often by a chief or some wealthy person who built up his prestige and family status by the gifts he gave. Potlatch is a Chinook word meaning "give-away." They gave away blankets, oil, dried fish, canoes, sheets of copper carvings, and even slaves. A gift was considered even more valuable if it was used up or broken — and then put back together again. I'm thinking this was the same philosophy behind the large number of broken pottery shards found near ritual sites such as Chaco Canyon in the Four Corners Area. Broken pots were precious gifts to the divine presence of that place.

Potlatchers gave a gift to the person who insulted him — back and forth increasing in value each time. Missionaries convinced the Canadian and American governments to ban these large-scale give-aways because they believed they stood in the way of the civilizing the natives. The ban has since been lifted.

"Gifts don't earn profit," Hyde said in *The Gift*, "They give increase."

After a year of selling my hats, I did a little inventory. I'd given away about two-thirds of them, and sold the other third. A friend said to me, "That seems about right." It does.

The ultimate potlatch would be to give someone an organ transplant, a gift of continuing life. What really happens when someone receives a kidney or a heart? How would you even begin to thank the donor's family, other than to encourage everyone you know to create a living will? An organ gift is wrapped up in total acceptance with no possibility of payback. In the movie, *Seven Pounds*, a dying

IRS agent, Will Smith, decides to give away his body parts to improve the lives of seven complete strangers. As this movie portrays, exchanging organs profoundly changes the recipient's and the donor's lives.

I met a woman from Boston at Maho Bay on St. John's in the Virgin Islands who told me she'd donated a kidney to a complete stranger. She met him at a party, learned he had a very rare blood type — hers — and after a long conversation said, "Let's see if I might be a compatible donor." She also told me that she felt guided by another presence and she just *knew* this was what she was supposed to do. How fitting, I thought, to hear this story on the very island where early Taino Indians settled and slaves later hid until the Danes freed them in the early 1800's. Between four and five hundred people then lived on this little island and survived through what they called "giveishness."

We usually use the word "save" rather than "give" when we speak of someone like Randy, a fifty-three year old furniture maker who lives in the next town east of us. He saved a life, but what he really did was *give* someone his life back. It was nearing midnight on a snowy -4° Vermont night when he drove home from his shop (where they played music one night a week). He noticed some tire tracks where there shouldn't be any so he stopped. What he found was a Toyota Camry upside down in Broad Brook with the motor still running and the headlights on. The trapped driver had only his head above the liquid ice. Randy spent a few minutes trying to get him out the door, but the door wouldn't open. The driver was conscious enough to tell Randy who he was. Randy propped him up through the door to keep him from drowning while he climbed the bank and ran to a neighbor's for help. Icy water was running through the car by the time the two men returned. By now Randy, too, was dangerously cold. The neighbor said, "I just grabbed the door and ripped it. The adrenaline gets going." They laid the driver on top of the car and tried to keep him alive until the rescue unit could lower a ladder. In spite of severe hypothermia, the trapped man lived.

Randy's grandfather had saved a man back in the 1920s who was trapped under a tractor. He had impressed upon his grandson, "When you see someone in trouble, you always stop." You don't think of exchange.

When I was side-swiped by a hit-and-run driver on a Boston rush hour freeway, within minutes three women appeared out of nowhere. I looked up through my tears and saw a sturdy off-duty policewoman from New York on her motorcycle who assured me everything was fine and she'd stay with me until the local police arrived, a young woman who put her arm around me asking if I was hurt and an older woman who immediately had her cell phone out. They were my "three Marys." They took over and kept me safe. Leaning against the crunched guard rail, I noticed an SUV pull over and then take off. Later the young man driving it pulled back in behind my crunched Saab, got out, and gave the police a full description of the car that had hit me, including the man's address. "My girlfriend was in a hit-and-run once and I swore if I ever saw another one, I'd follow the escaping driver." We give gifts for so many reasons — but usually it's because of an earlier prompting. That night the young man and his girlfriend had a dinner on me, but that check didn't begin to cover the gratitude I felt.

A gift-economy demands a high level of trust to make it work. For instance, consider the ceremonial trading of the Melanesian people who live among eighteen islands off the east coast of Papua New Guinea. They practice a very complicated Yin-Yang system. One is purely ceremonial and the other is a very practical approach to bartering and selling market products. Combs for coconuts. Colorful feathers for red ochre. Boar's tusks for pots. But no one was supposed to sell the valuable ceremonial gifts. This complex giving-ring once involved thousands of people and close to a hundred ceremonial canoes and, to a lesser degree, it's still going on today. A ceremonial gift could take from two to ten years to make the complete ring cycle. Everyone trusted everyone else to give a gift equal to the value of the gift they received. White armbands, considered to be female, made from shellfish, were ritualized gifts to men. They traveled counterclockwise around the islands. Red necklaces, considered male, were crafted from red shells and traveled clockwise as gifts to women. No one ever receives a gift from the same person he or she gives it to.

A HEART-BASED ECONOMY

Joel and I had driven through miles of gorse and grass only to find ourselves on a grey promontory south of Galway Bay called *An Boirenn*. The Burren. Aptly named, it means "a stony place." It's cushioned on one side by green Kerry and on the other by the purple Connemara mountains. We said at the same time: "We're on the moon!" The people who once lived on this austere landscape built numerous stone forts and galley graves. They followed Brehon law, not the laws of the English which later became our own.

People were paid for their labors in flax and wool, in weighed-out silver from their mines and in milk cows. A "set" of treasure was valued as half an ounce of silver, and one milk cow equaled one ounce of silver. They clearly defined who should and who should not be given loans. They couldn't have imagined a time when people would put their treasure in flimsy derivatives and futures. They recognized seven kinds of marriages and didn't waste their time disputing loving unions. People who committed crimes were fined or had to pay honor prices to those they'd injured; there was no need for prisons. They held their judges to very high standards — judges who spent decades studying law. They believed three things can cause a kingdom's ruin: a judge who takes bribes, an unlearned judge, and an unjust judge. Whoever stole a needle from a poor embroidery woman had to pay a higher fine than someone who stole a queen's needle. And, most importantly, perhaps, they believed that words mattered. Even satire. Because words can maim, the penalty for unjust satire or mockery was equivalent to a person's honor price. It was considered the same as if that person had been killed. It's obvious they weren't burdened by greedy lobby groups, hate media, or fear-mongering talk radio hosts. How these Celts lived, I thought, sounded a lot like Sophianomics. It's a word I coined to mean "living by Sophia's standards." If we lived in a heart-based economy — one centered more on giving, caring and helping, rather than hoarding, clutching, and storing up — we'd find ourselves enjoying a sustainable economy run on heart-math and head-math. We already practice Sophianomics a little bit. For instance, instead of selling our blood we can give a pint in exchange for a cookie and little glass of juice. We have the free use of internet search engines in exchange for seeing an ad or two. Unpaid volunteers build houses and restore communities in the hopes that someone else might do that in their community if they ever needed it. Some communities offer free books, such as at the "Read and Ride" I discovered one day at the Porter Square T Stop in Cambridge. But what if our entire society were more in tune with sharing their gifts — not as something special, but as a normal way of life?

A big and getting bigger question looms — not just in Florida, but on all our horizons: How do we care for our elders and others who need a little extra help in a way that honors them — and us? John and I are part of a Neighbor-to-Neighbor program in our community which aims at keeping people in their homes as long as possible. We do various tasks: picking things up, moving things, taking people to appointments — whatever is needed when we are called, but we don't keep track of our time on a formalized exchange basis. We just know that if we needed something, there would be someone ready to help. And the wonderful part of this neighborly program is that you get to know people better. You establish valuable relationships — something the Balinese knew all along.

The Abenaki people of Vermont tell a tale of four men who ask Gluskabe, a heroic figure, to grant their wishes. Each received a pouch with the instruction not to open it until they were with their people. Three of them couldn't wait. One, who wanted to be tall, opened it and immediately became a tree. One, who wanted to live forever, opened the pouch and became a stone. One, who wanted material goods, opened his as he was canoeing down a river and drowned under the weight of his pouch. But the fourth waited until he was with his people. His wish? May we never go hungry. Abundance followed him and his people wherever they went. Gluskabe-Sophia generously shares when we are generous.

The Cathedral and the Bazaar

I aspire to be an internet hacker. Not the criminal type — real hackers call them "crackers." But one like Eric S. Raymond, who wrote *The Cathedral and the Bazaar*. I was drawn to his book, not for all the computer stuff, but because of the title. To me, it suggests that we, as a culture, operate in one of two ways. To Raymond (who, by the way, gave away earlier versions of his book's draft on the internet), the cathedral represents the orderly commercial world — secure, closed, safe, dogmatic, proper and "right."

The Linux community he writes about was more like a great babbling bazaar, as open as it could possibly be. The cathedral method sets rigid parameters and is more yang. The bazaar is where anything goes (Yin). The "and" between them suggests we need them both.

I love the metaphor of living in open-space and open-source relationships that build on what other folks know. That's what the software developers, such as the people who built the Internet, Unix, and the World Wide Web, did. I couldn't *do* what they do — I just want to be like them: they're enthusiasts, artists, tinkerers, problem solvers and experts. Lisbeth, the girl with the dragon tattoo (that will make sense only if you know Stieg Larsson's books) is a hacker, a member of a smart tribe dedicated to problem solving by helping each other. Usually for free. I'm as different from Raymond as anyone could possibly be. I don't have a mustache. I don't own a gun. I'm a techno-peasant. But like him, I enjoy doing things that are fun, but that take a lot of effort. Like writing a book. Hackers know the world is full of problems just waiting to be solved. Amen to that. Hackers believe that nobody should ever have to solve the same problem twice because creative brains are a valuable resource. They believe other people's thinking time is precious so you share what you know. Hackers find boredom and drudgery evil. Hackers also believe freedom is good and there's no substitute for competence.

Raymond, who calls himself an accidental revolutionary, prefers abundance over scarcity and freedom over control. He also believes software and operating systems can be made better through the "Delphi Effect." In other words, a *group's* informed judgments are better than *individual* "expert" judgments. The term came from Rand researchers during the Cold War who were charged with helping the military forecast the impact of technology on warfare, a complex subject indeed. It's been used for many reasons since then — to mixed degrees of success. Naming it after the priestesses at Delphi is an ironic twist. Imagine big burly guys in military uniforms sitting on three-legged stools over fumes wafting from a mountaintop, trying to predict the future. But why should we be surprised to witness this "takeover" by the military, of something intended for the benefit of all? There is, of course, a precedent for Delphi-takeovers. After all, Apollo "took it over" from the Pythia women.

The bazaar metaphor implies openness and sharing over secrecy and a commons rather than fenced property. Tesla may not have been successful in making electricity free for all, but open-source techniques seem to be doing it.

Raymond and others struggle with the age-old question: What do you give away and what do you sell? My artist friends and I talk about that a lot. What's the business model for creativity? I had a publishing colleague who was a book designer and a very fine artist. She told me once that she would never rely only on her art to live. "I honor my art too much to ask that of it."

Children are little adaptive machines. Children don't "own" things because as far as they're concerned, everything is theirs. They live in open-space and spend all their time at the "bazaar." They survive in an abundant "gift-culture" where things are traded and enjoyed, rather than being anyone's property. Three-year-old Kaitlyn brought Josie a birthday gift but really wanted it herself. Her mother patiently explained that the gift was for Josie to which Kaitlyn replied: "But Mommy, Josie would want me to have it."

How do you license a bubble? How do you copyright a sand castle? You don't. There's always more where they came from. A larger question is: How do we make a living if we give everything away? Who gets the royalties on something a lot of people create? How much is intellectual property really worth and how can we be sure it's fairly compensated? How do artists live if their art is free? When it comes right down to it, how do we place value on a *thing*? Raymond points out that there is "use value" and then there's "sale value." They may be quite different. Something may be "worth" a lot more to me than anyone would ever pay for it.

In Welsh mythology, Sophia is called Ceridwen and her big cooking pot can feed anyone who is hungry. It never runs out. Is it magic, or is it like the Stone Soup pot that nourishes everyone because everyone contributes a little something.

Her Demurrage

A demurrage is a fancy term to describe the payment made to a ship owner when somebody keeps a shipload of "stuff" tied up longer than contracted for. In other words, the ship-holder receives an extra demurrage fee for the extended use of his vessel. Railways charge demurrage if you don't unload the cars quickly enough. Banks could also be charged if they hold money longer than agreed upon. Demurrage encourages circulation. It's not a bad idea, and if it were ever to materialize, the Terra would be a demurrage-charged currency.

It seems like an idea Isis may have come up with since it was practiced in Egypt. We know a bit about it from the story in Genesis beginning with Chapter 37. Joseph, the one with the technicolored dream coat, dreamed about his brothers' sheaves of wheat all bowing down to his wheat. This was not appreciated by his jealous brothers who decided to kill him. His brother Reuben argued against actually killing him, but opted for leaving him in a pit to die, and smearing his coat with goat's blood so their father would think wild animals had killed him. After further discussion, they decided to haul him up out of the pit and sell him to some traders coming by in order to make some fast money. Good economics.

So, that's how Joseph got carted off to Egypt. As luck would have it, he was bought by one of Pharaoh's officers. The ruler soon noticed how smart Joseph was so he put him in charge of all his storehouses. Joseph was falsely imprisoned on a rape charge and put in jail, where he befriended the chief jailor. He began interpreting people's dreams and word got back to Pharaoh that he was good at this. Since Pharaoh was having some particularly vexing dreams that no one could make any sense out of, he brought Joseph back to the palace. Joseph explained that the Pharaoh's dreams about seven fat cows and seven skinny cows, and later, seven healthy stalks of corn and seven withered ones, meant Egypt should stockpile food for a coming famine. If you want to know how the story continues you can read about it yourself, but the reason I bring it up here is to point out the Egyptian economic system in place at the time.

Stored up food as a monetary system most likely goes back to Mesopotamia's earlier agrarian revolution. Loans and advances were made to people from grain storehouses. They did their bookkeeping on small bits of fired pottery. Lieatar points out that there was a time-charge on those receipts. This system left no room for hedge funds, market manipulation, or cooked books. "For instance, if someone wanted to redeem an *ostraca* of ten bags of wheat after six months, he would only receive nine bags. This demurrage charge reflected the costs of guarding the depot and quantities lost to rodents. So we can understand that Egyptian farmers would never hoard this currency, but would rather invest in what was most handily available to them: improvements on their land and irrigation systems."

After the Roman takeover, the Egyptian system gave way to Roman currency which encouraged charging, as we do, positive interest rates, rates that encouraged storing up. As long as the negative interest rates were charged, and resources moved around, Egypt was able to build monuments and pyramids lasting for eons, as well as export wheat and bread to the ancient world. Once they were forced to adopt the hoarding Roman model, their economy tumbled.

A Sophia Gift: Generosity

"We are the Generosity-of-Being evolved into human form." That's how Briane Swimme sees us in *The Universe is a Green Dragon*. It is because of Sophia's generosity that we even think of giving.

My uncle Albert died at 54, but during his short life, he was known all around our small Wisconsin community for the gifts he gave. Every year around Christmas time, he'd butcher a cow, get it wrapped and frozen, and then spend a whole day driving around the community delivering meat to folks he knew could use a little extra on their table. He gave money, time, himself. He loved food, so he, as we all do, enjoyed giving what he loved. When people asked how they could repay him he'd smile and say, "Oh, just pass it along." He would have loved the 2000 movie, *Pay it Forward*. A young boy comes up with the idea for his school project of doing a good deed for another and then asking the recipient to "pay it forward." They didn't use the phrase "gift economy" but that's what it was.

Mother Teresa's hospice in Calcutta was called *Nirmal Hriday*, The Place of the Pure Heart. It had no doors. Constantly open, as she was herself, the house somehow managed to have enough resources to continue to care for the people who came. She never gave money a thought. "It always comes," she said.

Nipun Mehta, a U.C. Berkeley graduate with a dual degree in philosophy and computer science, worked for years within Sun Microsystems. He was interviewed in the Winter 2009 *Parabola* magazine, where he said it's a myth that you have to have things before you can give. He and some friends formed CharityFocus, where projects aren't planned, they just emerge. A few of his friends got together and said, "What if you just blew somebody away with kindness, somebody who's going through a rough period and just everybody sent them cookies, thank you cards, chocolates. Just flood them with goodness and they wouldn't even know who did it." You can download Smile Cards for free that say, "This is an experiment in anonymous kindness. You've been tagged. You don't know who did this so you can't pay back, but you can pay it forward."

Mehta defines "gift economy" as carrying a gift forward with no strings attached. If you have something of value, he says, put it in motion. Some cities have "Karma Kitchens" where you can eat and the bill will read zero because someone else has paid for it. If you'd like to do the same, you can leave some money to pay it forward for someone else. It's similar in some respects to the "Honesty Cafes" in Indonesia where customers pay what they feel the meal's true value is.

Mehta and his friends plan to start what they call "Compassion Labs" involving a cadre of entrepreneurs dedicated to birthing the gift economy in all it's true potential. He reminds us that there are three kinds of intelligence (Sophia Quotients): IQs, which we all know a lot about; EQs which we're just learning about — our Emotional Quotients; and now a third emerging one: CQs, Compassion Quotients.

A man who has given us a little glimpse of what a gift economy might mean for us is Edgar Cahn. He wrote *No More Throw Away People*. The book's point is this: if you can't compete in a dollar-based community, we just throw you away. Cahn came up with "time-dollars," a currency built on a system of caring for people and sharing what we each can do.

Lewis Hyde, in *The Gift*, described a traditional gift economy as being based on "the obligation to give, the obligation to accept, and the obligation to reciprocate … it is at once economic, juridical, moral, aesthetic, religious and mythological." Gifts can be "true" gifts or "obligatory" gifts. Who hasn't given someone a gift because that person gave you one first? A gift binds you to the giver in ways purely buying something does not. It can set up a web of gratitude — sometimes helpful, sometimes manipulative.

Let's play Sophia's "What if" game. It stimulates the imagination. What if *everyone* had enough to eat? What if homeless people no longer haunted the underside of our bridges? What if people no longer had to sleep in their cars because their houses were confiscated by the bank? What if people had better health and dental care? What if we *did* operate from a gift economy?

ENNEAGRAM NUMBER 3

Number Threes are competent and efficient. They are high performers and achievers and try to please everybody. But underneath their veneer of success, they can at times feel worthless. They can confuse their sense of who they are with what role they are playing. Number Threes are often driven and have to be careful not to burn out. They place a high priority on truth. Their intense feelings and emotional depth can come across like that of high-strung drama queens: moody and self-indulgent. They like to know what the plan is and need to feel in control.

SOPHIA'S MYSTICAL DANCER:
HILDEGARD OF BINGEN (1098-1179)

When she was three, a dazzling light made her shudder. For eighty-one years, Hildegard lived with that brilliance, but she was forty-three years old before she built up enough courage to realize the divine nature of that light. Later she would write: "All living creatures are, so to speak, sparks from the radiation of God's brilliance, and these sparks emerge for God like the rays of the sun."

When she was eight, Hildegard's parents "tithed" her to the church. She was their tenth child so they made her an oblate — a give-away. As a result, she spent her growing up years walled up inside a church with Jutta, an anorexic nun and loving teacher. Hildegard became a Benedictine nun herself at fifteen. Hildegard had visions all her life. Three times she heard: *Write what you see and hear.* But she didn't think she was worthy enough to do that. Then she got very sick. Finally, her "voice" instructed: *"Write this down — not as your heart is inclined but rather as my testimony wishes. For I am without any beginning or end of life. This vision has not been contrived by you, nor has it been conceived by any other."* She did ... and her energy and health returned. Eventually she became strong enough to call herself "a small sound of the trumpet from the Living Light."

For about 700 years, her writings on science, health and medicine, prophecy, art, ecology, politics and theology, together with her music, were virtually unknown outside Germany. Even within Germany, she was not widely recognized until recordings of her music reached a wider public. *Feather on the Breath of God*, one title, is an apt metaphor for the breath-taking, breath-giving music that floated from her imagination.

Volmar, her good friend, agreed to be her scribe. She could write, of course, but not as elegantly in Latin as Volmar could. Her first book, *Scivias*, took her ten years. Bernard of Clairvaux was her first reader; he passed her book on to the Pope.

In the preface to *Scivias*, a word she coined by combining *Sci Vias Domini* or "Know the Ways of the Lord," she wrote: "...the heavens were opened and a blinding light of exceptional brilliance flowed through my entire brain. And so it kindled my whole heart and breast like a flame, not burning but warming ... and suddenly I understood the meaning of the expositions of the books, that is to say of the psalter, the evangelists, and other catholic books of the Old and New Testaments." She wanted to taste their understanding.

The original manuscript was lost during World War II. Fortunately, the nuns at Eigbingen had a copy. Hildegard said, *"I write this, not for our time, but for the time when the air is no longer breathable and the water is no longer drinkable. Then they will heed my words."*

She lived through much of the 12th century along the Moselle and Rhine Rivers where the grapes and other crops stayed green and luscious. People, too, she said, *"are showered with greening refreshment, the vitality to bear fruit ... I am the breeze that nurtures all things green. I encourage blossoms to flourish with ripening fruits. I am the rain coming from the dew that causes the grasses to laugh with the joy of life."* She wrote about how science, cosmology, and art are all connected. Every creature, she taught, is linked to another and every essence constrained by another.

She created words and music for seventy-seven songs. People who sing Hildegard's music often have their own mystical experiences. To sing them, they must breathe differently — some singers actually faint. Hildegard believed the act of singing words, the vowels and the consonants, embeds the meaning of those words right into your very soul through your body's vibrations — sophisticated quantum physics for an "unlearned" woman of the 12th century.

Hildegard managed several religious institutions, often tangling with members of the church bureaucracy, kings and the pope. Still, she found time to write all those songs, nine books, over seventy poems, one hundred and forty-five letters, a morality play — and she painted or supervised dozens of mystical mandala-like images. Some of her art shows animals breathing and nourishing circlets of water ripples, along with trees, and angels all around, drawing life from all that lives, and returning it. She saw Sophia! Her paintings show Sophia wearing a red long-sleeved dress and embracing the entire earth.

No head-in-the-sky esthete, this Benedictine nun. She carried the word "justice" deep within her belly. True love, she said, *"tramples upon all injustice that is convoluted by the countless vices of dissention. Injustice is also dreadful in its very nature, poisonous in its temptations and black in its abandonment."*

Shortly before she died, on a bright September afternoon in 1179, two streams of light appeared in the sky and swept across the small bedroom where her frail body lay. Her trumpet was silenced, but the overtones of her words keep ringing. That light still illuminates the paths of many. We all have round souls, she said. Symmetrical and beautiful. Love is at work in the circles of eternity, and we're all brilliant in the dawn.

ONCE UPON A TIME:
Little Red Riding Hood

My grandmother loves to sew. She made me a red velvet cap which I wear all the time. Today my mother said, "Will you take this gift-basket of goodies, a little cake, and a bottle of wine to your grand-mother? She's not feeling well and it will cheer her up. But, stay on the path."

I pull on my cap and head for the path. Just as I enter the forest I see a shadow ... a big wolf! "Where are you going, Little Girl?" he growls. When I get scared I talk too much. So I tell him exactly where Granny lives. Not a good idea. The wolf must think he'd rather eat Granny, so he leaves me alone, but not before suggesting I pick some wildflowers for my grandmother. Being the obedient girl that I am, I bend over the daisies without realizing that now he has a few minutes to reach her house before I arrive. I hope he gets lost!

Knock. Knock. "Granny, I hear you're not feeling well. It's little Red Cap with a basket of cake and wine for you." A husky voice says, "Come in."

Granny must have a bad cold, I think. But once I get to her bed, I realize she is sicker than even Mama knows.

"What big ears you have, Granny." "The better to hear you, my dear."

"What big hands you have, Granny." "The better to grab you with!"

"What a terribly big mouth you have, Granny." "The better to eat you with!"

The wolf jumps out of bed, swallows me whole, and now he's sleeping. And snoring!

It's very crowded in here so I figure he must have swallowed Granny first. Then I hear the door open and a man's voice saying, "Granny? I was out hunting and I hear someone snor— wait a minute!" The voice got closer. "I've been looking for *you* for a long time."

I hear "snip-snip" and then I see Granny's sewing scissors. The hunter carefully cuts the wolf's belly open. "What's this? A red hat?" I jump out. And then I pull Granny out. As we hug each other, the hunter skins the wolf's fur. Granny shares her cake and wine with the us and I put her daisies in a vase. She is obviously feeling better so the hunter and I leave together, he carrying his new fur pelt — and me, my empty basket. My mother will be so amazed to hear this story!

A gift basket can be filled with trouble depending on who's giving it. Sophia seems to be saying through Little Red Riding Hood that motives need to be fully assessed. But this is much more than a story of naiveté. The huntsman is the hero of this story. Like Randy the woodworker, he doesn't hesitate — he jumps right in to help. And, like Randy, he's a careful helper. He knows his tools. As well as the potential drawbacks. He would have gone for help if he had needed it.

Here we have a tale of the (little) virgin, the mother and the crone. Three aspects of womanhood. The girl is dressed in earthy womb-red — like red ochre and blood. Red epitomizes the root chakra that grounds us to the earth. The story reminds us that our health and abundance lie at our very rootedness. Sophia's return depends heavily on sensitive, caring, skillful men who can "snip" through all the "harmful fur" and allow all women, young and old, to breathe again.

SOPHIA'S SPECIAL GEO-SPOT: EPHESUS

Once, Ephesus perched on the rim of the blue Mediterranean. At one time, 300,000 people lived in "Her Holy Port." Now the Cayster River has silted up and you have to travel inland about three miles from Kusadasi to visit this amazing archeological find. Unlike most old sites, nothing has ever been built on top of the original buildings in this old city in Turkey.

Amazons were likely the first people who lived here. Then the Greeks came, fueled by a story about a boar. Wherever the boar stopped, they were supposed to build a city. They found one caught in a thorny bush and began building what became this magnificent urban landscape.

You see marble everywhere. If you walk down the main street toward the two-story columned Celsus Library (named after a Roman named Celsus, who is buried there) you'll see the inscription: "In the primal beginning was the Word" and four female statues stare down at you. Their names are Wisdom (Sophia), Knowledge, Intelligence and Virtue. Behind them, wall niches once contained up to 12,000 scrolls. The Pergamon library, only eighty miles away, had 200,000 "books." Priestesses of Isis carried scrolls back and forth from the Mother Library in Alexandria to both libraries. The theater sat 24,000. Our sons climbed the seats way up to the top to hear us whispering from the stage. We proved it still has perfect acoustics.

Leto bore her twins, Artemis and Apollo, on the island of Delos, but that island became known only as *Apollo's* birthplace. Artemis became the heart of Ephesus. Pythagoras is said to have had a hand

in building her first temple in the early 500s B.C.E. It had three platforms, the longest side equaling the dimensions of Cheop's pyramid. It was intended to be a miniature universe, dedicated to the moon. Seven times it was destroyed by fires, wars, floods, earthquakes, and six times it was rebuilt again. A mentally ill man named Herostratus burned it on the very day Alexander was born. People say that happened because Artemis was away attending to his birth. Alexander rebuilt it. Then the Romans came, followed by the Christians. Paul preached against her and her temple; the disciple, John, called down God's wrath and split her altar in two — or was that particular destruction a well-timed earthquake? Mary likely lived out her last days in a house a few miles east of the city in pine-covered hills.

Sophia statue outside the library at Ephesus, Turkey

Artemis' temple was opened only twice a year during festival season;

pilgrims slept in tents. But the porch was always open as a sanctuary and haven for women and children. When anyone managed to cross her threshold, they were safe. At one time, Ephesians knotted ropes to her temple columns and ringed the whole city of Ephesus. The entire city became a safe haven. The temple was the heart of the city which was multi-lingual, multi-cultural and alive with art, metal crafts, dance, theater, athletics, music and storytelling. Many women ran their own businesses and donated baths, fountains, ceramics, and sculptures to the city; they sponsored games and theater events and maintained libraries. Imagine the agora filled with sights, sounds, smells from perfume sellers, purple dye, wool and fabric vendors, bakers, cobblers; Artemisian priestesses, who loved music, art, and luxury. And children who gave gifts called *artemas*: gifts of wholeness. People sang: "Hail to you who conducts the opposites to unity; hail to you who has woven maidenhood into motherhood.... Hail, Oh hope of eternal blessings.... Hail to you who are the healing of my body."

Statues of Artemis show her wearing a zodiac necklace. The seven stars of the Pleiades were her companions. Images of fecund figs and all sorts of animals and bees adorned her body. A sacred meteor stone (perhaps the very one later taken to Rome that now lies under the Vatican) was kept in her temple. Her priestesses were called worker bees: Mellisae. Her priests, Essenes, a college of drones, were asexual. Sacrificial animals were fed to the poor in a ritual called "dining with god."

Her temple became the bank of Asia when other countries' economics were in ruin. Her priest bankers — as many as 400 at one time — oversaw the funds, made mortgages, loaned on interest and supervised repayment schedules. Her coins have been found in over fifty Anatolian cities. Stamped on them are the words: "Artemis does not lie." Wrongs were avenged by dividing the gold — half to the wronged person and half to Artemis Ephesia. Justice was her calling card.

Sophia protects and nurtures us whether we realize it or not. Choosing to live in abundance rather than in scarcity is a matter of what we carry in our hearts, not in our bank balances. And what we spend is linked more firmly to our energy than our credit cards. Her gift-economy is ours for the unwrapping.

FROM SOPHIA'S NOTEBOOK

Don't worry. There are hot stoves around, but you need not touch them. There are deep gorges you might fall into, but I will guide your feet. Faith holds you at night when you can't sleep and says: "You're cushioned. You're pillowed and quilted and held. Sleep and then be awake. Totally awake so you can see faith in action all around you and within your awakened self."

That's what faith does. It's your Christed-gift. Your Sophiaed-gift. Faith is your companion when you think you are alone. Faith in your own abilities, your own strength, and then faith beyond that when you feel your own falls short. There is no limit to faith. It is one of your metaphors for abundance. Never-ending. Self-sustaining. Overflowing. It keeps. It's the gift that keeps on giving.

My well goes deep and holds water for a very long time. There may be two sides to a sword, but there is only one blade. And one purpose for it: to sustain life, wholeness, completeness. Life is a series of stages and opportunities. Having faith is feeling full; knowing the table is set and ready and holding delectable treats all the time. You only think the covered dishes may be empty. They're not. Food exists in many forms. Thanksgiving every day. Dishes beyond your slender gourmet attempts. Dishes no human cook could dream up. But chefs await in other guises to assist you, to continue to feed you. Bon Appetit. Enjoy!

part two

Sophia in Our Families and Communities

· ·

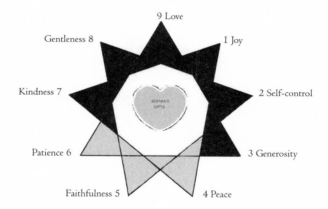

9 Love

Gentleness 8

1 Joy

Kindness 7

2 Self-control

SOPHIA'S
GIFTS

3 Generosity

Patience 6

Faithfulness 5

4 Peace

chapter four

SHE NAMES US PEACEMAKERS

Crop Circle: Honey St. Wiltshire, July 8, 2000

- -

"I am the Queen of Peace."

> ~ Medjugorje, Yugoslavia
> beginning June 24, 1981

MOUNTAIN JOURNAL ENTRY

Gulls stand sentinel along the ocean's edge like still grey and white painted carvings. It's low tide but they're not fishing; like me, they're just being one with the morning. Boston lies back over my left shoulder, and off my right arm, the cape curves out like a crescent moon beaming toward Provincetown, perched on the final strip of sand.

The sky hangs low this morning, its blue-grey gauze brushing Brewster Beach. Maybe it will rain. Maybe not. It's Boston, after all. Anything can happen. For now this splendor is all mine. My toe nudges vitamin-rich seaweed furrowing the sand. I squint. The ocean is so vast. A flock of birds suddenly comes alive and another walker in a red jacket jostles my periphery against the dunes. A fishing boat rumbles far off, another small boat crosses a wave in front of me and voices fill the space behind. My inner peace is broken.

Interesting verbs we choose to describe our interactions with peace. We break it, we make it, we agree to it, we forge it, we wage it, we offer it, we pass it, we broker it. We think it's something we can bring forth or squelch all on our own, when all we can really be is a channel for it. To do that, I need to be quiet. Really. Quiet.

HEARTBEAT QUESTIONS

What nurtures my spiritual growth? What impedes it?
What is "real" in my life?
How do I experience peace?
Who are my "doves"?
Where has Sophia turned up to offer me unconditional love?

GENTLE QUIETING

It's no accident the word *medicine* and *meditation* both come from the same root word meaning "to cure" and "to measure." When I meditate, I take measure of myself. I measure my breathing, my feelings. I sometimes ask, "How am I doing?" Although meditation can't "cure," I know it can reduce my distress and help me face whatever comes.

Jon Kabat-Zinn, the professor of medicine who founded the Stress Reduction Clinic at the University of Massachusetts Medical School, claims in *Coming to Our Senses: Healing the World and Ourselves Through Mindfulness*, that meditation doesn't catapult you anywhere, nor does it make your mind blank or relaxed. "It's a bodily gesture that inclines your heart and mind toward awareness of the present moment — just as it is." Mindfulness allows us to be exactly *where* we are *as* we are. Surely there is no better definition of non-judgmental love! But accepting things as they are doesn't mean we can't change ourselves and the world.

We can reach this peaceful state with practice but, as Kabat-Zinn points out, it's not necessarily about technique. You don't have to "Om" yourself to some other state. Mindfulness is the opposite of being sleepy. It's being wide, wide, wide awake.

I use St. Francis' prayer to reach a quiet, deeper meditative place. The one that begins: "Make me an instrument of your peace." I learned from Eknath Easwaran that it's good to take a prayer from your own tradition, whatever spiritual tradition that may be. Try to choose something you can easily learn that won't bore you by repeating it. For me, repeating just a one word or mantrum puts me to sleep. I find it interesting that "om" comes from "Ogham," the Celtic word for "Word or Logos." I know it's a powerful word. However, repeating any word over and over just encourages my mind to fly off to more interesting places. But when I memorized the "The Prayer of St. Francis," I was able to establish a word-rhythm in which, as Easwaran suggests, I can cast each word like a pearl dropping slowly into a bowl of oil. One after another after another at just the right pace that keeps my mind from going off into its usual questioning mode: "What do I mean by peace? What does it mean to be an instrument. To be used? To be exploited? To manipulate? What does "your peace" mean? Is it different from "my peace"... and on and on. Instead, I can quiet my mind and focus only on the next word and the next and the next in a way that brings me to an inner mental space of no space.

I begin by saying "Sophia." You can call the divine by whatever name feels right to you. "Lord" felt right to Francis. "*Make me an instrument of your peace. Where there is hatred, let me sow love; where there is injury, pardon; where there is doubt, faith; where there is despair, hope; where there is darkness, light; where there is sadness, joy. Grant that I may not so much seek to be consoled as to console; to be understood as to understand; to be loved as to love. For it is in the giving that I receive, in the pardoning I am pardoned and in the dying I am born to eternal life.*"

For Easwaran, who comes out of the Hindu culture, meditation is a systematic technique for guiding and concentrating our latent mental powers. Through it, we train our minds. He notes that a modern Indian mystic explained our mind's activities like this: A mind that is fast is sick; a mind that is slow is sound; a mind that is still is divine.

So I find a comfortable quiet place, shut my eyes, and breathe into the St. Francis prayer word by word by word. My thoughts no longer wage war with each other. Instead I find a place of peace. It's always there, but I'm usually too noisy or preoccupied to feel it.

A Womb Place of Unconditional Love

Two stone circles, a constructed mound called Silbury Hill, once covered in white stones, and an avenue of "male and female" stones, stand near the West Kennet Barrow. It's a long narrow Neolithic mound. Once, when I was alone, I crawled in and sat very still. I cleared my mind and got that it wasn't a tomb at all, in spite of a few bones archeologists found there. It seemed to be a birthing place. A place where a woman could go to anticipate her pregnancy. Or pray for fertility. A womb-space. I felt a pregnancy of peace. I picked up a small stone from a slippery smooth place where my thumb rested. I hold it whenever I wish to recreate this peaceful Avebury feeling. I've since learned there are more chambers beyond. As in my "Abundance Dream," more treasures await.

Frederick Buechner reminds us in *Wishful Thinking* that the Prince of Peace, even though he once said to his disciples, "Don't think I've come to bring peace on earth; I have not come to bring peace, but a sword," he actually meant he had come to bring peace to our hearts. We'll still have struggles and wars — that is, until we all grow up a bit. But peace, he said, comes through the presence of love.

Unconditional love was the overwhelming presence I felt inside the Kennet Barrow. Earlier, a group of anthropology college students had been touring the barrow. Several were smoking. When I sat down after they'd gone, the cigarette smoke lingered in the air and I thought: "Geez! Who would smoke in a cathedral?" But then Sophia reminded me that it's not a peaceful stance to constantly judge the world, young smokers or anyone else. When I view everything from only my perspective, I forget that other people don't always think the way I think, or value what I value.

"To oppose unconditional Love is to permit judgment, intolerance, possessiveness, jealousy, hypocrisy, and fear to overwhelm you. To practice unconditional Love is to focus all desire toward serving the greater good of all beings through loving, compassionate understanding. Unconditional love perceives from the other's viewpoint. It practices discernment so precisely that it becomes next to impossible to intentionally overstep another's will. One knows beyond a shadow of a doubt that nothing is between individuals and that everything is between the individual and God."

~ Patricia Pereira, *Eagles of the New Dawn*

HER GIFT: A PEACEFUL NATURE

Edith Wharton called this peaceful "barrow place" a "noble attitude." The Sophia in each of us recognizes deep community when we see it, and we desperately want things to work together. In *The House of Mirth*, "What [Lily Bart] craved, and really felt herself entitled to, was a situation in which the noblest attitude should also be the easiest."

But it's not easy. We're pulled in too many directions. We think we don't have enough time. Not enough resources. Not enough, period.

Sai Baba, the Indian guru to many, used this acronym for peace: Perfected Ego Acknowledge Christ Everywhere. I like that. And if we could spell it "pease" I'd suggest: Please Everyone Acknowledge Sophia Everywhere.

Most Celtic spiritual practices are rooted in peace. I wanted to tell the young man I met at the Veteran's Hospital not long ago about the Frank Mac Eowen book I was reading. But I put it down when I sensed that he wanted to talk. *The Mist-Filled Path* could wait. He told me he was suffering from "polytrauma," a new word for me, but one I suspected means *everything* hurts. He had spine and leg problems from an IED (Improvised Explosive Device) in Iraq, along with Post Traumatic Stress Disorder (PTSD). "I can't get a job. If my wife's folks hadn't taken us in, I don't know what we'd do." This young man was anything but at peace. I thought, *OK Francis.... "Where there is despair, let me sow hope." Let me at least try.* We spoke about the new wing of the Vet's Hospital in White River Junction and how wonderful the PTSD staff was. We spoke of Obama's increased budget for veteran care; we spoke of his wonderful family supporting him. He tried to smile a couple of times. I thanked him for his service. As soon as I said it, I realized it was as hollow a phrase as "I am sorry for your loss."

In the Celtic tradition, our souls have three cauldrons and if one suffers, they all do. The belly is the life force and warms us; the heart and solar plexus call us to what we have passion to do; the head provides our wisdom. All three of the young vet's cauldrons were dangerously close to empty.

We know what peace feels like, we just aren't sure how to create it. A loving action feels very much different than one of disrespect. We know when we enter a room or building if it's "at peace" or not.

Sophia Icon, written by Katriina Fyrlund of Varberg, Sweden

ICONS: WINDOWS INTO HEAVEN

My Sophia icon radiates peace. I believe she "writes" us just as iconographers "write" her. That's how colorful icons — *eikon* — are made, you know. They're written, not painted. The iconographer prays before picking up a brush. Katriina Fyrlund of Varberg, Sweden, prayed for my continued health before she started this icon, a most amazing Christmas gift from my son. A few Decembers ago we took the train to her house where her living room was lined with sparkling gold and colorful images — vibrations caught in color.

Katriina gets all her materials from Russia where the monks, who secretly continued to paint in spite of the Communist laws against it, truly know about icons. Once she's completed an icon, she seals it with a liquid the monks concoct from ox gall, crushed blackberries, crushed rowan berries and linseed oil among other "secret" ingredients. It creates a surface that will last for six hundred years.

Icons are not realistic images, but stylized fragments of a deep spiritual reality — a pathway into the invisible. They are codes, painted with great attention to detail. My Sophia sits with Mary to her right, John the Baptist to her left. They both stand on platforms which is a recognized icon symbol meaning they were humans who once "stood" on earth. Christ is above. And in the original icon, angels hover above it all.

Most icons are copied from older works. The original of my Sophia icon hangs in Moscow's Sophia Ascension Cathedral. Like her, "my" Sophia wears a Byzantine robe, which is common since most icons were first painted during that period, and even though she's not an angel, she has red wings. She reigns over the cosmos with the earth as her footstool. In one hand, she holds a staff; in the other, a scroll as a symbol of the Word, the Bible. The red is cinnabar. The background is 23.8 carat gold leaf.

According to iconic legend, Luke the Evangelist painted a dark-skinned Mary caressing her child. He painted it on a large piece of the table from Mary's home that, legend says, Jesus built. As a result, icons ever after have been created onto wooden planks. Mary took the icon with her when she went with John to Ephesus; then it found its way back to Jerusalem where it gained a reputation for protecting the place where it resided. Constantine wanted it to protect his new city of Constantinople, so that's where it was for years. It was called a "palladium" after Pallas Athena. Among other things, the silvery-white metal by the same name protects our air, as it's used

in catalytic converters and our groundwater's purification and treatment. She continues to protect.

A subsequent copy of Luke's original icon eventually made its
way to Russia to protect Moscow from Tamerlane, and, in 1395,
it took up residence in the Dormition Cathedral in the Moscow
Kremlin. It currently resides in a Moscow museum and is called
Umilinya, Mother of God (See p. 242.). I saw it on exhibition at the
Clinton, Massachusetts Russian Icon Museum and the hair on my
arms stood up when I entered the room it dominated. It's big! She
is big. Her love is big!

After they are painted, icons, traditionally, are blessed in a worship setting, as mine was on July 28, 2008 in an historical Episcopal
church near Randolph, Vermont. It's then that icons "come alive."
And indeed she did, as brilliant summer light streamed through 18th
century windows. The congregation prayed:

*O Lord our God, Who created us after Your own Image and Likeness; Who
redeems us from our former corruption of the ancient curse through Your human
befriending Christ, Who took upon Himself the form of a servant and became
man; Who having taken upon Himself our likeness remade Your Saints of the
first dispensation, and through Whom also we are refashioned in the Image of
Your pure blessedness; Your Saints we venerate as being in Your Image and Likeness, and we adore and glorify You as our Creator;*

*Wherefore we pray You, send forth Your blessing upon this Icon, and with the
sprinkling of hallowed water, bless and make holy this Sophia Icon unto Your
glory, and grant that this sanctification will be to all who venerate this Icon of
Saint Sophia and send up their prayer unto You standing before it;*

*Through the grace and bounties and love of Your Only-Begotten Son, with Whom
You are blessed together with Your All-Holy, Good and Life-creating Spirit; both
now and ever, and unto ages of ages. Amen.*

Icons can open up the inner senses, unveiling for a brief time
the dazzling brilliance of Sophia's beauty inside everything and everyone. After the blessing, we sang a hymn, part of which describes
Sophia's birthing of creations out of chaos: *"From the nothingness of*

space, *kindling life where all was empty, turning chaos into grace: when we feel confused and fruitless, dawn upon our restless night; give us faith's imagination, hope's renewing, love's delight."* (Carl P. Daw, Jr.)

While icons are extraordinary, all art has the potential to invite her in. As Arthur Versluis said in *Egyptian Mysteries*: "Any work of art is ultimately an entry-point into the transcendent, revelatory of not only subtle, but celestial beauty and power, and if the given work is not so, it cannot be properly called art at all ... all works of art ... are religious, sacred or nothing."

Christopher Alexander, an architect, thinker and writer dear to my heart, said in an essay called, "A Foreshadowing of 21st Century Art": "It is as if the thing, the bronze, or the carpet, establishes itself in its own belly as a voice, speaks with my voice, exists with my own force and forces my awareness of an ultimate mother ... of which I am a part — which exists in me." She is *immanent*. Inside. *With* us.

"The icons of old are the codings of tomorrow," Jean Houston said, "And tomorrow holds the promise of forgotten wisdom.

Enneagram Number 4

Number Fours typically are romantics. They're lovers. They strive to be authentic and unique — real individualists. They can be high-strung and self-indulgent and moody at times, especially when sadness threatens to swamp them. They like to have a script, a plan to follow, and rather than ask, "Who am I?" they are more apt to ask: "Who am I with?" Fours have to keep moving. Energetic! They're very creative and have intense feelings. They value staying connected to people and can readily recognize others' talents. They appreciate and foster beauty, but they have to watch themselves because they can run down and spend themselves before they know it.

HER SPECIAL GEO-SPOT: IONA

Iona, *I Chaluim Chille* — the island of Colm Cille — is three miles long, one mile wide, and bobs off the west coast of Scotland like a holy buoy. It's both austere and welcoming. Celtic and modern. *Ione* is "her" word — a feminine word related to yoni or vulva.

Joel and I caught the ferry to Mull, and then made our way on foot, as all pilgrims must, to Iona from Finnphort. Iona is such an old piece of earth that it predates living creatures — no fossils can be found there. There is a prophecy that says: "Seven years before the day of judgment the ocean will sweep over Ireland but the Isle of Columba will swim above the waves."

I picked up a small egg-shaped stone. Purple heather on the moor had turned yellowish green and sheep peppered the knolls. We walked around the cliffs and bays and up to Dun I, the highest point, which we climbed in ten minutes. I wanted to see Ireland, but it was too hazy. The sea was "machair" green — Iona green.

When Columba's hide-covered coracle landed, he knew it was her dove-place. Prince Columcille, later St. Columba, was of the Conaill Clan, born in 531C.E., ninety years after Patrick arrived to be Ireland's bishop. Columba is called "the dove of the church." An intense young man, he founded sixty monasteries at such places as Durrow, Kells, and Derry. He loved books. So much so that he once illegally copied a Psalter and was punished for it. Nevertheless, that act established copyright law. "To every cow, her calf." One copy allowed. A warrior by training, it was natural for him, when one of his monks was killed, to take up arms. As a result he was exiled to Iona with twelve of his faithful brothers. Eventually they numbered one hundred and fifty. Nothing remains of his original

Iona monastery. My Viking ancestors murdered sixty-eight monks down by the jetty in 806.

Queen Margaret restored the monastery for the Augustinians, then it was rebuilt for the Benedictines and dedicated to Mary. Joel and I entered Oran's pink granite chapel where I lit a candle for my mother, Ellen. Sixty kings are buried on the grounds. Forty-eight from Scotland, four from Ireland and eight from Norway. They include Kenneth MacAlpin, who unified Scotland, Macbeth, Duncan, and many highland chiefs.

Columba forbade cattle on the island; the monks who cling to rocky spires in Greece forbid chickens, even today. Why? Because they are female. Columba said, "Where there are cattle there are women and where there are women, there is mischief."

Tall standing stones once spiraled around Iona. There's no evidence of them now; no doubt they were all used in various religious constructions. The Stone of Destiny is said to have come from Iona. That's the stone Irish kings sat on to be crowned at Tara and later it rested under the Coronation chair in Westminster Abbey. Recently, it returned to its rightful home in Scotland.

Wise as a Serpent, Gentle as a Dove

We bumped over the Apian Way, a tiny old Roman road, in a bus that had no shock absorbers. Our destination: St. Sebastian's church. That was where a young Roman Christian guard was buried after he was tortured and killed with multiple arrows. Below the church lay the catacombs. Peter and Paul were buried here first, and then later moved to St. Peter's. It was where many early Christians hid out, prayed, ate together, and, surrounded by all these graves, anticipated their own deaths.

Catacombs dove from a wall drawing, c. 100 C.E., Rome, Italy

This hideout is only a few miles from downtown Rome and its infamous bloody coliseum sporting events. Early Christians left clay graffiti-prayers on the walls to remind us of who they were. We walked underground for what seemed like miles, listening to underground stories written on soft stone.

Prior to the 300s, Christians allowed women to be priests. They believed, as I do, that the Holy Spirit was female, in the guise of Sophia — often depicted as a dove. Burial niches called columbaria — from the Latin for "dovecotes" — honeycomb these underground passageways once sacred to Venus, whose name also means dove. The olive branch, like the one Noah's dove brought back to the ark, symbolized her peace. Solomon called his lover his dove — his perfect one.

Up until the thirty-year-old man named Jesus was baptized by John in the Jordon River, he was merely human. Then Sophia-The Holy Spirit, in the form of a dove, came to the Jordon River on his baptism day and in a motherly voice said, "This is my son!" It was then he became "Christ." Man-God. And he remained so until his death, and after, for he is as present to us in ethereal form as he ever was as a human. Fifty days after Easter, something else important happened. The disciples were gathered, with Mary, and a big wind blew through the house. At that Pentecost-point, Sophia became one with Mary. Just as Jesus was "en-Christed" at his baptism, Mary was "en-Sophiaed" at Pentecost. Up until then, Mary had been just a human woman — like us. And just as her son is present every-where — every minute, and to everyone who wishes to be with him — so is she.

It was Sophia's sense of humor, no doubt, to arrange for Co-lumba, the Irish prince, to be tutored by Druids, and then land on an island which, like his name, means "dove." His express purpose was to launch Christianity into Europe. I find it no coincidence that he landed on this island of standing stones, Dove-Island, on Pente-cost, May 12, 563 C.E. Columba returned to Ireland from Iona, at least once, to plead the cause of the bards — Druid poets. He said, "Don't banish them. Just widen the circle. Teach others what they know." Unfortunately, for all of us, they were banned. And like So-phia, they went into hiding. We suffer for not widening our circles.

Doves permeate our heavens. Pleiades, for instance, is called the "flock of doves." White birds have long been associated with the divine feminine. And like women, they have often been sacri-ficial figures. When Jesus cautioned his disciples to be (like Sophia) as wise as serpents and harmless as doves, he was referring to her "serpent wisdom" — the one depicted in so many ancient mystery cultures. Serpents, along with winged serpents or dragons, are cos-mic images deeply imprinted in us. Some say our genes remember serpentine-bird-like dinosaurs. We hold a primordial memory.

The serpent and the dove is a combined metaphor for the cre-ation goddess, and you'll find her all around the earth. She appears as the Grandmother who wraps the Australian continent, and in the images in Yucatan temple ruins called "the house of doves." Early creation myths tell of a dove brooding on the waters, finally laying an egg — the earth — and then a serpent coiling around the egg seven times to give birth to everything in the world. The Adena earthen Serpent Mound in Locust Grove, Ohio winds seven times — an egg is enclosed in its mouth. As we've seen, Ix Chel wears a serpent on her head, and female figures found in Crete's women are shown with serpents wrapped around their arms and heads. Serpent figures symbolize feminine wisdom.

Then a strange thing happened. Male compilers of the Old Testament morphed Mother-serpent wisdom into evil Satan in the garden and everything bad in the world became Eve's fault. It wasn't just Eve who was thrown out of paradise — Mother, Virgin, Crone were all thrown out of the garden. Despised. Rejected.

ELISE BOULDING: MODERN MOTHER OF PEACE

Like a Norwegian "Druid," Elise, the mother of our modern peace movement, spent her whole life calling for Truth. She was born in Oslo in 1920, and three years later, her family emigrated to New Jersey. When the Nazis invaded Norway, she realized there was no safe place on earth. "And I knew that I had found my life's mission," she said.

Elise died the year this book was written. I like to imagine that she would have enjoyed reading about the strong cadre of women

Elise Boulding, photo kind courtesy of the Boulding family

willing, along with her, to change the course of our planet's history. "It's been proved in all peace organizations that when women are in a coordinating role, it works better," she said. "I don't think this is a genetic thing. It's cultural. Partly, I think, it's because women's culture involves a lot of listening." Another time she said, "We need more women in decision-making positions, both in government and in the public sphere. Especially in the United States." But she also, as a mother of five, realized that — "If one is mentally out of breath all the time from dealing with the present, there is no energy left for imagining the future."

Women are better equipped to handle conflict in ways that don't involve bombs and guns. Early on, she condemned the use of napalm and the destruction of homes and crops in Vietnam. Elise longed for the day America would no longer be a "superpower," and instead, returned to a more modest role in the world community. She supported China's role in the world community and called for poverty to be abolished, along with discrimination, so every member of our world community could reach his or her fullest potential.

Elise Boulding believed that peace cultures thrive on, and are nourished by, how we envision the world. Include all ages of people in your work, she implored. Remember the women and children in any situation you face. Include art, music, dance, poetry, and theater in all you do for the human spirit needs it. And remember, she reminded us, to have fun. Truly, she was Sophia's voice.

SOPHIA'S MYSTICAL DANCER:
JULIAN OF NORWICH (1342-1416)

Since we don't know her given name, we call her Julian because she chose to live in an enclosed space within the church of St. Julian in the busy port city of Norwich, England. She was a contemporary of Chaucer's. After she recovered from the deadly plague, she had her first vision, her "showings," in May of 1373.

Christ, to her, was "our Mother from whom we are endlessly born." She also called him Christ-Sophia and taught that he doesn't take suffering away — he enters it with us.

As an anchoress, Julian anchored herself to the world by praying and meditating within her cell. She had a little window to the outside street, so even from the confines of her dim candle-lit room, she could talk to people who came by. "Remember," she said, "the world is criss-crossed with the footprints of God." And God, she explains, is not necessarily masculine, but rather a loving parent who, like a warm woolen shawl, daily wraps us in love. "The high might of the Trinity is our Father, and the deep wisdom of the Trinity is our Mother, and the great love of the Trinity is our Lord: and all that we have is in nature and in the making of our substance." She made a point of saying God is happy because he is our Father, he is our Mother. He is our spouse and our soul is his beloved wife. Julian could see the whole world in a little hazelnut balanced on her outstretched palm. T.S. Eliot borrowed her famous phrase and inserted it into his "Four Quartets": "All shall be well, and all manner of thing shall be well."

ONCE UPON A TIME:
The Velveteen Rabbit

I am a fat rabbit, but nicely made. My body's velveteen and my ears are satin pink. Once Boy said, "It's Christmas now." The other toys knew "Christmas" but I had to wait to figure out what that meant. It was very dark. I remember that.

But even in the daylight, I'm not always sure of what I'm seeing. Nana rules the nursery. One day she said I wasn't a real rabbit.

"What is REAL?" I asked the Skin Horse who seems to know everything.

"It's a thing that happens to you. When a child loves you for a long, long time, not just to play with, but REALLY loves you, then you become Real."

Oh. If you are wondering how long this takes, I found out it's a long time. I guess it's when most of your hair gets loved off and your eyes droop.

Once when Nana was flying around tidying up, Boy couldn't find the china dog he usually slept with. So Nana threw me onto the bed. "Here, take your old Bunny!" Boy held me and talked to me and we played. Pretty soon Boy couldn't sleep without me.

One summer day as Boy and I were playing outside, he dropped me in the grass and wandered off. Then the most amazing thing happened. A couple of hopping rabbits came by. I couldn't see their seams. "Come dance with us," they said. They sniffed me, then hopped away saying I wasn't real. But I knew I was.

One day Boy became very ill. Scarlet Fever. Nana said all his toys had to be burned. I was stuffed into a sack with all the other toys and carried out behind the chicken house. Lying there on the ground in a most un-rabbity pose, I began to shiver. A single tear ran down my shabby nose. And where it fell, a flower sprouted. It was the color of emeralds and there was a golden cup in the center. It opened and out stepped a tiny fairy with butterfly wings. "The toys this boy loved, I have made Real," she said. But I was confused. "Wasn't I real before?" "Only to the boy," she explained. And it's true! Now I have strong hind legs and I can dance! Off I hopped to find the other rabbits.

When Boy got better, he was looking out his window one day and he said, "Look!" He saw his rabbit bouncing along — a rabbit with the exact same markings as ... me!

Sophia, disguised as a fairy, offers the velveteen rabbit life. Sophia disguised as Nana cares for the boy and protects him — sometimes with tough love. She's wise, like the Skin-Horse, and as the hopping rabbits, she offers friendship. Her unconditional love makes the little rabbit, and all of us, *real*.

Graham Greene said: "Hate is just a failure of imagination." What makes "true love" *true* is that it isn't based just on hopeful thinking. What we can imagine, we can create. Underneath our scruffy bunny suits, as Margery Williams, author of *The Velveteen Rabbit*, well knew, we are specially marked velveteen and silk.

We are *real* lovers and peacemakers.

FROM SOPHIA'S NOTEBOOK

There can be no peace without love. Love does, indeed, manifest in toughness and difficult choices sometimes. Building boundaries for self-safety and well-being, and helping others to build their own, is never easy. But when love is the force that forges these boundaries, then love can also forgive and erase the guilt that enjoys creeping in.

Love is a force stronger than any other. Love is the cushion around life's sharp edges. Love is always present; families are formed to manifest love in very real ways. Love comes when relationships ask it in. Love is ready — every second — to ease the burdens. With love comes trust — trust in tried systems, trust that choices, however difficult, are undergirded by love. Love is greater than fear. The dark forces of fear creep in to separate and drive wedges between. Love erases those fears; it binds, bonds, holds, supports, bridges, balances, and reassures. You may think there are limits to this force, when in fact, there are no limits to love. It is truly boundless. Fear tries to draw limits; love is outside every box fear tries to draw. Love is endless. Children, when they find themselves in loving homes, learn this fact as actual experience, day to day to day. And when parents tend to forget, momentarily, the children are there to remind them of this universal love-truth. No end, no limit, no rules can be set up to force or contain love. Love will always creep in.

chapter five
SHE KNOWS US

Crop Circle: Roundway Hill, near Devizes, Wiltshire, July 25, 2010

· ·

*"Our Mother thou who art in the darkness of the underworld, may
the holiness of thy name shine anew in our remembering."*

~ Robert Powell, *The Sophia Teachings*

MOUNTAIN JOURNAL ENTRY

I long to hear spring's song birds. Winter's silence wraps me tight.
Bare poplar and white birch branches poke the sky like nervous gan-
glia. War hangs heavy. I ask Sophia: *Why are your children scrabbling in
the dunes? Why do your children keep hurling missiles and threats? Why are your
children so lost, so scared, so lonely? All we need do is look up into the night sky
and see your handiwork. You have handcrafted, knitted, and knotted constellations
in place. What right have the little lost boys to try to rearrange your stars?*

It's midnight dark. Unsure. Shadowy. Things lurk. All my emotions are caked over in ice. Tamped down. Quilted over. Tacked and
held. Frozen rain without the beauty and lightness of snow. Heavy
tears. Grey drops holding somberness. Not terror. That's much too
strong. No, they're Saturn-drops of lead.

My spirit soared with what I thought were birdcalls yesterday.
But today they, like me, seem frozen. What do birds use to de-ice
their wings?

HEARTBEAT QUESTIONS

How do I let hardships "go"?

What do I most fear? What are *my* shadows?

Have I allowed "ugly stepmothers" to come into my life to teach me something? What?

What keeps me from becoming the "royal bride"?

How would I describe my limitations?

HEARING THE CATARACT

In Norse mythology, Grandmother Goddess Fjorgyn is most alive and active during the dark wintery months. Frigg is the "mother," a summer presence; Freya is the "daughter" and most active in spring. But it's Fjorgyn of the night and of the earth that grants us solitude, security, protection and comfort. By December of a fateful year, I grew to know Fjorgyn well.

On March 6, I began to notice serious gas pains in my chest and stomach. Not the usual kind from eating cabbage or beans, but unkind ripplings. An ultrasound showed no problem with my gall bladder or liver. My doctor cautioned: Watch for a fever. None. Just gas pains. I tried over-the-counter gas-relievers and different foods, but the soreness and mild pain just sort of shifted around. When I breathed deeply I got a "catch" in my side like I used to get when as a kid I ran too fast. Finally, in August, a CT scan sent me off to see an oncologist.

Allen Wheelis, who wrote *The Seeker*, described my state of mind perfectly. "Then one day it's not someone else. The name on the report of malignancy is your own ... you clench your teeth and try not to hear the cataract. You had thought it was twenty miles downstream, but it's just around the corner."

People look at me differently now. Not so much in pity as in awe. I'm in "another place." A not-really-*our*-dimension place. I see words in their eyes: "Oh, no! This could happen to me!"

We say cancer "strikes" as if it's a snake coming out of no-where with deadly fangs aimed your way. But cancer doesn't strike as much as take up residence. Cancer settles in like an unwelcome guest demanding attention. I concentrated on my chakras — especially the orange one. I read dozens of books, some happened to be about women whistleblowers in corporations and government and I thought: we "ovarians" and "breasts" have learned how to lance pus from all sorts of infected wounds.

I meditate. I hear: *Humbly accept your challenges.* I know she knows me. Admission. Remission. Submission.

Frederick Buechner wrote about a man named *Godric*: God's Wreck, in Anglo-Saxon. I feel great affinity for that little wreck of a man whose best friend was Roger Mouse. "I needed Mouse for his strength and mirth and daring. Mouse needed me for my mettle and my wit." Godric speculates about prayer. "It's shooting shafts into the dark. What mark they strike, if any, who's to say? It's reaching for a hand you cannot touch.... You beg. You whimper...."

Standing on our western deck, under an August finger-nail moon the night before my ovarian cancer surgery, I finally moved past whimper into a quiet place of rest. The moon whispered, "You're now at the beginning of something new." I asked my Sophia-circle women, my "Roger Mice," to hold me, visually. "Wrap me in the Milky Way." Up here in the middle of Vermont, the Milky Way powders the midnight blue sky in bold streaks. I scanned its white lacy arms looking for that pointer sign from my National Geographic map that says, "We Are Here." I longed to feel the Sagittarius Arm and the Orion Arm hug me as I prepared to stilt-walk across the universe.

"Let me learn what it is I'm supposed to learn from all this." What I soon learned was that pain tells you where there isn't any pain, just as the dark shows you where there isn't any light. As soon as I turned out the lamp by my bed, my eyes popped open. Fear gnawed my chest and ground my spine. Doubts tiptoed in. What happened to my faith in God? In medicine? In Sophia? In my body? I drew some small amount of consolation from Frederich

Buechner who said in *Wishful Thinking*: "Doubts are the ants in the pants of faith. They keep it awake and moving." I doubt I'm up to this. I doubt I'm strong enough to handle what might come after surgery. I just plain doubt.

People with cancer number in the hundreds of thousands. Some say we are one out of every seven; others say one out of every three. Anyone who has experienced this particular challenge knows the extreme fatigue, the aches, the digestive track troubles. The depression. Cancer is commonplace. But I hadn't experienced it before, so it was all new to me.

On one of my first appointments to the infusion suite of our nearby Dartmouth Medical Center, I was struck by a theophany. That's what theophanies do — they sneak up behind you, clunk you on your head and say, "Hey! Get it now?" Suddenly I understood why Christ had to incarnate in a human body in order to "understand" humanity. Until it's *you* hooked up to that IV stand, with bags of poison dangling over your head, dripping into your veins, you can't really know what it's like to have cancer. Loved ones and visitors, as well meaning as they are, simply can't completely understand. Christ had to push Jesus' human IV stand around long enough to truly know *human*.

I marveled that my body could tolerate something as deadly as Carbo Taxol — yew tree juice. One day, one of my suite mates smiled and said, "You, know, this is like drinking a can of Drano!" We mirrored macabre smiles. The yew tree is so deadly poisonous, in fact, that all animals know enough not to even go near it — and they are not for one minute seduced by those little red berries with the pretty death knell bell-stones hanging inside. Since animals don't eat them, hardy yew trees live for centuries. Celts called them trees of immorality. When monks appropriated various earlier Druid sites — usually near springs or wells — they overlaid them with their Christian structures and the yew trees that grew there became part of their cloistered cemeteries. As in underpainting, the earlier energy never goes away.

Great, I thought, I'm being infused with cemetery trees. But then, in my peripheral image, I saw Sophia winking at me. Yew trees are also a symbol for warriors, she reminded me. Long bows were made from their strong branches. The Rune "yr" or "eur" governs journeys and quests, searches, transformation, the higher law, and the soul. I was engaged, it seems, in some serious soul-making.

Strange how the words "cancer" and "cemetery" can become the loudest words in your vocabulary. Like a drifting boat, my soul rocked every time I stepped through those oncology doors. I was dizzy, even with steady John at my side. And he *was there* — every time. When I passed through the same oncology doors a few years later for more treatment, in a strange way, I felt I had come back home. I was surrounded by the same IV stands and ministered to by many of the same *wonderful* oncology nurses. I sat in the same recliners and I kept asking the same questions: Why can't we spend a few more research dollars on finding new cures? How can we continue to say goodbye to so many of our friends and family members without demanding that we turn our attention away from war and toward healthcare? When are we going to address the real causes rather than go on treating (or failing to treat) symptoms?

My infusions lasted about as long as a trip across the Atlantic, with just about the same tired food served and the same efforts to get to the bathroom. But it's a nurse, not a flight attendant, who finally announces your destination. You unhook your seat belt, put up your tray table, teeter down the aisle through the double doors into the waiting room and enter a new country.

I reread Madeleine L'Engle's *Wind Through the Door* to remember how mitochondria and farandolae dance in my cells. They're little immune furnaces and they need stoking. I eat protein. I munch bright colored vegetables. I try to avoid caffeine and drink gallons and gallons of water. And, miracle of miracles, I continue to live. My farandolae somehow know the next dance steps.

And through it all, I meditate, I draw great sustenance from people in my little church, people in my e-letter chain, neighbors on our little mountain, from my gardens, and most of all, from my sons and husband who always seem to know the right timing. And how to keep me laughing. How did they learn when to step in and when to let me step out by myself? "Angels" drop in just as I need what they have to offer. All of this has taught me to ponder "all the company of heaven."

I began making a list of my "angels" and the gifts they brought. Dawna with Reiki, Diane with prayer, Margaret offering harp music, my "Sophia Circle" with visualizations of the Milky Way wrapping me in healing stardust, Jenny's chakra healing, Sherry's biofeedback balancing, Barbara's healing stones, Julia's watercolors, Mary Ann's stories, Karen's star-filled lap quilt, Callie's star card, Sharon's rituals, Joe with his e-jokes, and a host of others, all holding me in light. But most of all, John, who picks up Netflix, gives me massages, manages my wound care, goes to the library, gives me hugs, prepares great meals, engages me in long talks.

A cancer-survivor's life takes on the numbers game. Are they up? Are they down? You learn lab routines by heart. And, like *Jaws*, just when you think it's safe to get back into the water, you hear that awful monotone music again. And you walk through those same "Oncology" doors, again.

My husband has given me several buzz cuts. When hair begins to fall into food, you know it's time ... as he tossed my hair over the railing of our deck, my husband said, "Here, Chipmunks. Use it to line your winter nests." Our taller son, Nathan, affectionately kisses the top of my head and calls me "Chia Head."

I've been so lucky! My appetite's been with me the whole time. My bones have remained strong and I've tolerated most foods without being nauseous. I've drunk my share of wine; I've had no mouth sores. I've managed on most days to walk around a grocery store without feeling overwhelming fatigue, but John's been by my side to push the cart when it got too heavy. But make no mistake about it, chemo-patients need help to carry, to fetch, to support, whether they ask for it or not.

One day as I was hooked up to my IV stand, a little six or seven year old girl ran past me playing some game of her own creation. She was as bald as I was. Sophia seemed to be sending me a message: *You can deal with all this toxicity if you continue to giggle.*

More surgery was required in 2009, and as I recovered, I noticed a black bunny hopping across the April lawn outside my window. I hoped to be home for Easter, and the black rabbit may have been Sophia's way of saying: *Maybe. Maybe not. Not all rabbits are white. But, remember, the black rabbit's mine as well. Black-white, sickness-health, up-down, life-death. It's all part of this earth-game you're in.*

You learn to rejoice in small things. One trip around the quad turns into strength enough for five and then ten. You pass people who are undergoing various sorts of treatments and you wonder if they'll be home for Easter. You overhear snippets of last-stages of life planning and you think: it's always resurrection time in this part of the hospital.

A strange thing happened several days into my stay — and I use the word "days" because in hospitals there are no "nights." No one sleeps — staff or patients. On four separate occasions I saw a frame at the foot of my bed — like a flat screen TV, but in shades of grey and white. Within the rectangular frame, mist swirled. Beautiful swirling patterns morphed into new patterns. At first I thought it was mechanically caused by a humidifier exhaust. Of course there are no bacteria-laden humidifiers in a ward that doesn't even allow real flowers because most patients are severely immune-deficient. And it's not likely it would have appeared within a perfect frame. My drugs had been cut back. I couldn't come up with any rational explanation for this rectangle of perfectly formed mist that appeared in the same frame in the same spot at the foot of my bed. And it wasn't only confined to one room because, after a few days, I found myself in a different room and there it was again. Each time it appeared for only four or five seconds — I counted. And it always had the exact same moving, swirling pattern. I heard nothing, nor was I disturbed by it. I interpreted it as a *presence*, a Celtic mist that didn't need to be defined or explained. It just was there. And then it disappeared as quickly as it came. It seemed to be telling me something. Or playing games with me. Sophia's presence, along with cancer in your cells, I've since decided, can feel misty. It comes and goes.

OUR SHADOW-SELVES

The other night we watched Jamie Foxx and Robert Downey Jr. in *The Soloist*. It's the real-life story of a homeless musician, Nathaniel Ayers, who is befriended by a Los Angeles Times journalist, Steve Lopez. One night-scene shows a segment of the 90,000 homeless people who wander the streets of Los Angeles. It could have been straight out of a Brueghel painting of any dark, demonic, smelly medieval city. But it wasn't. It was in America, and it was now.

Homelessness is only one of the many shadows we face as a country. Racism and hatred of "the other" are a few examples of what Carl Jung called our shadow-sides. Unless we recognize these "darker" towering places within each of us — and within our culture — and name them, face them and integrate them, we won't heal and we won't grow. Shadows cripple. They stalk. They masquerade as half-truths. The more we open up our cobwebby corners, the faster we'll heal. My oncologist has helped me "name" and face up to the "truth" about ovarian cancer. As much as I'm the "Queen of de Nile," I am stronger for it.

The Japanese have two concepts for "truth." *Honne* and *tatemae*. The first is "real," the second is just the façade of truth. Barry Eisler, in his 2010 book — a thriller called *Inside Out* — claims society needs *tatemae*. One of his characters says: "Think about Gitmo. What was that all about?" Not about having a place to put the bad guys, the other guy answered. (That's a *honne* answer.) "The real purpose of Gitmo was to make the public feel safe.

Whether it was actually making anyone safe was a secondary consideration at best. Hell, the truth is, we didn't even know who we were putting in there, we just wanted a big number so we could announce to the pubic that we'd captured eight hundred of the 'worst of the worst.' Who wouldn't sleep better at night knowing so many of our enemies had been taken out of the game? But we knew most of them were innocent. But it didn't matter. We needed the number."

We like to think we're a shining beacon to the world, but as Goethe said, "Where the light is brightest, the shadows are deepest."

And no one is exempt. "Everyone carries a shadow," Jung said, "and the less it is embodied in the individual's conscious life, the blacker and denser it is. At all counts, it forms an unconscious snag, thwarting our most well-meant intentions."

My Sophia-friend, Penny Hauser, has written a book called *Broken by Addiction: Blessed by God*. It's about women in recovery, but, as a psychiatric nurse, she knows we all have some "black bunnies" hanging around. She says, "Anger gets triggered when the events in our lives do not match our values."

I find my own anger triggered when I expect people to be treated with respect and love and then realize they're not. I'm angry to learn that if you lined up ten women and said, "OK. Those of you who have never been physically or emotionally abused can sit down now," only one or possibly two women will be able to sit. The women still standing ask themselves, "How can I ever forgive what happened to me? Will I ever forget?" Penny says maybe not, unless they can feel the embrace of a gentle, loving God. She quotes Bishop Tutu: "Forgive and forget is what we are often encouraged to do. But that is not possible — at least the forget part. In fact, we need to remember."

We need to remember.

When my husband and I visited Greece and trudged up to Delphi, I had already read a lot about how people climbed these same steep inclines to visit female seers. The "Pythia" were hard-working women who warned, prophesied and diagnosed people's ills. They were the *bone* — the real truth-tellers, but people often needed to transform the truth into something more palatable. Then, as at all of her sites, a male took over. In this case, the male figure was Apollo and it was his temple that usurped hers. But Apollo's priests still kept a few women around to sit on their tripod stools to access earth's "dark wisdom" for them because they couldn't. They needed women to be their mouth-pieces. Until men realize that her wisdom is available to everyone, misogynists will continue to fear women as "the other" and our shadows will only lengthen.

We need to remember.

Prior to American women getting the right to vote in 1920, women could vote in sixteen other countries where discriminatory shadows had lightened a bit. Susan B. Anthony fought for over fifty years before the 19th amendment was finally ratified. Have you heard all the reasons women shouldn't be able to vote? Suffering Suffragettes! Let me tell you. Pamphlets were 1917's answer to the blog. I've taken the liberty of rewriting this a bit, but one pamphlet scattered and tacked around in public places stated women shouldn't vote because:

Husbands, fathers and brothers already represented them. If laws need to be changed, women can indirectly correct and influence (Now this argument ironically proved to be true as Harry Burn, a twenty-four year old Tennessee state legislator, changed his "no" vote to "yes" after his mother urged him to do so. Tennessee became the much needed 36th state to ratify the amendment and Harry Burn's mother could finally vote.).

Women shouldn't be given the right to vote because it would double the ignorant vote; bad women would outvote the good ones; men know more about business than women do; women would cease to be respected; women were already overburdened and have "higher" duties and shouldn't have to be bothered to vote as well; it will lead to family quarrels and increase divorce; it will destroy chivalry; women are too emotional and sentimental to be trusted with the ballot; it would only double the vote without changing the results; we already have too many voters. And finally, it would turn women into men!

The amendment was signed into law with no fanfare whatsoever. The leading women warriors weren't even invited to attend the ceremony, for there was none. I can vote in Tunbridge, Vermont now because of one vote by a Tennessee youngster named Harry Burn.

In his book, *Evil*, Roy Baumeister says the Ku Klux Kan didn't begin as a violent organization. Six bored young men after the Civil War couldn't find work and they wanted some action. So in 1866 they started a club. "Let's dress up in costumes, just for fun." The bedsheets came out and soon new members, like frat boys, were assigned hazing tasks. Wouldn't it be funny to go spook some black people? And play a few pranks? How did boys in goblin costumes turn into an organization that even well-known politicians joined? A terror organization known for lynchings and burnings? Is the explanation as simple as: People drink. They lose control. They cross "the line." They get away with it. People they look up to endorse it. It wins votes?

We're good at using euphemisms to hide what we're really doing. Baumeister lists a few: *ethnic cleansing* (Bosnia), *final solution* and *special handling* (Nazi Holocaust), *relax* (Spanish Inquisition) *bush clearing* (Rwanda). People who *torture* never use that word. Instead, they use expressions such as: tea party, dance, birthday party, the telephone, the submarine, the swallow, the airplane. Innocuous words, right? We don't send people to foreign countries to be harshly questioned and most likely tortured, we "rendition them." We like to Latinize our words; we add "ate" to them. We don't kill, we "exterminate," we "eliminate" and we "amputate." And we rationalize: "It's for their own good." "We had to do this for our economy." "If we hadn't, they'd have ruined us."

For too long, Christians have dealt with the "shadowy side of things" by simply calling it Satan — a convenient tag — and claiming we humans have no responsibility. "The Devil made me do it." All of America is called "The Great Satan" by radical Islamists. We humans are prone to fall for clerics who tell us *we* are strong enough to eliminate evil just by our actions. *We* can attack or avoid Satan.

Well, I know I'm not strong enough! I call on Christ-Sophia for help. And I regularly ask forgiveness for "things I have done and things I left undone."

Once a year, early Christian churches set aside one playful reversal-Sunday for the "lowly" to be raised up and the lofty to take their places. The homeless became bishops. The outcasts, priests. The vested, wore sackcloth. "Sacred fools" help us see life's paradoxes; they remind us of birth and death and rebirth. During Mardi Gras, people let their "shadow side" speak.

Back in the late '70s, Ruth Beebe Hill wrote a fascinating book about the Lakotah people called *Hanta Yo*. She was a full-blooded Santee Sioux and had a brilliant grasp of their dialects, rituals and songs. From her, I first learned about the *heyoka*, the camp clowns or the contrary ones whose job it is to jest, to act upside down, to reverse the normal order of things and to show how absurd things are. John G. Neihardt, in *Black Elk Speaks*, says that only those who have had visions of the thunder beings of the west can act as *heyokas*: "... *In the heyoka ceremony, everything is backwards, and it is planned that the people shall be made to feel jolly and happy first, so that it may be easier for the power to come to them. You have noticed that the truth comes into this world with two faces. One is sad with suffering, and the other laughs; but it is the same face, laughing or weeping. When people are already in despair, maybe the laughing face is better for them; and when they feel too good and are too sure of being safe, maybe the weeping face is better for them to see. And so I think that is what the heyoka ceremony is for."*

The *heyoka* is the "black bunny" that hops across our line of vision. Sophia lives in "the other." I told my Sophia-friend Laura about my hoping to write a book about gift-giving (which due to some excellent editorial advice by Michael Wiese, expanded and became this book). Laura said, "You really have to read Lewis Hyde's *The Gift.*" Laura had encountered it first at Oberlin and it's remained one of her mentors ever since. Hyde says that the "outsider" is always used as a catalyst to arouse nationalism, and when times are hard, he will always be the victim as well.

It's hard to generalize about who the "other" is because there are so many. For my mother, it was the Catholics. Back in Sand Creek as I was growing up, we all seemed to be Lutherans, therefore, "they" were the people who didn't go to our church. For the Europeans, the shadow-outsiders were the Jews. For the Vietnamese, it was the Chinese and for the Chinese it was the Japanese. For my Norwegian relatives it was the horrid Danes and the swaggering Swedes. For the Hindu, it's the Muslims and for the Muslims it's the Christians. For the French in Quebec, it was the English. On Crete it could be either the Turks or the Greeks, depending on which side of the arbitrary line you lived. And in Turkey it's the Armenians or the Kurds. Elsewhere in the Middle East it's either the Shi'ites or the Suni. Take your pick. Unless we name, integrate and welcome the "black bunnies," we'll continue to suffer.

Buddhist meditation practices teach how to recognize all our dark states and how to let the suffering go. The *Abhidhamma,* a Buddhist text, lays out three models or types of shadows: *The Greed Type,* those motivated by accumulating more and more; *the Hate Type,* those who see life as a battle to be fought and won over other losers; and *The Delusional Type,* those who are not paying attention.

Over the years I've watched people living and dying by degrees. It's a great long spectrum and our place on it changes. Some of the most alive people I've ever known are like the elderly woman who wanted to learn Aramaic. Or our dear friend, Tres Powers, who at 100 is nearly blind, is having hearing problems, and still plays the piano. Some of the half-deads I know are in their teens or early twenties. I look into faces in supermarkets and I see the nearly-deads like struggling members of an endangered species, pushing their carts past me, hoping they have enough money left in their checking accounts or over-extended credit cards to get through the checkout to the parking lot. They're all searching for something. Anything. The almost-alives sit in front of TV screens hoping to be stirred by reality shows. Maybe knowing the intimate details of somebody else's life will give them some small pleasure. The almost-alives sit in infusion chairs as well as meeting chairs, school desks and church pews. Sophia knows them. Sophia calls them to wake up. She won't intrude on their lives any more than my misty-hospital "visitor" at the end of my bed intruded on my life, but she's there and she's swirling. She's unexplainable, but she's real. She patiently waits.

THE "OTHER" DARKNESS

A group of creative women met at my neighbor's house the other night to swim in the silky water of her spring-fed pond, celebrate our giftedness and eat great food. Sara, another writer, asked me what I was writing now. I struggled for a few seconds to come up with this book's "elevator speech."

"I'm writing about the feminine face of God. I suppose you could call it my spiritual memoir."

"How does Sophia show up?" she asked.

I knew she was writing and editing a memoir by a group of older people in our community so I replied, "Well, for instance, she shows up in *you* every time you focus on telling the stories of the elderly as you are doing, every time you affirm their lives, every time you write! Every time someone creates something. She IS you, and she's me and she's all those other beautiful women — and men — around us. She offers a deep, dark, fertile place within each of us with which to create and affirm life."

Sara could have said to those elderly storytellers, "Write your own stories. I'm too busy and I'm not interested." If she had, she'd have chosen to exhibit that "other darkness." Not Sophia.

Everyone has their own definition of "evil" but it's usually described as a controlling, denigrating, abusive, hateful force. It's the opposite of being awake. It's life all spent. Bled out. Used up. I believe demonic hormones lurk in our food, mercury in our water, pollutants in our air and cancer in our bellies. It's everything Sophia isn't. Instead of being creative, compassionate and energetic, evil is greedy, destructive, and debilitating. Evil freezes us. Is evil simply something in our lives that is unbalanced? Or is it far worse? Evil seems to stagnate and move in the opposite direction of evolution. It also kills.

All this leads to my speculation about whether or not Satan, Lucifer, the Prince of Darkness — whatever name we choose to call this anti-Sophia force — is also redeemable. Is evil necessary to show us goodness?

John Milton reminds us in *Paradise Lost*: "The mind is its own place, and in itself can make a heaven of hell, a hell of heaven." If Lucifer is the Dawn-Bringer and the Light-Bearer, does he actually turn good people into evil? Heavens into hells? And can hells morph back again into heavens?

John Caruso, who works at the hospital where I get my lab work done, has written about Lucifer. He's a wonderful writer. I found his book disturbing, but I'm convinced disturbing books, like disturbing people, come into our lives to teach us something. His book, *Lightbearer*, begins with this question: "From the mind of the creator to the hand of the creature, from the maker of the pipes to the singer of the song, what essence imbued creation — dormant in the dark beneath its genius fields of invention — so vital it had to be passed on, so exalted it had to be cast down, such that God could not bear it any longer in himself?" Lucifer-Lightbearer and Michael battle, but what John has omitted from this modern-day Miltonesque epic, is what Milton himself also overlooked: We aren't encompassed by a dyad, but a triad. Sophia's there too.

Origin, who lived in the third century, believed that at the end of time *all evil* will be redeemed. In the midst of this whirlwind, I try to figure out my own responsibility for how this wisdom-drama plays out. Will I always be facing swirling mist — as in my hospital experience? Or will it one day "clear up"?

THE LUCIFER EFFECT

Philip Zimbardo, a sociology professor, wrote a book a few years ago called *The Lucifer Effect: Understanding How Good People Turn Evil*. When I first read it, I was searching for how evil tests our souls. I learned many things, including the fact that the *Witches Hammer*, that horrible manifesto against women, was required reading for inquisition judges. The author conducted his famous "prison experiment" at Stanford in which some students played the guards and others were prisoners. The guards adapted to their roles so thoroughly that half of the student "prisoners" had to be released early due to severe emotional disorders. His conclusion was that good people (like our soldiers) "can be induced, seduced and initiated into behaving in evil ways." *Lord of the Flies* choir boys can turn into killers. On the other hand, tell people they are altruistic and kind, helpful and compassionate and they will be.

Zimbardo's definition of evil is that which "consistently behaves in ways that harm, abuse, demean, dehumanize or destroy innocent others — or using one's authority and systemic power to encourage or permit others to do so on your behalf." Like Jesus' forty days in the desert, evil tests us and it is our job to prevail.

The entire Hutu-Tutsi Genocide in the spring of 1994 began with one rape. Mayor Silvester Cacumbi raped his former friend's daughter and then invited other men to rape her as well. "We won't waste bullets on you," he told her. "We will rape you, and that will be worse for you." And, of course, it was. Evil, as it always loves to do, escalated from there. Within a few short months, weapons of mass destruction — machetes, nail-studded clubs, gasoline fires — killed a million Rwandans. These numbers and the intensity of violence are simply staggering. Two hundred thousand women were raped in a few short months. Three-fourths of all the peaceful Tutsi people lay bleeding in ditches and fields. Pauline Nyiramasuhuko, who was a social worker, actually provided gasoline from her car to burn a group of seventy women and girls. Women were penetrated with spears, gun barrels, bottles, stamens of banana trees; sexual organs were burned with boiling water or acid. Women's breasts were cut off. AIDS still continues to wreak havoc. The hatred between these two groups may stem from how German and Belgian colonists divided them up, fomenting the idea that "the other" was the cause of all their troubles.

Rape is at epidemic proportions in the Eastern Congo, according to a UN spokesman, the worst in the world. We haven't figured out how to stop this kind of rampant evil. We send in UN peacekeepers. We threaten sanctions. We shake our heads at the pictures of whole villages being destroyed. But violence begets violence. Men with guns beget boys with guns. Rape begets rape.

In 1937, during what is now called the Rape of Nanking, Japanese soldiers butchered up to 350,000 Chinese people and thousands and thousands of women were raped. The "final solution" in Nazi Germany toted up millions of lives sacrificed. The solution of what? Zimbardo reminds us that British soldiers killed and raped Americans during the Revolutionary War; the Soviets raped up to 100,000 Berlin women. American soldiers rape as well — we just don't usually write about it in this country. Violence against women and children continues wherever war is waged. When 500 civilians were killed at Mai Lai, surprise, surprise, we all suddenly realized Americans, too, are capable of unspeakable evil. In May of 2004, images of Iraqi prisoners being tortured haunted worldwide media. Everyone remembers the trophy photos from Abu Ghraib. Donald Rumsfeld called it abuse, not torture. Is there a difference? Rush Limbaugh called it an emotional release. People were just having a good time. It took a twenty-four year old Reservist named Joe Darby to blow the whistle and call it like it was: *Evil*.

Sophia reminds us that even evil can be redeemed. Systems *can* be changed. We can demand *just* authority. We can decide not to sacrifice our freedoms for illusions of security. When we make mistakes, we can find ways to genuinely say "I'm sorry." And then not do it again. We can be much more vigilant in listening for ways language seduces us and pulls the hood over our eyes. We can find new ways to express ourselves without using sexually de-meaning words. When we can name it, we can change it. We can monitor our bullying and hate. Sophia will help us.

Whenever we refer to "the other" in derogatory terms, it's a slippery slide into deeper muck. If the person who is being called names is considered worthless, then killing can be "justified." The Tutsi were called cockroaches; Jews, voracious rats; Blacks, niggers; Iraqis, towel-heads and hajis; Vietnamese, gooks; gays, faggots. Listen for the slurs and watch how you react. Edmund Burke, an English statesman, said, "The only thing necessary for evil to triumph is for good men to do nothing." And for women to ignore what's happening.

Tolkien's Elrond, the Elf-King, warns that evil is empty, a cheap copy, a counterfeit. Frodo decides evil was what twisted the Orcs. We see that every grouping of beings in Tolkien's universe, just as every human in ours, carries the capacity for good or ill. He said, "Goodness is frightfully vulnerable to fraud." Hence, "The old saying: the corruption of the best is the worst."

But, take heart. Evil must eventually reveal its sinister nature and even the dullest of us will catch on. The evil Ring maintains Bilbo Baggins' youthful body without apparent physical change for fifty years, but he begins to feel it's "all thin, sort of stretched if you know what I mean, like butter that's been scraped over too much bread." Samwise Gamgee learns how to be on the "right" side of the story — if we are ever to have real hope. "The Ring" enslaves a victim's will by preying on its pride. It promises redemption. But real freedom means to be able to choose to do the good and very best thing. We are free-will beings and we always have the choice.

It would be easy to spot evil if it were always vicious and horrible. As graves are unearthed in a serial killer's backyard you might hear, "But he was a good neighbor. He seemed like such a nice guy!" Evil can be not only banal, but as smooth and as charming as that granny-and-little girl-eating-wolf. It still intends to kill, to entrap, to suppress, to stifle. We've seen all too often how evil can snap on a clergy collar or put on monk's robes. It was monks, you may remember, who flayed Hypatia, a brilliant fifth-century mathematics professor in Alexandria. They used oyster shells. Then they tore her corpse apart.

"But that was long ago. Bad things used to happen." Excuse me. That's acedia talking. Acedia leads to a feeling that "it's not my problem." When I choose not to see the evil in my neighborhood or family, I'm tricked into thinking it doesn't exist. And I can convince myself that all my troubles are caused by the homeless or immigrants, or gays, or women. Or all those lazy people who take our welfare money and drain our health care system. We hear: "It's the socialists. It's the communists. It's got to be some sort of "ist" because certainly it's not *me*."

The young boys who killed their peers and teachers at the Columbine high school had been disengaged for some time. One of their friends actually said, "Well, at least they finally *did* something." Our hearts can easily become anesthetized; our thoughts muddled. That's when shadows thicken. Injustices pile up like corpses in our morgues. We have to do something about them or the stench will overwhelm us. No amount of Vicks under the nose will staunch the odor.

Yes, there are suicide killers and "heaven addicts," but much of the killings resting on our own American shoulders result from greed. Follow the money. America has much to answer for.

Memories of slave manacles still bite into our wrists and ankles. Between 1450 and 1870 we bought and sold ten million people! Our economics depended on it, many of us believed at the time. We wrote into our Constitution, "All men are created equal," which was true if you weren't black, brown, yellow, a child or a woman. The people who argue for "taking back America" might well remember what "take back" entails. We embedded smallpox germs on blankets given to Indian babies. We drop bombs on innocent people. E.L. Doctorow put it this way: "The bomb first was our weapon; then it became our diplomacy. Next it became our economy. Now it's become our culture. We've become the people of the bomb." As someone whose life work led to the making of our bomb-culture, Einstein said it is appallingly clear that our technology has surpassed our humanity. How right he was. We write books on the "art" of war. What could be more oxymoronic than art and war?

Why is there evil? Evil requires three things, according to Roy Baumeister. It requires the deliberate actions of one person, the suffering of another and the judgment of either the second person or an observer. If evil falls in the forest and no one is there to hear, is it still evil? If there is a victim — yes! There are four root causes of evil, Baumeister says: (1) material gain, such as money or power; (2) someone's ego is threatened; (3) idealism; and (4) sadistic pleasure.

My Sophia Circle recently spent some time thinking together about the willfulness of children and a caregiver's need to draw boundaries. Then we moved on to our own fears and how evil manifests. "How do we hold the balance when so much hatred swirls?" "It's been with us since Cain and Abel." But, I wonder, is that just an excuse? Can we move past Eden's fratricide to a *different* humanity? A Sophiaed humanity?

DEALING WITH THE BOGEY MAN
We love to create imaginary monsters that hide under our beds or

scratch at our windows. I, like most kids, grew up believing they're real — and might "get" us. Since they're created by our childish minds, our adult minds can delete them. Fear is simply how we hold, or refuse to hold, those "scary hairy monsters." I find rather comforting the fact that "Fear not" or "Don't be afraid" appears in the Bible 365 times. One for each day of the year. Fear comes when we forget. My Swedish friend uses this acronym for fear: Forgetting Every Available Resource.

The morning the World Trade towers collapsed, I could no longer watch endless video loops of planes crashing into buildings, so about eleven o'clock I went out to walk my labyrinth. As often happens if you hold a question while moving toward the center, when you get there, you get an insight you didn't have before. As I entered, each footfall kept asking, "Why? Why? Why?" The answer came at the center: *They're afraid. Afraid we're ruining their religion, their culture. They're afraid we'll annihilate their very way of being.* But who was fearing whom here? Many years later, we are still forgetting our every available resource.

Sophia's Gift: Faithfulness

Sophia offers many gifts, many resources we can draw on. One is her faithfulness. She won't give up on us. She won't go away, even when we ignore her. She won't disappear even when our holy scriptures write her out. She'll be there for us when we ask her to be present. As a child, I learned the table prayer, "Come Lord Jesus, be our guest." Now, I include: "Come, Lady Sophia, be our guest. Let this life to us be blessed."

Enneagram Number 5

Number Fives make great analysts. They love to observe and collect data. But because they are so focused, they can appear cut-off and alone. They strive to be competent in all that they undertake. Sometimes, as a result, they seem hyperactive and aloof. They seek safety in their inner world and cling to truths — they know what's right. They work on big ideas. They can appear as youthful dreamers, but, on the other hand, can also be extremely confident and decisive. Fives are the ones "in the know," and if you're not, they may not care to spend much time with you.

SOPHIA'S SPECIAL GEO-SPOT: NEWGRANGE, IRELAND

Triple spiral, c. 3000 B.C.E., from New Grange, County Meath, Ireland

It's so well-constructed that, in over five thousand years, no major stones have jostled loose from the interior of this huge kidney-shaped mound that stretches over an acre of County Meath on the eastern side of Ireland. It's called *Brú na Bóinne* — the dwelling place of the Boyne or *Her people*. In Irish mythology, the river Boyne was created by the goddess Boann. It's her wisdom-home, site of the famous Irish legend of Finn Mac Cumhail, an orphan who was raised by the poet Finnegas and became Ireland's greatest warrior. Finnegas had longed most of his life to catch the "Salmon of Knowledge." One day he caught it with a hazelnut and he asked Finn to cook it. As it was frying, Finn touched it, licked his finger and received the salmon's blessing. Sophia's wisdom.

Newgrange is the anglicized title of this World Heritage Site. It was discovered in 1699 by a farmer and his wife who were out walking around an old Cistercian abbey that was built in the 1100s at the New Grange farm of Mellifont. Estimates are, it would have taken forty years to built this mound — interestingly enough — about the same amount of time it took to build Chartres' cathedral. It rose up out of the mists of Irish history so long ago no one knows exactly when. Older than Stonehenge. Older than the Pyramids.

To reach the entrance, you walk up about two meters. The entrance has been modified so you no longer have to crawl over the huge entrance stone. Once inside the carefully constructed passageways under its corbelled roof, you know you are on holy ground. This cairn is perfectly positioned over intense water and energy flows. Like the West Kennet Barrow in England, it's not a tomb, for only the ash remains of five humans have ever been found. Some speculate that bodies may have been taken in for a short time and then removed to somewhere else. It's likely been a ritual spot for centuries.

Our guide turned out the lights and described, using her flashlight, how at 9 a.m. on Winter Solstice the sun comes gradually down the shaft from the perfectly positioned "window" or opening on the side. It illuminates the triple spiral and stays there for seventeen minutes. Carved at least 2500 years before the Celts reached Ireland, it's only twelve inches in diameter, but may be the most famous image in Ireland. It was discovered by Professor O'Kelly who, in 1969, sat in the darkness and waited to "re-witness" this light show.

Around the mound, nearly a hundred slabs of huge "kerb stones" follow the contours of "her holy hill" and mark this place as truly important. Eighty-five of them are elaborately decorated with megalithic symbols, including circles, spirals and "cups." The entire exterior was covered with white quartz stones. Mica, which makes up granite and quartz, acts as an insulator, a container of energy. There are 240,000 tons of stone in this mound alone, with more in the equally large adjoining mounds of Knowth, with its 150 giant kerb-stones, and Dowth, which is still being excavated. Legend has it "she" shook all these stones out of her apron.

There are "towers" built into the Newgrange cairn — of the same height and structure — with varying leveled doors. Chanting inside sets up vibrations, as if it were a great organ sending out "her voice" into the surrounding earth and sea. Given that there are very old towers around Ireland whose origins no one can explain, this makes for an interesting early energy "radio-transmission" theory.

There is a similar passage tomb in Brittany called Gavrinis. Like Newgrange, it also has elaborately engraved stones inscribed with zig-zags, concentric circles, herring bones, and labyrs ax figures.

After our tour of Newgrange, Joel noticed, as we walked back across the bridge of the Boyne river to our car, that the eddies in the water seemed to echo the ancient swirls etched onto the rocks. Energy indeed swirls in the zig-zag meanders seen everywhere in this special place so close to Tara, Ireland's holy center.

Michael Poynder, who has studied constellation placements over time, believes early astronomers etched star maps on some of the kerb stones at Newgrange. The "cup" marks are stars in the constellation Draco-Dragon. Draco is another name for the north star around which all systems evolve.

Rudolf Steiner tells of a polished rock crystal that was placed in each of the two cups carved into a particular rock near the triple spiral. When the sun came through the shaft, the light was "split" by the crystals and the meditating person within was transformed into a "light-bearer." She experienced an initiation-vision of her own creation. She became the "grail," the cup-bearer.

SOPHIA'S MYSTICAL DANCER: JACOB BOEHME (1575-1624)

Jacob Boehme was born close to the Bohemian border in Goeritz. His German Lutheran parents were farmers and as a young boy he had a vision while tending the cattle. He wasn't robust enough to farm, so eventually he became a master shoemaker.

His first vision as an adult came when he was twenty-four; he saw Sophia on the shiny surface of a pewter teapot. It changed his life forever. He described her as a shiny mirror of God's will — God made visible. It is she who summons the uncreated into creation — she is the Divine Chaos wherein all things lie. Jacob Boehme called her the "ground and the unground." *Ungrund*. The Abyss. Others quake and call her chaos. There's no doubt about it. She's unpredictably deep. Deceptively dark. And available to everyone. Within her all freedom lives, all ideas take shape; it's where her wild power swirls.

When Boehme wrote his first book, *Aurora*, he hadn't intended for it to be published, but it got around and found its way into print two years later in 1612. He was labeled a heretic, imprisoned, then, fortunately for him, released. "Not I," he said, "knows these things, but God in me." All things, he wrote, are born of desire and there cannot be light without darkness. Later he wrote *The Signature of All Things*, which included the idea that Hermetic mysteries have always been couched "under shadows and figures, parables and similes." They're obscure, yet clear. Those who do understand have, as Boehme put it, "tasted of the Feast of the Pentecost."

Whether openly or covertly, he was an alchemist. He used symbols of gold and silver to show how we might develop into fully conscious beings and unite with God. With Sophia. He equated spirit with sulfur, love with mercury and essence with salt. He is, in fact, considered to be the creator of symbols. He thought of himself as the prophet of her dawn. For that reason, he's known as the father of Sophiology. Likewise, Hildegard of Bingen, who called her the Voice of Wisdom four hundred years earlier, might be called the mother of Sophiology. Hildegard described "source springs" where everything, including animals, angels and humans, participates in divine creation. Boehme pointed out that divine powers operate on every level of the cosmos. "The outer sun longs to be the inner sun," he wrote. We each hold, as Jacob Boehme put it, the "gold in the stone," our transforming creative power. Good and evil, love and wrath, can be found in people, of course, but also in earth and elements, Boehme wrote. If he's right, then even my mind and body hold alchemical secrets. Sophia grants us "Cinderella Power" to turn ashes into golden slippers.

Once Upon a Time:
Cinderella

Before my mother died she said, "Ella, remember you are good and pious and kind. I promise to watch over you from heaven." I wept every day over her grave. When father remarried, my two new step-sisters moved into our house and they were anything but kind to me. Or good. And certainly not pious. Nor was their mother! They took all my dresses and then laughed at my shabby shifts. "You're so dusty and dirty, from now on your name will be Cinder-Ella!"

When father left for the fair, he asked his girls what they wanted. Pearls said one, a new dress said the other. But I asked for a hazel twig to plant on mother's grave. It grew, and each time I visited the grave a white bird perched on a branch.

One autumn, the king hosted a festival and invited all the young women in the kingdom so his son could choose a bride. My two step-sisters dressed in their finest. Then my step-mother threw lentils and peas into the ashes and said, "If you can pick them out in an hour, maybe you can come along."

I couldn't do it alone so I called out to the birds for help. Pigeons and turtledoves flew in through the window and within an hour all the lentils and peas were stacked in neat piles. "Oh. But you don't have any suitable clothes and you don't know how to dance. So you can't come." Off they went.

Heartbroken, I walked to my little hazel tree. The birds heard my plea and suddenly I was wearing a gold and silver dress with silk slippers to match. I found my way to the palace where everyone thought I was a foreign princess. I danced with the prince far into the night, slipped away, changed into my grey smock and was sitting by the fire when everyone returned. They were all abuzz about the beautiful stranger.

The next night I wore an even lovelier gown and after the ball, sneaked back to the hearth once again. On the third night of the great festival, the little bird presented me with the most gorgeous gown in the kingdom and golden glass slippers to match. After dancing the night away once again, I ran off, but the prince had covered the steps in pitch to catch me. I had to leave one of my shoes behind.

"A-ha! Whoever fits this shoe will be my wife." So the prince traveled up and down the kingdom holding my one golden glass slipper out in front of him like a magnet.

And now, the trumpets are outside our door. My step-mother drags her oldest into the kitchen and hands her a knife. "The prince is here. Your feet are too big. Quick, cut off your toe so the shoe will fit! You will be queen!" My step-sister swallows her pain and the shoe fits! She rides off with the prince. They pass my mother's grave. A dove in the hazel tree cries out: "Look! There's blood all over, and her foot's too small; she's not the bride you met at the ball!"

So the prince brings her back and my other step-sister gets to try. But of course her foot is too large, too, so my step-mother hands her the knife. "Cut off your heel! You will be queen!" Again, the prince rides off with a bleeding woman and again the truth-telling birds let him know she's not the right woman either.

I overhear him from the kitchen. "Are there no more daughters under this roof?" My step-mother spits, "Only the dirty, deformed girl by the hearth." He stands at the kitchen door. "Take off that wooden shoe and try this slipper, maiden." Of course it fits perfectly. "You shall be my wife." We ride past my mother's grave and this time the birds sing: "Looky look, look. Her foot's just right and there's no blood at all. She's truly the bride you met at the ball."

While the Disney version of this tale has some similarities, including a good Sophia-like fairy godmother and helpful birds, this Grimm version of Cinderella is certainly more — well, grim. It ends at the wedding where Cinderella's birds pluck out first the right eye and then the left eye of the evil step-sisters so they go through life — blind.

Cinderella plants a hazel twig on her mother's grave. Druids used hazel twigs for divination. It was because of the hazel tree that the salmon of wisdom was caught in the old Irish folktale. And remember, it was in a hazelnut that Julian of Norwich saw the entire world safely held.

Marko Pogacnik calls this a tale of human evolution. It's about our growth into wisdom. He likens the prince's invitation to the castle to Christ's invitation. Like Cinderella sifting through the ashes to find the peas and lentils, we too, must distinguish between what grows within us and what's dead and left over from the past. Cinderella's help comes from Sophia, epitomized by the white doves. It's not a story of revenge as much as it is about getting rid of the dualities that bind us. Like the wicked stepsisters, we are blinded first on the left and then the right.

She knows who we are under our dusty clothes. Once we call on her for help and actually *see* Sophia, we can all become a "royal bride."

FROM SOPHIA'S NOTEBOOK

My story is always your story. You are my face. You are my hands. You are my heart. I stand ready and waiting to be of assistance. When women "wake up" they know I have always been there. From the very beginning. Time is your construct. When you are more ready to notice, then you sense me, feel me, for I am of experience. Mystical for many. Less ephemeral for most. I am the cushioning hen-like image Christ painted. The one who births and keeps on birthing. Who creates and keeps on creating. Who sings and keeps on singing and dancing. And playing.

I am on the fringe of the fires, on the edges of water, in the center of ice. I am where nature breathes clear and easy. I leave places that are polluted with chemicals or thoughts. I am rarely in war rooms. But you'll sense me in birthing rooms. Where people concentrate on their breathing, I am there. Inspiring. When people die, I am there, helping them expire, when they exhale this life to go on to another.

Tell them I wait for them. There is no rush. Each comes at her own pace. Wisdom holds all patience. Keep your faith. Faith in each other. Even those whom you do not trust. They have their roles to play now. Rest assured. Every baby lamb is held in the family warmth. Each

one. Ewe lamb — you lamb. You, too, are warmed and fed and tend-
ed. Fear not. I am with you. You shall not be cast away, discarded,
even though your wool may be carded. Your plenty, more evenly dis-
tributed. Your gifts put to better use.

I have other lambs. Capable lambs. And shepherds aplenty. With
crooks and staffs and savvy knowledge of the desert places. Both are
there in the desert. The wolves and the shepherds. Fear not.

chapter six

SHE MAKES US STRONG

Crop Circle: Cley Hill, Warminster, Wiltshire, July 14, 1997

· ·

"Listen with inward ear to the music of her wisdom, teaching all creation. With inward eye visualize her brilliant name, flowing across your heart in letters of molten gold."

~ Ramprasad, the 18th-century Bengali poet

MOUNTAIN JOURNAL ENTRY

A throaty call floats through my open window. Athena's owl perches somewhere in the dark forest that surrounds our house. Surely sound must be an important part of alchemy — it can't be all just sulfur, mercury, salt and lead ... and gold. Her energetic vibrations spin the straw-me into star-stuff. I know her vibrations somehow web us to planets and galaxies. How else could there be celestial music?

Venus and I rose this morning at the same time. Bathed in bright light, I face a new day by listening to *The Schola Gothia*. I'm betting these women get their vocal affirmations from the reverberations they hear in Bridget's cathedral where they recorded this CD in Vadsteena, Sweden. The very place where Bridget, a 14th century woman who married at thirteen and had eight children, was "called to be God's mouthpiece." During her lifetime, Bridget had 700 visions of social and spiritual reform. In one, she got the architectural design for her blue granite church — it should be square rather than rectangular, and there would be four altars, not just one. The nuns would worship from the upper balcony and the monks would worship down below. Imagine the balanced energy swirling around during meditative rituals in that space!

HEARTBEAT QUESTIONS

When do I feel most powerful? *Where* am I the most powerful? When do I feel the weakest?

What's the wisest thing I've ever done?

Where is the place I can go where I most feel her presence? Who am I with?

What makes certain places "sacred" for me?

ARTEMIS STARSHAPERS AND EARTHSHAPERS

I am sitting on a dock, lazily splashing my feet in the water. I don't swim; neither did my mother. I suppose I inherited my fear of water from her. Or from a past life involving fishing boats. Off in the distance I see a bear lumbering toward me. Closer and closer. So close I can smell it. It ignores all the other people around me and comes straight for *me*. I freeze, thinking that if I am very still the bear might not notice me. Not a chance. Instead, it comes up behind me, and with a very big hot nose, pushes against my spine and I fall into the water. My heart races because I think for sure I'll drown.

Then I wake up laughing because the dream-water only came up to my knees. I can still feel her steamy nose on my back.

Artemis the Bear Goddess always comes along to push me into doing what I don't think I'm strong enough to do. While I had learned I could write passable publishable articles, and a few small children's religious books, I didn't believe I had what it takes to write a *book*. However, when my archeologist friend, Jim Mount, approached me with the idea of writing a young people's book on the early effigy mound-building Indians who lived in the Mississippi River Valley from 650 C.E. to 1200 C.E., I thought hmmm ... maybe I can.

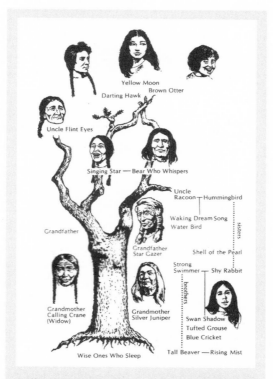

Yellow Moon's family tree, by George Armstrong, from The Earthshapers

The Earthshapers, I decided, would be set 900 years ago in the Upper Mississippi River valley, right across the river from Prairie du Chien where we lived at the time. It would be after the time of "The Ancient Ones," the Hopewellian and Temple Mound people who'd lived farther downstream and had established a complex trading culture. Within "The Great Gathering Place," now called Iowa's Effigy Mounds National Monument, there are 191 mounds, 29 bears and birds, and the rest are conical burial mounds. One bear effigy, in particular, is 70 feet across the shoulders and 137 feet long. It is roughly three and a half feet high. The only human burial remains that have been excavated are at the bear's "heart." What are the mounds telling us?

Jim and his park crew invited our family to join them one Saturday to spread lime around the mounds so they could be photographed from the air — the only way you can really see their shapes. It had to be done after the leaves fell off the trees and before the snows came. It was our first close-up experience with the bears. They seemed to be teaching us something, but we weren't quite sure what.

Thinking it would be a book for our sons, I started writing in a young boy's voice. Then Jim asked me, "Why? Why not make the story about a girl?" A girl growing into womanhood. Of course. Perfect.

I started out by drawing a tree. At the top I wrote "Yellow Moon." Her name just came to me. I didn't know at the time that Artemis was known as the Moon Goddess. The crescent-shaped moon is Artemis-Sophia's most powerful phase, her most fertile symbol. Ironically, it's also the one that appears today on flags of some countries where women are just coming "into their own." Waxing strong.

The bare skeleton of Yellow Moon's family tree hung above my typewriter, daring me to fill the branches with names of her family members and how they related to one another. Once I knew who they were, I believed they'd lead me to Yellow Moon's story and ultimately help me understand what the mounds were for. I labeled the roots at the bottom of the tree: "The Wise Ones Who Sleep."

Later, I realized another writer in Portland, Oregon was at the same time researching and dreaming about a young woman also connected to bears. Yellow Moon and Ayla were both "born" in 1980, albeit twenty-five or thirty thousand years apart. Jean M. Auel began her research around the time our family helped to lime the Effigy Mounds. She originally approached an editor with her idea for a short story. As all good editors do, hers saw greater potential. It grew into the very popular Earth's Children five-book series beginning with *The Clan of the Cave Bear*. Along with many other readers around the world, I devoured each with relish. But I didn't know Ayla existed as I stared at Yellow Moon's family tree. Ayla's huge Ursus Spelaeus, the cave bear, outweighed by three times "my" black bears loping across lazy Iowa fields. In one scene, Ayla calls the log-caged cave bear "Winter Sleeper," "Honey Lover," "Big Furry Baby." It's easy to anthropomorphize bears — even towering ones like Ayla's — because they look like shaggy humans.

A black bear visited our Vermont gardens one dusky July evening, flipping heavy rocks in search of ants and grubs. I spotted her broad backside just as she was leaving. She sauntered past our garage and down our driveway. My "sitting on the dock dream" returned and I again felt a big moist nose against my spine. "Mother Bear," why don't I ever see your face? It was then that I got the image of Sophia as an iceberg. Her power lies in the ninety percent we never see. We just see the little bit of her in what's been *barely charged* with her divinity. We can't even begin to imagine what lies below the deep and vital surface of her waters.

After my little historical fiction for young adults was published, reviewers called it "an archeologically authentic novel about an ancient Native American culture ... a moving and sensitive piece of fiction." I was pleased, although my royalty checks and Auel's must look quite different. Still, I count myself not only rich, but blessed by the whole experience. Jim helped me, as did Clark Mallum, another renowned archeologist. Thanks to careful research, I could weave into my story artifacts and trading history: obsidian, copper, gold, inlaid shells. My "extended family" grew along with Yellow Moon's. After the manuscript was finalized, George Armstrong, a Chicago-based artist and folksinger who was known to play his bagpipes to the rising solstice sun on the shores of Lake Michigan, masterfully wielded his drawing pen. Soon the faces of her family appeared on the family tree. He saw them even more clearly than I. Writing that book was far from a solitary venture. Like monks who never sing alone, I raised my voice in the good company of Yellow Moon's whole family: Brown Otter, Daring Hawk, Bear Who Whispers, Singing Star, Juniper, Calling Crane, Uncle Flint Eyes, Uncle Raccoon, and of course her beloved blind grandfather, Star Gazer. And when I look back, I can see Sophia-Artemis' hand in it all.

Even if we don't know much about the night sky, most of us can find the big dipper and the north star. That's where Ursa Major lives. Seven stars form the great She Bear. It's as if she says, *"Don't fear the 'empty' darkness. I'm here keeping an eye on all my cubs."* We depend on our "pole star," the *axis mundi*, to be the constant around which everything moves. The "Little Bear," Arcas or Callisto, which means "the most beautiful," is her daughter.

Caves around Europe hold "bear" memories of a Black Virgin who was sometimes called Isis-Artemis-Diana. And Mary. In Crete, a bear-like stalactite hangs from the ceiling of an "Artemis Cave" and it's called "Mary the Bear." I don't find it strange at all that Mary came to Ephesus, to this "pagan" Mother City, to live out her later years.

Artemis-Ephesia, with her bear, lion, deer and bee symbols, reigned for a thousand years before the Apostle Paul arrived in Ephesus about sixty years after Jesus was born. He spent two years planting a few Christ seeds, but saw little success at the time. Diana-Artemis was too well entrenched. The city had a population of about 200,000 and scholars estimate that Paul converted from forty to sixty people. In spite of the note Paul added to his first letter to his friends in Corinth: "...I will stay in Ephesus until Pentecost, for a wide door for effective work has opened to me and there are many adversaries," Christianity had no real toehold there until the end of the fourth century. All the city guilds, prototypes of later medieval guilds, were connected to her temple. Paul's tent-making friends, Prisca (Priscilla) and Aquila, who traveled with him from Corinth to Ephesus, were most likely guild members. Guilds supported the economics, not only of the city, but the entire trading arms throughout Anatolia (Turkey) and the whole thriving Middle East.

In early She-Bear festivals, a girl of ten and another of five dressed in saffron yellow moon-robes to act out the two sacred sky bears. The crane dance became her labyrinth ritual. The "Cauldron" dance is still danced in Morocco, mainly by women. It's called the "Guedra" and draws peace and blessings up from the earth, out into all the people present. Panpipe players and festival flutists, tip-toeing "bird" dancers, and parading children regularly reenacted her *rituals*, a word which means "to fit together." Her rituals wove together the financial, legal, educational, arts, civic, and athletic community of Ephesus. All things there were related through her. What maintains the wholeness of a place is always what people deeply honor.

Before her temple was built, and then rebuilt, people worshipped her at a nearby tree shrine on protective sheepskins laid out between two streams. She was the old, old energy under-girding the city, and the whole region, for that matter. She welcomed proper performance, diligence of duties, care of the weak, the hungry, the sick, the abused. She allowed no sexual activity within her sacred space. A boy's choir performed at her religious functions. Her priests sacrificed their manhood to her.

Independent and very patient, Artemis-Diana "waited" for all people at the threshold of her cypress grove-temple. It is from her grove we adopted the term "virgin forest." In *The Moon and the Virgin*, Nor Hall says: "The virgin forest is not barren or unfertilized but rather a place that is especially fruitful and has multiplied because it has taken life into itself and transformed it, giving birth naturally and taking dead things back to be recycled. It is virgin because it is unexploited, not in man's control."

During the first century, someone donated a huge building adjacent to her temple which housed the poor and the homeless of Ephesus. Sacrificial animals — sheep, goats, oxen — were fed to the hungry. Her hymns said she went "from strength to strength."

Three main Christian church councils met at Ephesus to try to settle internal theological differences: in 431 C.E., 449 C.E. and 475 C.E. At the first one, Mary was claimed to be a virgin, like Artemis, and the Mother of God. *Theotokos*. An earlier council decreed that priests should be celibate, just like Artemis' priests, the "Essenes." Monks retreated into monastic life not so much to scorn women, but to refuse a masculinity that had become too bellicose. Too violent. Too abusive to women.

When her temple was pulled down for the last time, John Holland Smith tells us that some of its magnificent red porphyry columns — the very ones I later lovingly stroked in Istanbul — were installed at Hagia Sophia. When I learned of *Ephesia grammata*, little prayers and writings about Artemis which served as charms, which were sewn into little bags and worn around the neck or shoulders, I sewed little velvet bags to give to all my friends. I figured they could add their own "magic" bits inside, for Sophia's magic permeates the world.

Artemis-Diana was frequently associated with Lucifer by later churchmen. In *Restoring the Goddess*, Barbara Walker speaks of our struggle to bring myths into some kind of harmony with how we perceive reality. "Goddess is not simply the female face of God. It embodies a different philosophy of life and death," she said. And Elinor Gadon puts it this way: "Until women can visualize the sacred female they cannot be whole." She is the Mother of All Creatures. Our psyches are overlayed with strong but elastic bear archetypes capable of stretching around the world and into the deepest caves.

I remember my mother telling me, as a child, how she and her twin sister Eleanor used to spoon in bed (as they must have curled in Julia's womb), just to keep warm in the chilly upstairs farm bedroom. They'd tell each other scary bear stories. "Tell me! Tell me, too!" I begged. "All right, but then you have to go to sleep. There is a bear slowly coming up the road, s l o w l y coming up the driveway, then up the stairs — one, two, three...." I knew how many stairs there were and I quaked, waiting for the tickles and giggles that would follow when my mother played the part of the bear who came to "get" me.

The Taoists value the Great Bear as Queen of Heaven. The city of Berne, Switzerland's capital, means "She-Bear." They still display her bear-symbols. The Bear, Artemis, appears in Celtic story as "Artio" or "Art" and nicely connects with the "Bear King," "King Arthur," and to the wonderful places all his stories led. She is connected as "Her Bear" to my friend Herbert, who has a wonderful collection of bear sculptures. We have my own "Teddy," whose one glassy eye is now missing. I got him when my dad worked on the Al-Can Highway during World War II. Joel's Pooh Bear, John's black and grayish-white Paul Bear, and Nate's jaunty feather-hatted Paddington Bear, join Teddy to faithfully watch over our bedroom from their perch on an upper shelf.

SHE'S OUR QUEEN BEE AND THE HONEY

Last spring, a black bear broke through the barbed wire surrounding the hives and ate thirty pounds of our friend's honey. As that winter-starved "Pooh" scooped up all that golden goodness, she probably didn't pause to ponder how all that "hunny" would improve her immune system, kill any harmful bacteria and promote healthy tissue growth. She ate it because it was sweet. When she had had her fill, she turned her busy snout toward the bird feeders. Artemis at work, I thought.

Sacred geometry surrounds bear-work and bee-work. Each of the hive's waxy cells is an exact 60° hexagon perfectly positioned. When we burn candles made of beeswax, we may sense something cosmic melting. Bees share their secrets with us, as Sue Monk Kidd reminded us in *The Secret Lives of Bees*.

Old Celtic beekeepers talked to their bees. They knew the bees listened. Bees, they said, come from the "otherworld" and can share starry wisdom with us mortals. Beelore claims the queen, who can lay up to 2,000 eggs a day, is connected to Venus, the planet of love. A hive knows how to build community and support one another.

When it comes time for their queen to do her waggle dance, they swarm and follow her. Otherwise, as Kidd points out, they all suffer from "queenlessness." They lose their dance rhythm. Collecting pollen holds no allure. They die. And when they die, our crops wither for lack of cross-pollination. Everything comes down to bees, it seems. And to the queen.

Sophia's waggling. We can no longer afford to live in "queenlessness."

Some ancient people spent decades searching for a land of "milk and honey." It was there all along. Demeter was the "Pure Mother Bee," and Artemis gathered the Melissai around her — her priestess worker bees. Her priests were called the Essenes or the drones. Egyptian kings were venerated through Her as "One of the Bees," and when people died, they "fell into the honey pot."

We're sticky-stitched to bees, cell by cell. They show us how to build community and relationships. How to "bee" whole. She's there, buzzing in the center of it all. Her dark wisdom permeates our hive.

URSULA AND THE *HOOLY WUMMEN*

The Catholic church designated October 21st as the feast day of a young girl who was surrounded by a legend of no small proportion. Ursula, a teenaged Cornwall princess betrothed to a guy in Brittany, begged not to be married until she'd traveled Europe. Ursula convinced her father to let her travel with her friends for three years. As the story goes, she invited 11,000 of her girlfriends — her handmaidens — and took off. But a storm blew her into the Rhine River and down to Cologne (filled with bad guys called Huns). She refused to marry their chief, was shot with a bow, and her whole virgin army were beheaded. This is not the first time, or unfortunately the last, when a woman dies trying to get away from a man wielding a weapon over "lost love."

Like most legends, Ursula's may have been founded on a scrap of historical truth. Thousands of women were, at one time, sent from England to Brittany to help populate their newly conquered territory.

Someone wrote an inscription of her story on a church wall in Cologne where some young girls had been killed. Two. Five. Eight. Eleven. The number varies. Like most urban legends and internet stories, this one, too, was interpreted in many ways. One account says the girl was named Ursula and she was eleven years old. Another called her Undecimilla. (You know how confusing those Roman numerals can be. A monk later translated that as 11,000.) The exact details don't really matter. The point was, women were killed. Back when Artemis was called Ursel, her temple stood on the very spot where this church was built. Bone "relics" were dug up from a local burial ground.

Women have long been considered property and Ursula's story continues to be played out. She is raped in Darfur. Murdered if she "dishonored" the male members of Islamic family. Beaten, stabbed, shot by a man she trusts. She continues to be burned in rural India where murder is far less trouble than divorce and a man can readily get another dowry-rich woman. Daughters cost more to raise so we shouldn't be shocked to learn that right after ultrasounds became available, in Bombay alone, according to Alison Jolly in *Lucy's Legacy*, out of 8,000 abortions, 7,999 were baby girls. When only two children were allowed in Chinese families, midwives kept a tray of sand close to the birthing bed. If the baby was a girl, chances were she'd be smothered before her first cry.

What are the statistics on rape now? One every five minutes? Every four? Rape is not about love — it's about power. It's about who has the right to f--- and who doesn't. "F-you" really means *I hate you*. Boys learn very young that they don't want to be called wimps or pussies. That's the "opposite from me," so many of them grow up believing from all they see around them that women are despised, and need to be f---ed and controlled.

In 1997, a group of New York police officers repeatedly raped and brutalized a man named Abner Louima with a broom handle. Why? Just because they wanted to treat him like a woman.

As I write these dreadful accounts, however, I am reminded of what Maya Angelou said: "The brutes and the bigots, the batterers and the bastards are also children of God." Sophia holds out hope for all of them! For all of us!

Ursula's story was off and running when the mystic Elisabeth of Schönau saw Ursula and the girls in a vision. She wrote about it in *Revelations Concerning the Sacred Army of Virgins of Cologne*. It was followed by another 13th century collection called *The Golden Legend*, and then in the 15th century, my favorite: *Legends of Hooly Wummen*.

Various sailors, no doubt heated up by the thought of all those lonely virgins, loved naming far-away places after them. Christopher Columbus sailed into a lot of islands in the Caribbean and called them The Virgin Islands. Ferdinand Magellan, sailing through "his strait," on October 21, 1521, named the cape, Cape Virgenes.

In 1506, a strong woman named Angela Merici gathered twenty-eight women around her (appropriately enough, that's the number of the moon-days of a woman's cycle) and said: "Let's teach young girls." It took forty years for the church fathers to sanction what they were doing, but finally, the Ursalines became the teaching nuns. Those She-Bears are still making a difference. As a result, more and more people are catching on to the fact that when young girls are loved, protected and educated, families become empowered. And whole nations benefit.

CIRCLES OF STRONG WOMEN

Stone circles create otherworldly spaces. People passed their sick children through one stone circle that still stands near Land's End on the west coast of England, believing they would be cured. Lovers came to these stones, seeking happiness. Women desiring to become pregnant passed a piece of clothing through the opening. Stone circles pull people into another reality — or perhaps they visit them to become more *real*.

When I was three years old, the Mills Brothers had a hit recording about wanting a paper doll to call his own — "not like a *real live girl*." I believe this song helped pave the way for sex toys. Life-sized manikins such as Real Dolls (with three orifices and articulated skeletons for "anatomically correct positioning" for only $6,500) come in ten body types, sixteen interchangeable faces and any wig you'd like. Websites, like the group of men calling themselves "iDollators," share "girlfriend" pictures. Men can totally control these "women" who are always compliant, never talk back and do exactly what men want them to do. Sadly, people who repair them say they're often mutilated.

I grew up wondering what a "real live girl" was. Did I have to be like my father or my uncles to be "real" and "strong"? Or could I be like my mother or Aunt Bertha? I was nineteen when Barbie was born, so I obviously skipped that "perfect little role model" who has taught many girls to be "real" by getting more matching outfits and prettier makeup.

Without any sisters of my own, I found myself, deeply into adulthood, still yearning to gather strong women around me. My circle, I thought, might resemble the Sand Creek Lutheran ladies' circles back in Wisconsin. They met monthly in homes, which provided a reason to wash the curtains and clean the carpets. They had Bible study, worked on quilts or other charitable gifts, talked a lot, made money for the church's mission goals, planned funeral lunches and picnics, indulged in "just a small piece" of cake, drank pots of strong Scandinavian coffee and then went home knowing that, if they ever needed to talk to anyone before the next month's meeting, someone would always be ready to listen. The message my mother's circle had engrained deeply within my cells was, "Like the moon, circles are important. Be in them."

I had a diverse gentle gathering of women in mind. We'd use tested dialogue principles. We'd be women who wanted to share spiritual insights. In other words, women who wanted to be wise Sophias together. Like mom's circle, we would meet in homes, talk and listen — deeply — to each other, express our own inner spirituality in whatever ways seemed authentic, drink herbal tea and wine and eat a simple dinner together. There would be no agenda and the outcome would not be pre-determined. It would be King Arthur's round table for champion "grail-girls."

Circles teach us many things: equality; harmony; balance. A place filled with nothing, yet offering everything. A safe place to play. Like cross-sections of trees, wheels, mandalas, sand paintings, sacred hoops, cauldrons, Tibetan bowls, medicine wheels and crop circles, they are all powerful symbols. Our world is filled with them.

Circles stitch us into sacred spaces whenever we sit down in the round. We draw circles in the ground. We edge them with stones and call them medicine wheels. We create kiva-circles around hearth fires. A consultant once suggested that if we got rid of rectangular tables and moved to circles, organizations would take on a different way of being.

What if *everyone* sat down in circles and looked into each other's eyes? Would our collective wisdom more likely surface? Would we find, as Aristotle suggested, that what is eternal is circular and what is circular is eternal? As Black Elk reminded us: "Everything the Power of the World does is done in a circle. The sky is round, and I have heard that the earth is round like a ball, and so are all the stars.... Birds make their nests in circles, for theirs is the same religion as ours."

This whole idea of growing spiritually together seems scary for some — rather off-putting. My idea of spirituality has nothing to do with *religious*. Nor does it mean pious. It's a deeper ecology; one we all can grow into.

Being spiritual or spirited is the process of allowing Sophia's breath to fill us. Not just with shallow Sunday or Sabbath breaths. She makes us everyday-strong. We all become mystics in our own ways. Mystics invariably feel God in them. Source. Cosmic spirit. The Universe. Whatever we call it, we are merged. We need not all be like Bridget. Or Hildegard. Or Julian of Norwich. Or Meister Eckart, who, incidentally, claimed that not just Mary, but our own *souls* are mothers to God. I'm talking *everyday mystics* here. Ordinary folk. Doing very ordinary things.

I talked to a few friends about my idea. They each invited a few of their friends and soon we'd formed a cohesive group. We called ourselves "The Sophias." Or as my husband would ask, "When are the Sophies meeting?" We decided to meet on the first Sunday after a full moon, so no one needed to send out a schedule.

Each of us brought an object — something that seemed important to us for some reason, so no one needed to ask, "What's the topic?" Our experiences guided us. We established a pattern of starting with a brief centering/meditation — time many in business circles call "checking in," "sensing" or "sourcing" by connecting with "Source." Then we'd tell stories about the object we'd brought. The visual metaphors deepened as we placed and replaced our "sacred objects" in the center of our circle.

The feminist author, Carol Gilligan, says: "Speaking and listening are a form of psychic breathing." We speak; we listen and the circle breathes. In this intentional space, we deepen, sharing things from our hearts, not from our heads. Round and round we go, like rolling down hilly grass. Safe. Easy. And powerful.

Before long, the Boston Sophia circle had settled into a consistent group of eight; we ranged in ages from thirty to sixty and we came from a variety of spiritual paths. Our goal was to play, to have fun, and to deepen our wisdom by listening to each other. We had no rules, but we did adopt a few guidelines: silence is fine; don't interrupt; listen deeply; don't try to fix anything — or offer advice; speak and listen from the heart. As we held several objects at the same time and spoke, our metaphors grew more complex and more meaningful. More mystical. Our conversations became deeply threaded and entwined. As the old saying goes: you had to be there.

Since Sophia is our creative source, it should have come as no surprise that we found ourselves encouraging and supporting each other's creative pursuits. Without necessarily planning to, we had become a creative clan, a tribe of active Sophia-women. In the space of a few years, we Sophia women had produced three books and as many art shows, a few new business ventures and the writing and recording of a musical play. In the midst of all this creative flurry, we also helped stitch our lives together as we grieved and celebrated. And, as women usually do when they gather, we laughed!

Hermes Trismegistus was right. God is a circle whose center is everywhere and whose circumference is nowhere. Because we were "together" even between meetings, we joked about tapping into our "Sophia Inner Net." Even when we weren't in a real circle, we could send each other messages. While meditating at home, one of the "Sophies" got a personal message for me, at just the time I was contemplating going off on a private work-induced stress-reduction retreat. "Go to the trees," she said. "By the water. Alone. Sit. Let the trees teach you. Feel the sap, know the rootedness and groundedness." I relayed this restorative experience in Chapter One's "Songs from the Sacred Grove."

When we're not speaking in our Sophia circle, we honor the silence. Like Quakers, we listen our souls into discovery. We listen each other into speech. It may, as the Quakers claim, be the greatest service one human being can do for another. Silence, like listening, is powerful. It is like a lake, Octavio Paz says, "Down below, submerged, the words are waiting and one must descend, go to the bottom, be silent, wait." Perhaps that's why being silent for any length of time is so frightening to some. People fear silence because they think they might get pushed off the safe dock into deep darkness. Or find nothing there — only the void. But by entering the silent circle, we dare the labyrinth's "minotaur-bull-man" and discover that whatever emerges will buoy us up and we float in her presence. We are not gored, nor are we bored.

Here's a portion of what Debra, one of our Boston Sophia members, wrote about Sophia after one of our gatherings.

"I could never tell if she was real or simply a fantasy, like the Druids, like fairy energies are only fantasies. But suddenly I knew they are real too, and so, likewise, the search for Sophia begins.... She is the wind that moves and she is the space that exists where nothing is. She is the glue to relationships that make us stick in there and learn to love with and through others. She is the knowing within that something is supposed to happen, and of course it does. She is also the receiver ... the one who listens to the inner knowing."

Supportive, inclusive, nurturing, loving circles now extend like grandmother-serpents around the earth. Jean Shinoda Bolen predicted in *The Millionth Circle*, her small essential guide to women's circles, that this would happen. Her title is based on the hundredth monkey theory, that there will be tipping point, a critical mass of circles at some point, and we'll all be in them — drawing on our inherent spirituality — all enjoying our Sophia state.

Circles inform us how to better care for each other. They mirror Sophia's deep, dark, delicious divine energy. When I look across the circle into another woman's eyes, I can see Sophia more clearly. When we speak our own truths, I hear her voice.

Being in one circle leads to being in others. So, when we moved to Vermont, one of my first self-appointed tasks was to start a "Sophia-north" group. Women in Sophia circles stay pretty consistent, I've noticed; perhaps that's because our hearts as well as our minds are so totally engaged. We seven Vermont-Sophias meet monthly. I know of some women's circles who meet once a year for an extended retreat. Other women's circles practice very deep self-awareness and transformative techniques over the phone or on Skype. I'm guessing any circle will hold if accessing the deep wisdom of Sophia is the reason for meeting.

In our Sophia Circles, we not only share in sacred play and wonderful food, but we form deep relationships and support our sisters' inner work from a safe place. We've learned over time that it's all right to be vulnerable, to be "real" when we come together. We gather, like priestesses, to honor Sophia in each of us. She sparks our memories so that, together, we remember more. And more. And more. And more.

We inspire each other. We con-spire to be more than we ever could be alone. The ordinary objects we bring to the center of our wisdom circles often take on magical auras as we hold them and speak.

Penny said she thought each time, long and hard, about what object she'd bring — that was how she prepared her inner self for the circle. Sherry likened her choosing of an object to a deepening. Holding our sisters' "soul-stones," we often speak more than we know we knew.

We spin ourselves, like Grandmother Spiders, from a simple "Y" shaped silk structure into an intricate, delicate yet extremely strong web, each of us hanging from a spinneret and trusting the whole design to hold. Each knows she is responsible for her own strand, which, if weakened and frayed, threatens the entire web.

ONCE UPON A TIME:
Charlotte's Web

"Where's Papa going with that axe?"

That's Fern. Her father is about to kill one of the runts born last night.

Fern names the pig Wilbur, wraps him up, and feeds him from a baby bottle. She says she loves him more than anything.

Now Wilbur is all grown up, and it seems to be my turn to save his life. I have often explained things to Wilbur, like the Latin names for the seven parts of my legs. I've told him stories every day and sung to him every night. But it's close to butchering time and it's time to do something spectacular to distract the farmer. I think humans will believe anything in print, so I decide to compose.

"Some Pig!" I write in thin spidery letters above his bed. "Hey, come look at this," somebody yells. "We have a very unusual pig out there in the barn." Now people come from all around to see Wilbur — the famous Zuckerman ·pig. I plan new messages. "Terrific." "Radiant."

I need new words, so I send Templeton out onto the fairgrounds to find some. Rats know how to find things. He comes back stuffed with fried food and carries a scrap of newspaper with the word "Humble." "Oh, good," I say. "That means not proud and it means near to the ground. That's Wilbur all over." I spin into the night.

Wilbur wins first prize; and now it's time for me to spin one last time for my own children. "You have been my friend, Wilbur. That in itself is a tremendous thing. I wove my webs for you because I liked you. After all, what's a life, anyway? We're born, we live a little while, we die.... By helping you, perhaps I was trying to lift up my life a trifle."

Hooray! Wilbur has won first prize. My chubby friend chokes up and tells me I've saved him. And he would gladly give his life for me if he could. I tell him as gently as I can that I am dying. I don't even have enough silk left to lower myself down. So Templeton has to climb up and carry my precious egg sac filled with 514 eggs, my magnum opus, over to Wilbur's bed.

"I'll watch over it for you, Charlotte. And when they hatch, I'll tell them all about you," he said. "And I'll name them." Good. I hope at least one is named Joy.

Communities and Neighborhoods

E.B. White wrote *Charlotte's Web* between 1949 and 1951, a story of a little scared pig, vulnerable, wistful, lonely and in need of protection. We meet Fern, the little girl who saves him. And Templeton, the self-absorbed rat, who admits he's a heavy eater and sounds like a lawyer. He knows how to spy and hide, but doesn't know the meaning of play. However, if a task is connected to food, he'll do his part. And of course Charlotte — a Sophia figure, like Fern, but on a spinneret. She's all-knowing, compassionate and willing to sacrifice — everything. Charlotte-Sophia cures loneliness and offers purpose. It's a Sophia-tale filled with life-affirming cycles of birth and death. And birth again.

White said he never intended there to be deep symbolism in his story — just one of friendship and salvation. But you can't write about a furry eight-legged creature capable of frightening "Little Miss Muffet" without evoking Spiderman myths, or earlier female archetypes, such as Arachne, the Fate-Weaver. She, as you may remember, won a weaving contest with Athena. Athena changed her into a spider so she could ever afterwards catch souls, like flies, in her web, and keep them safe for eternity.

Webs are amazing things. You can see (and buy) some in Williamstown, Vermont, if you visit Will Knight's spider web farm. He harvests a crop of them every morning, then sprays and mounts them to create web-art. I've heard spider webs can even staunch bleeding if you can gather up enough of them. We love and loathe spiders at the same time. A colleague of mine was so arachnophobic that when a spider appeared in her bathtub she called her husband away from work to deal with it.

Grandmother Spider, in some Plains Indian stories, spun a web-line from east to west, then north to south, and anchored the universe. Hanging from a spinneret, she crafted the rainbow. She is called "The Woman Who Holds Up the Sky" and wears a white cape of wisdom. Dream catchers are crafted replicas of how Grandmother Spider weaves and catches us up into life itself.

White wrote in a letter to the filmmaker who was about to turn his book into a movie: "I think it would be quite untrue to suggest that barnyard creatures are dependent on each other. The barn is a community of rugged individualists, everybody mildly suspicious of everybody else, including me." Sounds like the Vermont I've grown to know and love.

We live on the edge of a township called Tunbridge. On one road into town, a beautiful covered bridge crosses a busy little waterfall. The bridge is an apt metaphor for how communities can bridge their differences even if they are extremely independent. "Tun" comes from the Anglo-Saxon word "town" and people back then met in "tungemot" or town meetings. So do we. On the first Tuesday in March. So do all Vermont's 237 towns and nine larger cities. Tunbridge town meetings start at 10 a.m. sharp. Our town moderator, Euclid Farnham, makes sure of that. We break for lunch. It's hard not to talk to people you disagree with if you want the salt passed. My husband, an excellent pastry chef, is known for his "town meeting lemon meringue pies." We pass school budgets, we buy new graders, we support the library, we levy taxes and tend our cemeteries. Neighbors know neighbors. They know who's hurting and who needs help. Who's good at certain tasks. And who isn't. Who is seeking a cribbage partner. Who might appreciate some extra garden produce or blackberries.

With only about 700,000 people, all of Vermont is like one big community. John and I have personally met both of our Washington D.C. senators and (we're so small we have only one) representative, as well as our governors and state legislators. Most Vermonters have an opinion about how things should be run and we're not afraid to express our views in town meetings or even on the dirt roads when we stop and roll down our windows to say hello to a neighbor. We first learned our neighbors' names at a neighborhood pig roast. It was hosted by our neighbors, the ones with the white "Wilbur-like" mailbox. When we pass it, we take note. If there's mail showing through Wilbur's plastic tummy, that means our mail's arrived, too.

Many people around us are still named Ethan and Ira. I know a couple Priscillas and Felicitys. I could probably find a Zebulon and a Pamphille or two nearby, if I tried. I look at our stone fence and suddenly Robert Frost stands by my side. I see stacks of crumbling stone foundations and realize we once had many more neighbors up here on our mountain than our current seven families. And in a way I cannot begin to explain, when I walk past old stands of lilacs, waving gold tiger lilies, or the crumbling brick schoolhouse, the after-image of their presence makes my life richer. I've read that they used to call each other for parties with a horn or conch shell blown from their front stoop. Sometimes their echoes still float across the hills.

You can still hear people say, "I'm helping out so and so," rather than "I work for so and so." New Englanders work for themselves but readily contribute to others. Survival encourages sharing. It always has. When our farming neighbor Steve brings his big blue tractor with its back-end snow blower up our driveway after a major snowstorm, I no longer feel as if I'm trapped in Steven King's Overlook Hotel. I'm home. I'm safe. Steve's here.

Most of us work 2000 hours every year and spend another 900 at home. How do we have the time to find or sustain community? Some communities that we can unwind from our memory tapes were formed in the space of a weekend, a summer camp, a college dorm. When I lived there, Sand Creek had a population of 150. We had a post office, a bank, a couple of churches, my dad's store. We had a creamery, some gas stations, a barber shop and a car dealership. We celebrated the 4th of July with a big parade and an evening talent show. We raised money for the volunteer fire department, we had picnics in the park. We kept agreements. We built trust. We cared about each other and had fun doing it.

Now, we create online virtual communities filled with keyboard-people searching in dim light for others who will listen to them. To validate their existence. To play with them. But virtual people can't drop off a tuna casserole or fresh cinnamon buns. Or drive you to an appointment. Neighbors know who's hurting and who needs help.

Vermonters don't hang around your doorsteps. At least not the ones on our mountain. Everyone's too busy. But they're there when needed. Communities are rings of hospitality, concentric circles of people choosing to be "with" other people. Sophia seems to be moving us toward more intentional communities, co-housing and ecovillages. She knows we long to care for each other, old with the young, cantankerous with the sweet-hearts, the ones who long to say hello and the ones needing to wave goodbye.

SOPHIA'S MYSTICAL DANCER: JANE LEADE (1624-1704)

A 17th century noblewoman, Lady Jane Leade, heard a woman talking to her at a neighborhood Christmas party when she was only fifteen, and she was convinced the voice didn't come from the other *human* party-goers. *"Cease from this. I have another dance to lead thee in, for this is vanity,"* the voice told her.

Jane married. After her husband died, around 1670, she sat down and before long, Sophia spoke through her pen: *"Behold, I am God's eternal Virgin-Wisdom, who thou hast been inquiring after."* Jane described her as a woman with a very friendly and dignified demeanor. Her countenance, she said, radiated like the sun and her dress was fine translucent gold.

Lady Jane's book group studied Jacob Boehme's writings. They reveled in his descriptions of fiery realms of angels. Like him, Jane wanted to look deeply into the void and find the source of all ideas and touch her wisdom, for Sophia had told Jane she would have no rest until her Sophia-wisdom had been born in the depths of her soul.

But how does all this happen? What if you miss her voice at a Christmas party? What if you don't set your pewter pot in just the right light as Boehme did? Sophia, Jane said, is the original Wonder Woman, "the Wonder of all Wonders, which hath been since time's Creation." You'd have to be blind and deaf to miss her.

Lady Jane went on to found the 17th century Philadelphian Society for the Advancement of Divine Philosophy, a forerunner of the Theosophists. She also wrote several books on mysticism, as well as her diaries: *A Fountain of Gardens*, which was published in 1696. Among other things, she also "saw," in some future time, that Lucifer would be redeemed by Christ. Jane challenged us all to receive Sophia's instructions and learn her secrets.

HER GIFT: PATIENCE

Like a solitary spider, Sophia patiently waits for us to tap into her power line anytime, anywhere. It's her power we're channeling. And, in turn, we become more patient with people and situations. Our patience stems directly from knowing we're strong enough to deal, to wait, to endure. We can cope. And because we're strong, we can *feel*. We don't have to disguise our emotions any longer.

Poet Audre Lorde said in her autobiography, titled, in pure Sophia language, *A Burst of Light*: "We as women tend to reject our capacity for feeling ... because it has been devalued. But it is within this that lies so much of our power." By the time she died of cancer in 1992, Lorde had written seventeen volumes of poetry, as well as essays and an autobiography. She reaffirmed for me that there is great power in feeling! What *I* feel is real. What *you* feel is real. You can argue with anybody's reason, but you can't argue with what they're feeling. Oscar Wilde put it this way: "To deny one's own experiences ... is no less than a denial of the soul."

 ENNEAGRAM NUMBER 6

Number Sixes are often called the loyalists — they're troopers and love to fix things, and they get things done. They like to plan and can often get lost in the details. Sometimes they procrastinate because doubt can freeze forward motion. They're loyal and faithful, but question *everything*; as a result they often question authority. You could say they have trust issues. Or you could say they're just very brave. They try to cover up their anxiety by playing the devil's advocate. They love to scrutinize and look below the surface.

STRONG BUILDING BLOCKS: SACRED GEOMETRY

"In ancient times, the philosophers (lovers of Sophia) weren't thinking about weapons or apples and eggs and the grocery bill. They were finding proofs of divine order."

~ Alice O. Howell, *The Web in the Sea*

David N. Elkins, a psychology professor, says he believes in the sacred "because I simply no longer have the strength to sustain disbelief." He wrote about eight alternative paths to the sacred in *Beyond Religion*: the feminine, the arts, the body, psychology, mythology, nature, relationships and dark nights. Of course no one, not even Elkins, can know the true nature of the sacred. It's like trying to define a kiss. A kiss is more than lips meeting. It's a mysterious union that can't be measured with numbers. Or defined with words.

Still, our minds search for ways to understand. We ask ourselves, what's under and behind some places of power? Could it be "sacred geometry"? And what is sacred geometry, anyway? How can we measure the sacred? We certainly can't form, contain or define it with numbers and shapes, squares and cubes and triangles, circles and dodecahedrons. Or can we? And if, as Walt Whitman believed, spirit and soul are sacred, might the "spirit and soul of the earth" also be sacred? Can we rationalize the irrational?

THE FATHER OF GEOMETRY

Pythagoras, living in the late 500s B.C.E., wasn't the first philosopher (the Magi came before him) but he's the one we all remember. Preceding him was Thales of Miletus who thought all things held Sophia — all things hold the divine. But it was Pythagoras, living in the late 500s B.C.E., who bequeathed us geometry and called it the measurement of earth and the heavens. "Geometry connects us to the cosmos," he said. Some believed he was actually Apollo reincarnated. Numbers aren't merely counting sticks, he told his followers, but proportion and harmony. He spent twenty years learning ancient arts from the Egyptians. And then he studied with the Persians before going to Samos, the Greek island in the North Aegean Sea.

What we know of Pythagoras comes only from his disciples, and later, people such as Aristotle who really liked to scribble, because, like Thales, Pythagoras saw no need to write things down. He established ways of living that some monks and ascetics still emulate. For instance, he taught people to value silence, to be vegetarians, to wear linen. He practiced self-denial, used incense, music, and rigid cleanliness. The Essenes followed in his footsteps. In his *Timaeus*, Plato built on what he had learned from the Pythagoreans and brought us the term *world soul*. Gaia soul. Mary soul. Her soul.

We, too, can learn meanings hidden in music and geometry and signs. We are more than just earth, air, fire and water. We are, Pythagoras argued, justice, soul, reason and opportunity. He said whole numbers are the numbers to pay attention to. Zeroes and irrational numbers didn't hold much meaning for these early mathematicians. After all, odd numbers were feminine, irrational, and even numbers, rational and masculine. Except for One. The monad was the source of all numbers. The possibility that "One" could be feminine didn't get much traction from the Pythagoreans. Or for that matter, from most male writers. But now Sophia's time has come. She's our "one" golden opportunity.

What's the Square Root of Two?

Plato thought that the study of geometry was the most distilled expression of philosophy, of her wisdom. When you hear *sacred geometry* in the same breath as the word *architecture* you can bet it's being used as a way to describe a specific way of building sacred buildings that has been used from antiquity to the present. This way is based on the generative property of simple proportions. The diagonal of the square is the simplest one, so let's start there. Draw a square in your mind. Now imagine a line going from one corner to the opposite one. You now have all the geometry needed to build the Hagia Sophia in Istanbul or the Pantheon in Rome. Simple! Both of these buildings are based on the diagonal of the square....

My son noticed my furrowed brow.

"It's not that hard to understand," Joel said as he spread the paper out in front of me and instructed me to first draw a square. "We need a unit from which to measure, so now write "1" on each side of the square. Find a point on that square. Remember, Mom, this is all about proportions, not *numbers* so as much as you'd like to say the golden mean or the golden proportion is 1/3 to 2/3. It's not. It's a proportion. You divide a room or a wall or your square into two parts. You can't measure the divine order in numbers any more than you can really describe Sophia."

"But I know paintings are more pleasing if the sky comes two-thirds of the way down into the painting. Isn't that the golden mean?" I asked.

"No."

"OK. Let's go on." I had visions of being one of Pythagoras' students sitting on my haunches as he drew with a stick in the sand, saying things like, "There is geometry in the humming of the strings. There is music in the spacings of the spheres." Geometry is Sophia's model for the universe. I've got to pay attention.

"If you think back," Joel said, "to when you learned the famous Pythagorean theorum, you'll remember that the long side of any triangle can be found using **a** squared plus **b** squared equals **c** squared. Well, that diagonal turned your square into two triangles and the two short sides are both I. So the long side is the diagnoal, the square root of 2 (yes, I squared still equals I so I+I does equal 2.) The square root of two also represents the exact width of a circle that perfectly encompasses that square. But that circle's diameter is I.4I42I3562373095............ and on into infinity. It's a number you'll never describe. The square root of two is NOT a number, it is a beautiful wild untameable and indescribable proportion to the simple number I. And if you use this diagonal line to make a new square, you have a new shape where all the sides are in the same proportion to all the sides of that old square."

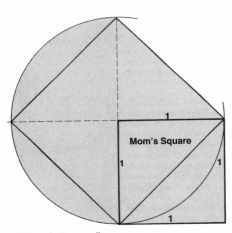

"Mom's Square"

Joel continued explaining that if you draw a new diagonal in that new square you have found the square root of two, and you are on your way to building a series of squares that are beautifully and harmonically related to one another, but impossible to describe in number. All it takes is a piece of string (or a compass) and a straight edge and a pencil and you can make the glorious facade of the Parthenon. Or construct any "sacred" space, the proportions of which makes you feel as if you've "come home." All from our mother square. In other words, from unity (one square) comes all things. Obviously we can't take in the whole universe, so we have to take little bits of it into our minds and understand how it all unfolds, origami-like from one square.

Now, we have the proportion that is the square root of two and we're on our way to building a series of squares and circles that are beautifully and harmonically related to one another. This is impossible to describe in numbers but easy to see once it's drawn out.

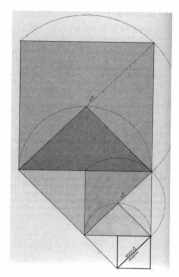

Squaring the Circle

The generating power of this alternation between opposites, between the irrational roots and the rational sides, is what György Doczi calls "dinergy." In *The Power of Limits*, he shows how this dinergy generates growth in plants and animals. The dinergy of a growing series of golden section rectangles maps out the spiral of a nautilus shell, for example. Albrecht Dürer showed the dinergy of the growing series of "square root of two" relationships that describe the sacred geometry of the human body. I think it is through this dinergy, this awesome power in the interaction between the rational and the rational, that Sophia slips into our world.

THE SQUARE ROOT OF THREE

The square root of three can be found by letting two circles of the same size overlap each other. If the width of this white overlapping area is I, then the height is the square root of three or I.732050807568877...........

Does this shape look familiar? The top half of the overlapping area is the same geometry as every gothic arch in every gothic window in every gothic church.

The overlapping white area shown here is also sometimes called the *vesica piscis*, literally meaning "fish bladder," and was a sign of feminine genitalia long before today's Christians began attach-

ing it to their cars. It even predated the early Christians who scratched the symbol in the dust to secretly write the code word for the Greek word *Ichthos*, which means fish. It was a clever secret anagram code for "Iesous Christos THeou Ouios Soter" ("Jesus the Christ, Son of God, the Redeemer"). Pisces ... "Jesus the fisher." By the sign of the fish, they knew who was a Christian and who wasn't, who they could safely

"Vesica Piscis," as depicted on the Chalice Well cover, Glastonbury, England

stay with or who might send them to the lions. But long before Rome's gladiator games, this sign stood for her almond, her vulva, her fertility. A Divine Wisdom underlies all sacred geometry.

THE GOLDEN RATIO

When we speak of the golden ratio, golden mean, the golden section, the golden number, the divine proportion, we are speaking *sacred geometry-eeze*.

The golden mean is found again and again in nature — tree branches, broccoli, sunflowers, seashells — as well as in architecture. This sacred proportion was used over and over by architects to make designs with shapes harmonically related to the original units of the design. It still is.

In the Figure, *The Square Root of 5*, we started again with a square where every side equals 1. If you draw a circle so that a square fits snugly in half a circle, the diameter of that circle is a little more than twice the original I of the side of our square. It is exactly the square root of five of that original I. The bit left over between the square and the circle along its equator is the golden mean of I. So in this illustration, A is the golden mean of B and B is the golden mean of A + B.

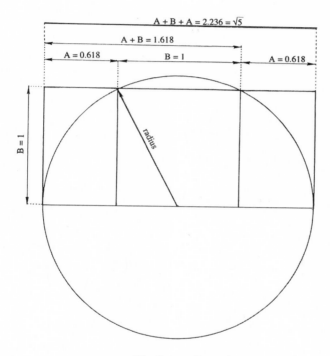

The Square Root of 5

Only 0 and I remain the same when they are squared. All the other numbers either grow or shrink. The golden ratio is, like Sophia, a both/and. It is a relationship between a rational number (I) and an irrational one (.618 033 988 749 894 848...........). It's known as phi, ø, and can be used in art to divide something that is whole, like a wall, a room, a sculpture, or a picture, into two parts. One larger, one smaller. In most pleasing paintings, for instance, the sky will come down about two-thirds of the way into the composition making the golden ratio between sky and landscape. We call it *phi* after Phidias, a famous Greek sculptor, who lived from 480 to 430 B.C.E. and designed Athena's bronze statue inside the Parthenon using (her own) divine proportions.

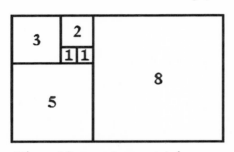

Fibonocci Sequence in geometric form

This gridded image shows us how to visualize this ratio using the Fibonacci sequence. It's a "sacred game" played by adding the two prior numbers together for the next number: 1, 2, 3, 5, 8, 13, 21, 34.... and so on to infinity. Each pair of numbers gets closer and closer to the ratio of the golden mean without ever reaching it. It's named after the 12th century Pisan Italian who grew up in Northern Africa and learned math from Hindu-Arabic teachers. In fact, he introduced the decimal system to Europe, which was, at the time, still using Roman numerals.

Fibbanici's proportions please most of us; they make us feel whole and at ease when we enter a space or view a work of art. When they're not there, we feel more fragmented and sometimes slightly nervous. We sense something's not quite *right*. The Parthenon's harmonious structure was based on this golden ratio. It's the ideal relationship between line and mass that says, "Come on in; you'll be at peace here. Enjoy the beauty." Sacred geometry uses the same simple proportions all over the world. Teotihuacán. Stonehenge. Jerusalem. The Great Pyramid. Every time you visit a sacred place you'll find these proportions embedded there.

Stephen Skinner says, in *Sacred Geometry: Deciphering the Code*, that the Fibonacci series also seems to determine how many petals a plant will have on its flowers, growing out from the stem at geometrically predictable intervals.

No wonder our kids, and our "inner children" love to play with spirographs and computer programs that build fractals and wonderful complex figures from lines and circles. Nature shows us how — with examples such as the chambered nautilus that grows in a logarithmic spiral. Or a fossilized ammonite.

Sacred geometry is literally a large, world-wide topic — one not all of us need to, want to, or will ever completely understand. But if you're seeking more, I'll point you to two books I have found very helpful. Like the golden mean itself, one is bigger, and one smaller. The big one is actually a textbook a Vermonter, Paul Calter, wrote called *Squaring the Circle: Geometry in Art and Architecture*. The other slimmer book by Robert Lawlor is simply called *Sacred Geometry*.

SACRED SITES AND SIGHTING THE SACRED

Old sites call to me. It must be her holy math. I prefer visiting temples of Isis and Artemis before they became temples of Apollo. Or later Christian sites. I want to stand next to her holy wells before they were surrounded by monastery walls. I look for Her signs on stones — spirals, meanders, eyes.

Leonardo da Vinci used up many notebooks trying to square the circle. Why? It was an intellectual game to see what complex and interesting designs he could make with circles and squares. From mandalas to domes, circles join squares to create beautiful space. It may be an attempt to join the heaven-without-end, as in a circle, together with the four-squared boundaries of earth. Jung thought the circle represents the super-conscious aspects of nature, and the square, the conscious rational aspects.

Sophia's symbols keep showing up. For instance, in a famous painting of "The Baptism of Christ" by Piero della Francesca painted about 1450 (next page), a dove hovers over Jesus' head and the entire painting is placed under a gold frame-like arch. If you were to use this arch to draw a circle in the larger square, Sophia-dove would be at the very center of the circle.

"The Baptism of Christ," Piero della Francesca (c. 1420-1492), used by permission, National Gallery, London/Art Resources, NY Imaged Reference: ART374312

The Roman architect, Vitruvius, who died fifteen years before Jesus was born, called his famous outstretched arms and legs image the perfect human body. It's male, of course, since female bodies at that time were considered much less perfect. The central point is the naval; arms and legs form a compass.

"And just as the human body yields a circular outline,
   so too a square figure may be found from it.

For if we measure the distance from the soles of the feet to the
   top of the head,
And then apply that measure to the outstretched arms,
The breadth will be found to be the same as the height."

(Vitruvius, *The Ten Books on Architecture*)

Geometric principles inspired Bernard of Clairvaux. He
founded the Cistercian order and sought to build "perfectly"
proportioned Christian architecture. "What is God?" he asked.
He answered his own question with: "He [sic] is length, width,
height and depth."

In order to discover King Solomon's old building secrets,
around 1130, Bernard sent Hugh of Payens (and eight other
men who eventually grew into the mighty Templars) down to
Jerusalem to scope out the Al Aqsa Mosque and what was left
of Solomon's courtyard and temple. He wanted to rediscover
the secrets of sacred geometry. Or to uncover the Ark of the
Covenant. How was that early temple constructed? *Bring me back
a description of the proportions, he instructed, because they are the sources of
form and energy in the world.*

Soon after the men returned, magnificent cathedrals sprang
up all over Europe like mushrooms. It's likely that the art of building sacred spaces was handed down from the Druids to a group
of companion monks who could sense alignments and flowing
energy in certain places. They would erect a pole and when the
sun made a shadow, they drew a circle around the shadow and that
became the center of the yet-to-be-built cathedral.

The biblical proportions of Solomon's temple are all counted
out in careful cubits; you can read about them in I King 5 and the
subsequent chapters. Solomon's father, David, was a good friend
of Hiram, an architect-builder in a nearby country — Tyre. That
was Goddess Country. So they pooled their resources and built
a stone-pillared building in the style of her temples that Hiram
knew so well. They lined the cedar paneling with gold. The Romans destroyed the temple shortly after Jesus was crucified. Even

the subsequent temple rebuilding is all gone now except for one wall — the Wailing Wall in Jerusalem.

People swarm to Jerusalem to visit what's left of the sacred sites. When a shaft of light during Winter Solstice hits the triple Newgrange spiral perfectly, and we witness it, we are deeply and profoundly affected. Often for life. It's also why thousands of people flock to Mayan sites, for example. Or travel to standing stones. Or gaze at Chartres Cathedral's windows that seem to open to the heavens. It's why people climb the internal chambers of the Great Pyramid that point to the stars. Or visit Cambodia's Angkor Wat's temples that square the circle again and again. "These places belong on our World Heritage Registry," we say. "They must be protected and saved for future generations."

Mircea Eliade, in *The Sacred and the Profane*, tells us sacred places break off the homogeneity of space. Through that break is "an opening by which passage from one cosmic region to another is made possible — from heaven to earth and vice versa; from earth to the underworld."

FOUR CORNERS

You can sense these "openings" Eliade referred to at Chaco Canyon in the Four Corners Region of the southwest. My friend Jim, who later came to Effigy Mounds and encouraged me to write *The Earthshapers*, was an archeologist there and told me many stories about that place. He described Navajo healing ceremonies for returning war veterans and told me about his blind adopted Navajo grandfather who became my inspiration for Yellow Moon's grandfather, Star Gazer. I wanted to experience Chaco for myself. Unlike Shiprock, which nature carved, communities of real people created this complex of pueblos and roads and petroglyphs that dot New Mexico, Arizona, Utah and Colorado.

If you unfold a map of the Four Corners area and draw a line from four sacred peaks: Wheeler, north of Santa Fe to the east; over to Humphrey's Peak at Flagstaff; Arizona to the west; then another line from Mt. Taylor up to Hesperus Peak, they would intersect at Chaco Canyon.

One day in early September, John, Joel and I bumped our rental car over the long dirt road to Chaco Canyon south of Farmington, New Mexico to see this "center of the earth," this sacred "Place of Emergence" for ourselves. "Seeing" is just one of the senses you call on when you approach this vast expanse of old pueblos strategically placed in relationship to each other. You hear the hawks overhead. You feel the dry heat on your skin. You thirst. You sit in the shadows of the T-shaped windows and experience the dark and light moving across the floor. You imagine climbing down a ladder into the round kiva prayer circle below the floor. No one actually lived here in spite of later attempts to label the rooms "homes" and the common areas "food storage places." Archeologists have found no garbage middens that would have piled up over the years if people had actually lived here. So it must have been an assembling place. A church. A conference center. A ritual center where people gathered, sang, danced, told stories and then went home. But not before leaving broken pottery-prayers in tribute to a divine energy that would accompany them until the next gathering. Pottery, for the Pueblo people, as for many First Peoples, are "her" cauldrons — containers created from sacred earth to hold and bless their food. Leaving shards behind was a thanksgiving offering respecting her bounty.

About 700 years ago, the "Chacoans" decided to abandon this temple complex altogether. Perhaps the spiritual power was so strong they didn't want it misused. No one knows why they left any more than we know why the Anazazi — the old ones — left Mesa Verde a few miles to the north. They carefully stoned up Chaco's windows to shut out the light, using the masonry skills it took to build these complex buildings in the first place. They dismantled the wood roofs. And, like the Classic Mayans in the Yucatan before them, they simply walked away.

But an important petroglyph remained behind on the southeastern cliff perched atop nearby Fajada Butte, a 330-foot-high lone outcropping of sandstone. In 1977, Anna Sofaer, an artist who was volunteering with a crew that surveyed all the petroglyphs in the valley for the National Park Service that summer, climbed this sandstone butte. When the sun was at its highest point at the top of a forty-foot cliff wall, she noticed a dagger of light coming through a ten-centimeter-wide opening between three positioned sandstone slabs on a carved spiral etched onto a rock. It happened to be near mid-summer and Anna "Sofia" Sofaer made a brilliant guess that turned out to be correct. The structure was an elaborate sundial that marked, not only the solstices and equinoxes, but also the 18-year cycle of the moon's orbit. Later, she surveyed the buildings in the valley and made a convincing case that all of them were built as giant sundials with walls that were so carefully placed, they were shadowless at important moments in the solar and lunar calendars. The huge cosmological system appears to include even outlying marker spots, such as Mesa Verde and Chimney Rock lying just north in Colorado. They were used as observatories of the day and night skies by early astronomers.

People of the area speak of a female presence who sometimes appears on the Fajada Butte. "She Who Dries You Out." A "Cloud Shaman." A woman who lives in the sky and can only be seen in the mist. One anonymous man tells of his encounter with her when he was ten. He calls himself Wanderling. Wanderling was born around 1938 when *The Yearling* had just been published, and his uncle, a desert plant researcher, gave him that name because the little lad seemed to "wander."

When he was ten, his uncle took him to Chaco Canyon. A spiritual elder had told his uncle to go to Fajada Butte on the winter solstice at full moon. The elder gave the young boy some "plant medicine" several nights in a row and he slept soundly. He remembers his uncle asking the elder how they would climb the cliffs of this formidable butte. "Eagles fly, they don't climb," the elder had said. The boy woke up with his uncle and the elder at the top of the butte, perched where only the most experienced rock climbers could reach. He was sitting just a few feet below the sun dagger, which he never actually saw, but his uncle and the elder had made their way up there.

Later, his uncle gave him some notes he'd written about the boy's experience as they talked that morning on Fajada Butte. The wind was gusty and three vultures circled overhead. The boy crawled into a cave where he was confronted by a woman who, at first, looked like an old lady with long white hair and a wrinkled face. But then she changed. Her face became smooth, her hair black. She carried a pouch. With her thumb and the first finger of her other hand, she spread open the top, put in two fingers, then pulled them out covered with white corn meal. She made three marks across the boy's forehead — each two fingers wide. Then she shook out the pouch. White powder swirled and she was gone. She may have been Hopi, they decided. She wore a heavy, woven one-piece white dress tied with a rope at the waist with a fringe at the bottom. It was clean, the boy said, but it seemed "old." She was barefooted and wore shell or bone jewelry — no turquoise or silver. She wore a shiny layered cape of black crow feathers.

Marie Battiste explained how aboriginals (and young boys on rock climbing trips with their uncles) understand perspectives of sacred places — and of life in general. They see them in four ways, she said in *Reclaiming Indigenous Voice and Vision*: as a manifestation of their language; as a specialized knowledge system; as a unity with many diverse consciousnesses; and as a mode of social law, order and solidarity.

When we approach a "sacred" place, we sense her presence, her clarity, her order and her strength.

SOPHIA'S SPECIAL GEO-SPOT: PARTHENON

After the Persians sacked Greece and destroyed her sacred ground, the Greeks prevailed and built a whole city in Athena's honor. In 447 B.C.E., work began on the top of their sacred rock — the Acropolis, their city on a hill. There, they constructed a mammoth temple to Pallas Athena, the Virgin Place — the Parthenos. I looked down, opposite the main steps leading to the Parthenon, into what must have been the city marketplace, and imagined Socrates followed by his students, walking around as it was being built. No doubt he was commenting on the construction and what it all meant.

The early Greeks wanted the inside of this spacious temple to be empty — except for the colossal brass statue, twenty-four and a half feet tall, designed by Phidias. The sun shone on her and sent her reflections far out into the harbor. Her war gear must have struck fear into the hearts of any would-be invaders. In the 600s, when Christians converted the Parthenon into a Christian temple, the original temple was torn down. Later, the whole space became a mosque, and finally, a Turkish ammunitions storehouse, and her columns were used for target practice.

The temple opens out to the rising and setting of the Pleiades, just as Chartres' main door does on the Western Wall. I was amazed to learn that Mayan structures open to Pleiades as well. Perhaps the builders wanted us to remember why the Pleiades is important to us. As Job said, "Can you bind the sweet influence of the Pleiades?" Not likely.

The Parthenon's main building proudly stands on three levels. It's cleverly constructed to fool the eye. The rectangular sides are slightly curved and the massive marble Doric pillars recede in size and placement.

One of the Caryatids holding up the roof of the Porch on the Erechtheion at the north edge of the Acropolis, c. 410 B.C.E., Athens, Greece

All the divine proportions make this massive building appear to feel airy and light. Carvings of war exploits progress around the frieze along with a possible depiction of a virgin being sacrificed so her father might win the battle. They were once colorfully painted. Marble moons wax and wane. Young virgins wove Athena's veil and walked the Sacred Way from the northwestern side of the city to the Parthenon to present it to her at appropriate festivals. And off to the north, I spied six beautifully sculpted women. The famous Caryatids still hold up the roof of the building called the Erechtheion, after the legendary founder of Athens. Their name comes from the young women from Karyai, who once came to dance before Athena. Now they're frozen columns standing in silent tribute to all load-bearing women, to all beautiful, strong supportive women. To all women around the world who carry and balance and support.

Athena's temple in Troy was called the Palladium after the small image of herself that Athena supposedly carved. People believed that as long as this wooden statue "from heaven" stayed, the city would be safe. During the war with the Greeks, the statue was stolen and Troy fell. Later, Romans carried it off to Rome to be installed in the Temple of the Vestal Virgins. When Rome fell, it was carted off to Constantinople where Constantine buried it in one of the Artemis-Ephesian temple's huge red porphyry pillars topped with Apollo's statue. He supposedly added some Christian relics as well: splinters of the real cross and nails which Helene, his mother, no doubt brought back from her pilgrimage to Jerusalem.

In 392 C.E., the church fathers pronounced the Olympian deities dead. As a result, all the female figures slid over to rest comfortably on Mary's shoulders. Then she became the Palladium — The One Who Protects.

SPIDERS, UNITE!
When spiders unite, they can tie up a lion.
~ Ethiopian proverb

All of us are created with divine proportions. How can we be anything but powerful and beautiful? Goethe sends Faust to "The Mothers." It's there, he was told, he would find ultimate beauty because her realm is one of formation and powerful transformation.

"The woman's place of power within each of us," Audre Lorde said, "is neither white nor surface; it is dark, it is ancient, and it is deep." It's older than Ireland's Burren rocks. Older than Iona stones. Thirty thousand years ago, people painted a particular womb-power image: nine women deep inside a cave in north-eastern Spain. To this day, they are still dancing. Three are young girls, three are women and three are thin, dark crones.

At her trial, Joan of Arc was accused of "acting against nature" as a woman. She was acting too powerfully, her accusers said. Our female cells remember the millions of "witches'" bodies curling up in church-fires. Don't claim your power. You'll be flayed!

But we won't.

We refuse to let it happen again.

Say "power" with emphasis on the first syllable — POW — and notice how it pulls at your diaphragm and rumbles your chest.

We are volcanoes set to erupt! I believe Sophia would want us to claim this power and use it judiciously. Lovingly. Carefully. And above all, wisely.

Susan Faladi confirms this sentiment at the end her book, *Backlash*, by saying that women seem "unaware of the weight and dynamism of their own formidable presence and of the vast and unstoppable vitality they possess." Indeed, most of us do.

Don Juan, a friend of Carlos Castaneda, calls the womb the "Perceiving Box," but only after it no longer reproduces. That's when it becomes a tool for evolution. The womb possesses direct knowledge and women simply take this for granted. We women think, well, that's just who we are. No big deal. But men *never* take this power for granted. Men usually find it much more difficult to *know* all the things that women do. Women, he said, have endless power at their disposal, but he never could understand why women have so little interest in gaining access to it.

Regardless of our gender, it's time we no longer shy away from our own power. Lynne Andrews defined our power this way: *"Power is the strength and ability to see yourself through your own eyes and not through the eyes of another. It is being able to place a circle of power at your own feet and not take power from someone else's circle. True power is love."*

We hear "hard" not only as a thinly veiled erection image but as the preferred route over "soft." We've been conditioned to value hard economics, hard facts, hard decisions, hard work. The sciences, we've been told, are hard; humanities are soft. Political parties are still categorized as the "hard" father party, the Republicans, who are not afraid to go to war and the "soft" Democratic mother party that cares for the little people and seeks equality. But we no longer have to live in dualities. Her message all along has been "both/and." But it will take more than Viagra to heal our erectile dysfunctions!

Robert McElvaine said that Darwin performed a sex-change operation on Mother Nature. He turned her into a stern, uncaring fatherly parent interested only in the strongest, the hardest, the fittest. Others later said: "Dominate nature! Control it! Make war with it!" And now, look what's happened.

Just *listen* to the phallic language we use. We like to "stick it to 'em" with penis-shaped missiles. "Screw you!" "Carry a big stick." "Give them the shaft!" And remember, it's girlie to "pull out." We "penetrate" enemy territory and soldiers everywhere are conditioned to believe, along with George Patton: "Them that does the fighting does the fucking." Losers get castrated. They get turned into "women." In Turkish prisons, the most cruel thing to do to male prisoners was to force them to weave, because that was women's work. It's a fact that men in America commit violent crimes ten times more than women. Call Hitler a sissy, a president a wimp or a king a "softsword" and see what happens. The Marine "pelvis" chant, "This is my rifle, this is my gun. This is for business, this is for fun" turns real men — the ones who really know how to love — into killers.

Real people don't need to get even. Strong men or women don't need to be hard. They don't need to rip vaginas open with bayonets and rifle butts or pull a trigger yelling, as a Mai Lai soldier did, "Fuck 'em to death!"

War makes people go "berserk." *Beri* means bear and *serkr* is a skin or shirt. Between the 8th and 10th centuries, special Viking warriors put on bear suits before going into battle and became rage-filled killing machines. Believed to be chosen by Odin, who borrowed the bear-costume from his female counterpart, they thought they were invincible. Whether their states were drug or ecstasy induced, the warriors would later again return to normal. By 1200, these uncontrollable gangs were banned. Ironically enough, now Scandinavian countries rank among the lowest in the world for violence.

We no longer need berserkers. When we partner with Sophia, we can see ourselves as powerful beings, equipped with safe ways to express our rage. She offers us her nine gifts, and its *our* faces that are reflected in the canopy of the entire universe. It is then we realize we aren't in bondage, and our perception of reality can change.

The strength of the Artemis "bear" was known even to the biblical writers. Paul describes a riot involving some of his friends in Ephesus in Acts 19. "Great is Artemis of the Ephesians!" the people yelled. Someone quieted people down by saying, "Citizens of Ephesus; these men are not blasphemers. Who is there that does not know that the city of the Ephesians is the temple keeper of the great Artemis and of the statue that fell from heaven?"

A stone from the sky? A black meteor stone falling from heaven onto the earth creates a pretty powerful symbol. One of her black rocks is still enshrined at Mecca. It's called the Ka'aba. The Sufi poet, Rabi'a, a woman on fire for love and truth who lived in Iraq from 717 to 801, described how it took Mohammad fourteen years to get to Mecca, and when he got there, he found priestesses guarding her stone and circling it seven times, as men continue to do today. But now no women do. This black stone was the symbol of the goddess of Arabia and it fell to earth at the spot, so it's said, where Hagar conceived Ishmael. Hagar was, just to refresh your memory, Abraham's consort, a handmaiden of his wife, Sarah. Sarah couldn't conceive, but Hagar gave birth to Ishmael, the founder of the Muslim faith. Then, in spite of her old age, Sarah gave birth to Isaac and therein lies a Jewish-Muslim rift yet to be healed. People forget that it was a *female* sphinx-like being who carried Mohammad in his visions, up, up through seven levels where he experienced God directly. In Sufism, God is The Beloved, the reconciler of all differences. We're waiting.

Another meteor-mother stone was carried from her sacred mountain in Turkey to Rome and placed in her temple, which now, ironically enough, sits exactly under the Vatican.

In thinking together about how powerful we are, take a minute to write down the "If I" stuff you've told yourself over the years. Here are some starter thoughts:

If I am too smart, the boys won't like me.
If I do this well, my women friends will be jealous and they
    won't like me.

If I outshine my husband, he'll no longer love me.

If I make more money than my husband, he'll feel impotent.

If I don't take care of my parents, I'll be a failure.

If I'm not perfect at (fill in the blank) my (fill in the blank) will disown me.

If I don't have a man in my life, I'm worthless.

Now create another list. This time assess your own strengths. Everything you're good at. "I am good at…." "I feel powerful when…." How does the length of each list compare? What have you learned about yourself?

Croning Wisdom

The word "crone" once conjured up for me long pointed chins, a humpback, gnarled hands, and skinny fingers curled around a knobby stick. Scary. Ugly. Now, when hairs appear on my chin, I just pluck them out. And thank her for helping me to age. I'm happy to claim my cronedom because I've learned from Barbara Walker, and others, that she's the third face of the virgin, mother trio. Virgin — the one who dares stand alone. Mother — the one who agrees to stand with children. And Crone — the one who eagerly stands for more than she may yet know.

The word itself most likely referred to Rhea Kronia, Mother of Time. But it's also connected to crows — *Coronis*. Carrion birds. Or vultures — as the huge images in very old sites in Turkey show. She cares for life and death, birthing and passing.

People who research passages and important decades claim that once a woman reaches her late fifties, she moves into a place of wisdom. Into that "Womb-Perception Box" which Don Juan described. First Peoples often place their female elders in an honored position. She no longer needs to be wise just for her family; now she can be wise for the entire tribe.

You have to be post-menopausal to "get" this wisdom, apparently. Women, it seems, become wiser when they no longer have to deal with those PMS, lunar-lunacy, twenty-eight-day moon phases of their lives. Wise, how? Do we have the wisdom to say "No" now? The wisdom to balance? The wisdom to continue to create? The wisdom to spend time in solid friendships? The wisdom to help heal? The wisdom to bravely speak? The wisdom to go where others perhaps do not dare to go? The wisdom to confront abuse? Head on? Or perhaps we carry just enough wisdom to not make things worse. Do we have the wisdom to realize what motivates people and the wisdom to know it's not always the same as our own? The wisdom to know how to give? The wisdom to know how to receive? The wisdom to keep stirring the bubbling cauldron? The wisdom to keep asking powerful questions, and to be strong enough to not always have the answers?

My friend Sharon Bauer, who lives in Watertown, MA, struck me as being a priestess the very first time I saw her. She was a member of the painting group I mentioned earlier and has been a psychotherapist, peace-activist, artist, and ritual guide most of her life. I was part of her own big croning celebration. One day I decided it must be time for me to mark my passage too. So I asked her if we could do it, just the two of us, in her beautiful urban garden.

One crisp November morning I turned up earlier than our agreed-upon time and sat for a few minutes on her front steps, meditating. Asking for a symbol, a totem for the day — for my life. A crow landed on a branch, just above my head. When Sharon came out bearing a beautiful gourd, I told her about the crow. She said, "Oh" and went inside to get a crow's feather and the Medicine Card for crow. "We might like to read about this later," she said. I still have the saddle-colored gourd she gave me, complete with a crow's feather attached to its lip. It's filled with bits and pieces of flowers and trees we gathered from plants and trees she had planted to honor each of the four directions. Circling, singing, we finally reached the western-most point in her garden where two trees grow together. Where they embrace, we placed the feather and the card and that's when the morning miracle happened.

I began reading aloud what "Crow" means from the *Medicine Card* book: teacher, word-smith, publisher — when forty or fifty crows flew onto branches overhead and cawed raucously.

Crow.... Are you "cawing,"
So I may know,
The Secrets of balance,
Within my soul?

Or are you sending,
Your sacred "caw"
Just to remind me,
Of universal laws?

The instant I stopped reading, they flew away. Every one of them. Some in pairs. Some alone. In the space of thirty seconds, Sharon's tree was no longer crow-winged black, but leafy green again. I turned to her with tears sliding down my Scandinavian-biscuit cheeks and whispered, "Nobody else would ever believe this!" She just smiled and nodded.

When I see crows now, and they caw to me often, I suspect they ALL know I'm a crone. I'm sure those crows in Sharon's garden chat with our Vermont crows because I daily hear them encouraging me to "...*speak in a powerful voice when addressing issues that for you seem out of harmony, out of balance, out of whack or unjust.... Be willing to walk your talk, speak your truth, know your life's mission, and balance past, present and future in the now. Allow the bending of physical laws to aid in creating the shape shifted world of peace."* (*Medicine Cards*, Jamie Sams and David Carson) Caw! Caw! Caw!

I just noticed for the first time that "ritual" is part of the word "spi ritual" — ritual is, then, one way to recognize "spirit." Some people court ecstasies with drugs or prayer and fasting or dance and ritual. The Tibetan lung-gompas run in a trance for days and nights without stopping to eat or drink, their eyes fixed on the horizon the whole time. Others, like Mohammad, who "surrendered to God" (for that's what Islam means), have ecstasies thrust upon them. They "fall into consciousness." Thomas Merton described it this way: "A door opens in the center of our being and we seem to fall through it into immense depths which, although they are infinite, are accessible to us."

Our stalwart, beautiful Sophia undergirds all we do and all we attempt to do. Many women have shown us how to be strong. Eleanor Roosevelt, for example, taught us this: "You gain strength, courage and confidence by every experience in which you really stop to look fear in the face. You are able to say to yourself, 'I lived through this horror. I can take the next thing that comes along.' We all must do the thing you think you cannot do." A young woman hoping to be our next state representative asked a group of us: "What would you do if you knew you couldn't fail?" What could we accomplish together, knowing Sophia will not let us fail?

FROM SOPHIA'S NOTEBOOK

Follow your best intuition. Intuit. Into it. Your deep knowing. Wise woman, you know when to be still. The call to speak the truth in love emboldens you ... to speak to all who would listen.

Relax and you will know. I spent long eons not-doing, but watching. Now is the time for all of us to "do." Welcome my abundant imagination. You know the value of community — as you call it — a common love-life. But like bored children, you expect to "have" and when your expectations are threatened, you whine and fall down, kicking your heels like a transient child, hoping your parent will set some limits to your behavior. "Chasten and punish me so I'll feel better." But love is not like that. Love allows. Love is fertile and builds. It does not tear down. It upholds, sustains and continues on even in the bleakest of moments. Love is what you are at your very core. When you know you are loved, there is no need for temper tantrums, for hitting back, for selfishly grabbing.

Humans grow by brushing up against sandpaper. It comes in many forms. Irritations smooth, form and polish. From the rough wood comes the shape of you. You emerge from your humanness into something else. Something even more beautiful. You continue to form yourself and life's irritants help you. You learn to use them for even a larger purpose. You learn to be thankful for them, not chafe at them. You learn to respect this living system of earth and beyond and how it all works together. Here and "beyond." But, of course, there is no "beyond" for it's all right here with you now. You set up opportunities for yourself and when you forget you did that, you whine, "Why? Why me? Why this? Why now?" Faith takes the "why" questions and turns them around to "But, of course!" Remember your strength.

part three

SOPHIA IN OUR UNIVERSE

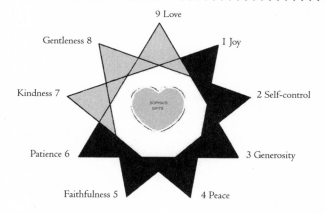

chapter seven

SHE INVITES JUSTICE

Crop Circle: Roundaway, Wiltshire, August 7, 2008

. . . .

*"She holds the sun and moon in her right hand and embraces them
tenderly…. She made everything … embraces all creatures and is
especially extended over peoples, kingdoms and all goods…. You
must be diligently on your guard so that the greening power you
have from God will not dry up in you."*

~ Hildegard of Bingen in a letter to
Abbot Adam of Ebrach

MOUNTAIN JOURNAL ENTRY

I count shades of grey in the sky: aqua grey, violet grey, mauve grey,
pinkish grey, rosy grey, quartz grey, almost black grey. The creek:
icy, frothing, burbles and hides. Why am I searching for flowers on
my path? I know there are none this time of year. Then the crazy
thought comes: it doesn't matter because it's all matter.

A strange combination of patience and impatience washes over
me and I yearn to move on to something, yet I enjoy just being in
stillness. I wait for the dove's fly-over.

I write:

> As frightened chicks, we scatter, searching
> For your warm wings.
> Circling hawks, greedy jaws snap. We hobble, harassed
> Battered, bruised, bleeding.

Oh, Winged One. Great Giver of Justice,
Let me soar with You.

HEARTBEAT QUESTIONS

Where would I never want to live? Why? Do I have work to do there?
What have I said or done that, in retrospect, seems to have been unfair?
What new memes might I foster?
In what ways might I be more gentle?
How does nature bring me closer to Sophia? Places where I "breathe" her?

NEW MEMES

We share collective memories; they're our memes, our cultural building blocks. It's how I carry my attitudes and beliefs back from when I was submerged in the Sand Creek meme pool. I float on the eddies of ideas I heard my parents, my pastor, my teachers, my friends saying.

Memes are like contagious brain-viruses that flourish on radio and TV talk-shows, Petri dishes and bloggy bacteria fields. They cling to slogans and bumper stickers. They creep into our brains through music, books and movies. Like little bugs, they mutate, recombine and we begin to think that we thought up those political phrases and religious platitudes and attitudes about people and places ourselves. Sound bites and catchy phrases stick because we "get" them.

Meme was coined by biologist Richard Dawkin, over thirty years ago, to define a unit of cultural information. It comes from the Greek word *mimesis* or imitation. They replicate in ways we can't predict. We might find some memes very attractive when we first encounter them, so we make friends with them. We may even adopt them. And then they take on a life of their own. They're hard to get rid of. And like genes, but less stable, they survive in the memories of successive generations.

Take the "flying meme," for instance. In his book, *The Evolving Self*, Mihaly Csikszentmihalyi says, "To soar above the earth was thought to be the privilege of superior beings: angels, dragons, spirits." Not anymore.

Or consider the "smoking meme." My dad always had a pack of Luckies in his left breast shirt pocket and one usually dangled from his lip. Actors and actresses blew smoke across all the movie screens when I was a kid. I married a man who'd smoked since his 15th birthday. Then one day ash from his cigarette dropped onto the blanket of our newborn; he put that cigarette out and grabbed for a new meme, a new view of himself that wasn't built around the old meme, "I am a smoker." To foster his "I am not a smoker" meme, he had to give up coffee for a while, as the old meme was wound tightly around that cup. And he no longer lit up every time he got into the car. Most people have finally adopted a new smoking meme: *smoking causes lung cancer.*

Now and then we play "the lottery meme." "If I win the lottery, all my troubles will be over." Half the people in the U.S. hold this creation meme: "The world was created 6,000 years ago." We also carry "weapon memes." First we had stone axes; everybody had to have one. Then it was swords. Only certain people could swash those buckles. Then people in the Tuscan town of Pistoria started carrying small guns around. Soon everybody wanted a pistol. Kalashnikovs. Uzis. We're now addicted to guns. There's a meme afloat in the current bacteria-rich Internet that says, "The government's going to take them away. Stock up on ammunition." Guns help us play the game most chimpanzees and other primates play. It's the "I'm more powerful than you" meme. Geneticists tell us that 94% of our genuine material overlaps with chimpanzees. I live in the quiet expectation that the other 6% of what makes us different from chimps will kick in soon and we'll actually begin to foster "the compassion meme." The "I'm not afraid of you" meme.

Ever since about 3,000 B.C.E. we've carried a "war meme." That's the meme that says war will always be with us and we'd better be ready to wage it or we won't survive. That meme had already attached to our son Nate who was about four when he piled a mountain of sticks onto his little red wagon. He came chugging by and I asked him what he was doing. He said, "You never know when somebody's going to drop in for a war."

Many men and women carry the "inferior woman meme," which says women are less than men and they must be controlled, protected and corrected. This meme was alive and well long before the Taliban moved into Afghanistan. Women were often kept in dark tents so long their bones and muscles were permanently damaged. In China, the bones in little girls feet were once broken and then bound so as women they would hobble and be more pleasing to men. Their feet never really healed. The men carried the "little feet are sexually attractive meme." The women carried the "I must do what the man wants meme."

In spite of our planet's need to view it otherwise, many of us still hold the "foul your campsite and move on meme." There's plenty of everything so just use it up. We've been burning oil and coal for two hundred years, why not continue? Shaking loose the "we'll never run out" meme is very hard to do.

Sadly, most of us harbor an "other meme." That's the one that says (fill in the blank) isn't us, so we want nothing to do with them. The "others" are just out to destroy our "right and better" way to live. "They" have to be defeated, killed, destroyed.

"Death to America!" "My way or the highway." "Take back America." Twisted memes create bent people. As a result, even without thinking, we cling to ideas that are false, harmful, and ineffective. Furthermore, because our resistance is lowered, we're open to accepting more memes just like the ones we've adopted. That's how memes spread. Political factions are masters at meme-spreading. No amount of hand washing or anti-bacterial agents can keep memes from infecting others.

Unless we're truly *thinking*, ideology will always trump imagination. Our cultural software is very complicated; there are never just two sides to any story. There may actually be as many as twelve. Rudolf Steiner stretches our imagination by challenging us to try to see everything from at least twelve points of view, like the number of astrological signs. I'm a Leo, a fire sign, for instance, so my chief meme says, "I'm strong; I'll just go for it with enthusiasm!" but a Sagittarius might say, "Wait a minute. I've got to think about that first" and a Gemini might say, "Let's just talk this over." When we are able to integrate *all twelve signs*, we're a bit closer to accessing Sophia's wisdom.

Memes propagate like bunnies unless they're challenged. Barack Obama challenged the meme: a black person can never be a U.S. president. The movie *Cocoon* challenged the meme: we're alone in the universe. Roger Bannister challenged the meme: nobody can run a mile faster than in four minutes. Koko challenged the meme: primates can't communicate. Reinhold Messner challenged the meme: you can't climb Mt. Everest without carrying oxygen with you, and Junko Tabei challenged the meme: women can't climb Mt. Everest.

Daniel Quinn tells this old story: Once upon a time in the land of broken legs, the inhabitants heard rumors of a far-away land where people moved around freely because no one's legs were broken. Everyone scoffed. How could that be? How could anyone get around without crutches?

Some of our old threadbare "justice memes" go like this — and we just keep hopping along on our "crutches," repeating them:

Welfare recipients or people getting unemployment benefits are lazy so they don't deserve help.
Some people don't deserve citizenship.
Homeless people just want to be left alone.
Rape victims are asking for it.
Women shouldn't work because their children will suffer.
Women don't need the same salaries as men.

Gays destroy the sanctity of marriage.

CEOs deserve huge salaries and we have to pay them that or we won't get competent people to run our corporations.

Jews are rich and they run our financial systems.

Poverty will always be with us.

How about spreading this meme: growing your own food is the best way to live. Or: not having a gun in your house will keep you safer. Or: gender doesn't determine love. Or: "apocalypse" doesn't have to mean "destruction." It can also mean "revelation," a new way of seeing.

JUST WORDS

A ridiculous wormy fish-like creature about three inches long squiggled into my dream consciousness. Then it morphed into a tiny unicorn/dragonfly. It followed me everywhere. Its large, luminous eyes blinked, and turned into television screens. Hypnotized, I watched. It brought with it way too much information! I longed to be alone, but it constantly hovered. It even flattened itself like a bat and sneaked under cracks in closed doors. Once it got tangled in my hair. It pursued me — "talking, talking, talking" — but I couldn't understand it.

I woke up thinking my brain was fried. But that dream made me more awake to *words* ... how I take them in, how I send them out, how I hold them. Words tumble off internet pages and pile up on our keyboards, they dribble and twitter. Why shouldn't we spell "wine" *Yn*? But it seems a waste to use only 144 characters when we all know so many more.

Logos was the Word of words — the first connection. Logos was the "Let there be..." creation-making word. Sophia was called the original Logos — then she became Sophia-Christ and then people who read the book of John attributed Logos to Christ alone: "In the beginning was the Word and the Word was with God and the Word was God." And Sophia was silent.

For many years, I've made a living either putting words to paper or onto screens and helping other people to do so as well. Diane Ackerman, in *Deep Play*, says writing is simply the process of "tilting tiny cogs and wheels into place." But then those cogs start turning. Once released, they can't be dialed back. It's the writer or the speaker's deep responsibility to know what wheels turn what cogs and what might be set into motion. Like mobile phones that can trigger bombs, before you know it, words, too, can go "Kaboom!" Or they can lie quietly like sleeper cells in our brains until we hook them up. Chemists tell us that when two agents come together to produce something new and different it is called *hypergolic*. Writers call it metaphor.

The Secret Service has let it be known that death threats to our president are now 400% higher than against any other president in history. Words can be as lethal as a knife in an ankle holster. "White Supremacy-Speak" and "Jihad-Speak" are "hypergolic bombs" set to detonate. Words pack explosives. Old Irish bards were invited to attend the kings at battle because they could raise blotches of skin on their enemies simply by reciting satirical verses at them.

We protect freedom of speech, unless you yell "fire" in a crowded room. We protect your right to publish most anything you're thinking and it's even easier if you, yourself, are the publisher. During Elizabethan times, "scandalous" and illegal publishing endeavors were called wagon-back presses because, as their name implies, an author's words could be quickly packaged up, and paper and press packed into a wagon and moved on in the dead of night — if need be, to another location. Today we call it the Internet. Hate blogs and myths can circulate faster than you can hit "send." If your spam protector is set on low, you'll find words floating into your head at a dizzying pace. And most of them prey on our fears. Eat this. Don't eat that. Don't flick your car's headlights at night or a gang member will kill you. Don't let sparks from your clothing get near your gas tank when you fill up, or you'll be set on fire. Coca Cola is an effective contraceptive. The ACLU plans to remove all crosses from tombstones.

"We were never born to read." That's how Maryanne Wolf, a Tufts childhood development professor, begins her provocative book with the unlikely title: *Proust and the Squid*. It's the story of science and the reading brain. The title comes from the reading insights we gain from Proust (reading as a kind of intellectual sanctuary) and the squid (reading by making neuron connections).

We were never born to read; we were born to tell stories and keep oral histories. Reading came late in our human development and "folks in the know" at various times said — don't do it! It will destroy your memory. When writing did dawn onto our collective scene, it was connected with priestesses and the royals. Hieroglyphics was called "writing of divine words" and sometimes ink was washed off with beer so people could "drink the knowledge" right from the papyrus. Moses, no doubt, could read hieroglyphics. Letters came alive. "A," in fact, was called one of three Hebrew "Mother" letters.

Given my great interest in writing, as well as in all things "goddess," I *loved* Leonard Shlain's book, *The Alphabet Versus the Goddess*. It's all about the conflict between word and image. Shlain is a vascular surgeon who knows how blood gets to the brain. And he's also interested in questions such as: "What caused the disappearance of goddesses from the ancient world? He postulates: because alphabet literacy reinforces the left brain hemisphere at the expense of the right hemisphere, the female divine began to disappear when writing replaced images. The more feminine right side is where we store, not only images, but ubiquity.

Webster tells us that ubiquity is omnipresence — being everywhere at the same time. It's the way I sometimes see the whole planet in Mother Turtle Rock. It's what enables me to hold a certain pink rock from my collection and again be in Isis' temple in Turkey, and then float with her down the Nile, and then become a part of "her" star, Sirius.

Annie Dillard wrote a short story once about eating soup, seeing carrots, meeting the farmers who grew the carrots, visiting the fields and moving from that landscape to the world and to the universe. Surely it's what George Washington Carver had in mind when he held a little peanut in his hand and said, "If you could understand this peanut, you would know God." Or Julian of Norwich who could see the whole world in a hazelnut.

It's hard to control ubiquity. Darned near impossible. Take the pig, for instance. Little Wilbur (or maybe a sow) was Demeter's sacred animal. Pigs were connected to the fertility of crops. Egyptian farmers encouraged pigs to trot along behind them as they sowed seeds in the fields to stamp them down. The Great Scandinavian Mother was sometimes called Syr (sow). Her chariot was pulled by boars. In the Buddhist tradition, Marici was called the Diamond Sow. Seven little pigs attended her throne. In Scotland her name is Orc and the Orkney Islands are sacred to her. Bagpipes were originally made of pig's hide. They were holy instruments, instruments capable of transformation. So, to conquer the Scots, the English banned bagpipes from Scotland at one time. And in an effort to destroy "her," pig meat was condemned, just as the Goddess was condemned from middle-eastern religions. Or was it because a buried meme was cautioning, "Like the horse, the pig is *her* sacred animal. Don't eat it."

A young Yale undergraduate's creation calls to everyone visiting Washington D. C's mall. Part of the power of Maya Ying Lin's Vietnam Veterans Memorial lies in how she balanced right and left brain perceptions of it. The polished black granite wall stretching off into the distance is totally understood and appreciated by the right brain. So is the sensation your hand feels as it passes over the names. But the fifty-eight thousand names that form this database in stone is a left-brained experience. The names are listed in the order in which the veterans died. Words to read, to touch, make rubbings of, to weep over. Ubiquitous words. Sophia words.

It was 8th century *literate* monks who caused artists to flee for their lives during what's called the "iconoclastic" movement. "Get rid of the icons!" they cried. "Depend only on words. Deface the Virgin!" But then Empress Irene came along and said, "Don't listen to Pope Leo. Bring back the church murals. Remove the plaster!"

Shlain reminds us that the human face is recognized by the right brain. When women's faces are veiled, they can't see each other; in effect, their right hemispheres are also veiled. Diminished. In other words, veils enhance the left brain — the linear, rational "masculine" brain.

Words aimed at denigrating women have piled up for so long we may never remove the stench. If she speaks out, crush her mouth with a hot brick. That one came courtesy of Mesopotamia. Thomas Acquinas wrote that women are defective and misbegotten. They don't have souls. Although he married Katie, Luther lumped women with vermin, plagues and wild beasts. Women, he said, are punishment God sent because of Eve. Small wonder he also jettisoned Mary. Here are a few phrases describing women written by other Christian church men: Satan's bait; poison for men's souls; the delight of greasy pigs; bad stem; evil root; honey and poison.

The Malleus Maleficarium, The Hammer of Witches was written in 1487 by Heinric Kramer and James Sprenger, two Dominican friars who taught theology at the University in Cologne. They were called by Pope Innocent VIII: "Heroes of their order." I have a copy; it makes for heavy reading in every sense of the word. They quote Aristotle a lot. They address as Question VI, "Why is it that women are chiefly addicted to evil superstition?" Their answer: It's well known that women copulate with the devil; women are weak. Women are idle; they have slippery tongues. They're defective — formed from a bent rib. They have weak memories and they lie. "To conclude, All witchcraft comes from carnal lust, which is in women insatiable."

It's filled with lurid, mostly North German, examples of what witches have done to good men. The devil, working through women, causes impotence. There's a lot of coverage about remedies for that. Many prayers and incantations. Lengthy and explicit instructions for judges examining witches — numerous actions they can take. Then we get to Questions XIII to XV: basically, how to torture. Trials by red-hot irons — that sort of thing. Copies flew off the printer's shelves.

People steeped in oral cultures believed books would short-circuit the work of critical understanding. In India, during the 5th century B.C.E., Sanskrit scholars decried the written language. Iona's Columcille went to the mat for the *filid*, the poets who spent twelve years memorizing stories. Some of those long Celtic tales took days to recite. When the Irish finally did write, Thomas Cahill tells us, the calligraphic strokes seemed magically beautiful. They "obeyed a prehistoric mathematics oscillating between equilibrium and imbalance, a harmony without a manifest center." In other words, divinely done. In fact, many people really believed *The Book of Kells* was written by angels.

The Alphabet Versus the Goddess ends with the author's hopeful conviction that we are entering a new Golden Age. "One in which the right-hemisphere values of tolerance, caring and respect for nature will begin to ameliorate the conditions that have prevailed for the too-long period during which left-hemispheric values were dominant. Images, of any kind, are the balm bringing about this worldwide healing." Dostoevsky may have been right — beauty will save the world.

About the time Irish monks were illuminating manuscripts, my old Viking ancestors came along, pillaging and burning. Lindesfarne, that slender finger of Christianity sticking out of the northeast coast of England in particular, attracted Norse attention. Easy pickings. They beached their *langskips* looking for gold and silver in the years 793, 801, 806, and again in 867.

That was about the time a little boy named Olaf Tryggvason was captured by Estonian pirates. He was taken to Novrogod in Russia, and, lucky for him, the people who bought him were a loving Estonian couple. The skald-poet, Snorri Snorkelson, who wrote down many of those old Norse tales about two hundred years after they happened, tells of how the boy's uncle, Sigurd, came to Estonia to collect taxes for the Russian king. One day he noticed a little nine-year-old boy who was obviously a foreigner. He questioned young Olaf only to discover that it was his nephew! His sister's abducted child. So he took him back to Vladimir's court where young Olaf learned warrior-craft. When he was just a teen, he was clever enough to command a Russian warship. Thanks to Valdimir's wife Rogneda, Olaf converted to Christianity and in 986 she helped him escape from some jealous Russians. He took his loyal men back to Norway, became king, and that's how I got to be a Lutheran.

Being a warrior, the king often converted people to the new religion with a sword — that's how it was usually done. Norsemen saw no value in colorful religious books, wooden churches or weak priests who hid behind altars. They didn't need crosses. They had "The Mothers," often in carved groups of three, offering bowls of fruit and other wonderful things to eat. Their rune-words were carved on stone.

Our three-year-old granddaughter pretends to read by sitting down and opening up any book, including her parent's big *Joy of Cooking*, to read all the Dr. Seuss words she knows. She will continue to ponder those little black squiggles until one day they will form *cat* and *kitty* and *meow* and *Riley*, their cat's name. Josie's fertile brain will have figured out how to read in milliseconds all those oral words she's been stuffing into her ever-expanding cranial word-cupboard. One day her parents might suggest that she read some of the books her grandmother has written. Perhaps my words will make a difference in her life or someone else's, for however long — a few seconds, or as long as it takes to change the course of the stars. That's the power of words. By the time Josie is five, she will have heard thirty-two million more spoken words than kids her age whose parents hadn't read to them.

When we name some of our war missions "Infinite Justice," as we did in the latest war in Iraq, we then know we have to reassess whether our words are *just words*. Or not.

To Sing, Dance and Tell Stories

Oren Lyons told Bill Moyers, "Life will go on as long as there is someone to sing, to dance, to tell stories and to listen." Lyons is the Faith-Keeper of the Onondaga Nations who belongs to the Turtle Clan of the Seneca Nation, a part of the Iroquois Confederacy. The "People of the Longhouse" declared that all the people of "the nations" were one people. Oneida. Onondaga, Mohawk, Seneca, Cayuga — all together. It provided our founding fathers with the inspiration to create a new world where individual states could become one nation. The Iroquois Confederacy realized that justice is part of our cosmic order and they raised a tree to remember they were one powerful group.

It wasn't always that way, however, because long before Columbus set foot on American soil, the tribes warred against each other. A Peacemaker came and worked among the tribes. We don't know his name; people just called him Peacemaker. He had a vision of how things might be. But it took a Mohawk woman, Jikohnsaseh, to put his vision into practical action. She established the powerful Clan Mothers and the longhouse became a symbol of their cosmos, for it had a sky roof and an earth floor.

Often a valued guest of the Swedish government, Oren Lyons was visiting Stockholm and agreed to join a dialogue circle at a World Café gathering which Joel and I also attended. It was a fragile time: late September of 2001. We helped each other quiet our nerve-wracked hearts. Joel played a clavichord he'd built and Leila, the Sami Minister of Justice, sang for us in her resonant alto voice a reindeer song, and her daughter's birth song. Oren, I remember, was very interested in the wood Joel had used for his small keyboard instrument.

We sat in a Sophia-wisdom-circle in a room made of oiled wood and stone. Flickering candles in sixteen beautiful bowls formed an inner circle of global unity that evening. We were far from the chaos of New York City, where unholy dust still filtered down around the rubble. Before leaving Vermont, I had picked up a bright maple leaf and tucked it into my journal. My heart was heavy as I boarded the plane, but the little red-orange leaf deep in my briefcase seemed to say, "Don't worry. You'll be safe." Crossing the Atlantic that night, I wondered why I had bothered to take a leaf with me, and I hoped it didn't constitute an "agricultural product" that needed to be declared at customs.

But sitting in the circle, I now knew why. Oren had earlier said, "A clear mind uses clear words." So it was with a prayer for clarity that I placed my humble leaf-gift before him at the center of our circle. I remember saying something like, "I offer this maple leaf in thanksgiving for your people's wisdom and in remembrance of the blood — red like this leaf — that has been shed — and for the sweetness of peace." I also told him that I was saddened that his voice was not as clearly heard in America as it is in Sweden.

During the course of the evening, he explained how the Onondaga people practice dialogue. Because they have an oral culture, no one takes notes at their circle meetings. The women stand behind the men to remember and speak back what the men have said. The Clan Mothers are the record-keepers and it is they who tell the children what has been decided in the council circle. People sit in silence for exactly as long as they intend to speak before they say a word. Nothing is decided until the message has been clearly given and clearly received. The person who "hears" the other speak, must repeat what he's heard. Then the original speaker repeats what he has heard the listener has heard. Everyone must be in agreement or the meeting continues — as long as it takes.

Days, weeks if need be. The circle has directional and elemental meanings: earth, air, fire, water. The one who sits in the place of "fire" is called "The Firekeeper." If Osama Bin Laden were in their circle, Oren said, he would be invited to be the "firekeeper."

What did that mean? If a terrorist is honored the same way everyone else in the circle is honored, he'll better understand his role in the world and how "fire" can be a good thing, or a very destructive thing? Justice is not so much about determining *who's* right, but *what's* right. Rumi once said, "I seek justice from no one but from this justice-seeking self." Can people sitting in Sophia-Wisdom circles change the world?

How do we live on one little fragile planet and honor our differences? All too often, like those wild Norse relatives of mine, we choose to destroy the "other." My 9th century relatives thought they were being *just* to their people back home when they collected what they called a nose tax on people they conquered. If you didn't pay, they'd cut off your nose.

"The Other" often sneaks up in ships. Maya and Aztec calendars and almanacs predicted the arrival of Cortez. To the very day! So they weren't surprised when white men showed up. What surprised them, however, was the awful cruelty those men brought with them. The lovely jade green, yellow ochre, and subtle reds of the Maya's long painted agave bark books, which the Spaniards hurled into bonfires, curled into ash before their eyes. Their precious carvings, destroyed; their sacred macaws and parrots slaughtered. Some Portuguese slave hunters actually crafted lampshades from human skin.

Pizarro climbed up 13,000 feet to unjustly trick and kill thousands of Incans. He captured the king and then agreed to release him in exchange for a room full of gold and silver. It took months for the Incans to haul in all that precious metal. Once delivered, Pizarro sentenced his royal prisoner to death by burning. Pizarro's priest convinced the Incan king that if he became a Christian, he could escape death by fire. The king did, so he was "mercifully" garroted instead of burned. Nine furnaces worked three months to melt the ransom into bars. Pizzaro wasn't alone. In the first hundred years, from 1520 to 1620, *seventy million people* throughout the Americas were slaughtered one way or another. And of course death didn't stop with the thanksgiving feasting of 1620.

We may never find peace on this continent until there is justice for the children's children of those so piteously treated.

STONE BOATS

After the Stockholm conference, Joel and I took the car ferry to Gotland — God's Land. The island floats out there on the salty Baltic, marking the direct trade route from Finland and Sweden to Russia and Poland.

Rock carving of a bronze age ship, c. 1600 B.C.E., Ostfold, Norway

The next day, in Visby's cathedral, I was thinking, we're so far from anywhere here, surely I can forget about 9/11 for awhile. I soon learned everyone has CNN. I was so touched by the prayers the children of the parish had posted on a bulletin board. Joel translated: "Help everyone in the USA," which was accompanied by crayoned planes flying into tall buildings. "Dear God, please make sure it's not like this ever again." "God, make it so everyone in the US gets the help they need." Through my tears, I wrote a short thank you note and tacked it to the board. I left the cathedral thinking about all the other prayers sent up in this part of the world. *O Lord, deliver us from the Norsemen. O Lord, keep us from Nazi ovens. O Lord, protect us from Stalin's wrath.* I added one more: *O Lady, show us the way.*

Novgorod and Beyond

In 1029, back when Gotland was called Akergarn, another Norwegian king named Olaf, Olaf Haroldson, known to all of us Norwegian Lutherans as St. Olaf, beached his "ocean steed" on this very island enroute to Russia. He was a Christian so he stayed long enough to build the first wooden church on the island and baptize a few people, then he pushed on, a man conflicted

Prow from a wooden ship, c. 850 C.E. Oseberg, Norway

and perplexed by life. Snorri tells us he was a strong man with piercing blue eyes. When he was twelve, his mother convinced a rich friend of hers with a ship to take him on as one of the rowers. A good rower could do five hundred strokes an hour. He grew up fast. Norse ships didn't need harbors, given their shallow drafts, so they skiffed up and down rivers and wave-raced through the seas. Olaf spent the rest of his life surrounded by clanging swords and bloody battles. On one trip, he broke down the London Bridge, scooped up a lot of gold and chased the Danes out of England so his friend, King Ethelred, could rule again. As his men rowed away from Gotland, he dreamed of giving up the life of soldier-king and becoming a monk.

There are 350 stone "boat" graves on Gotland. In Old Norse "boat" is the same word as "cradle" and "coffin." Joel and I chose to eat our picnic lunch near where Tjelvar, the first man who landed on Gotland, was buried. Stones formed the outline of a huge ship — eighteen by five meters. Munching our apples, we wondered if any of our relatives might be buried around here.

Sophia was teasing me but I didn't realize it at the time. Nine years later I began to seriously investigate the DNA my sons and I, and Josie, carry around. I began by trying to acquaint myself with the strong women in our family, starting with my mother Ellen and her mother Julia (of the black and white monkey fame), and her mother Carrie (Karen) for whom I'm named. Then came Karen Mathiasdatter, Sidsel Andersdatter, Maren Nielsdatter and Anne Thorgersdatter and a host of others who moved down from Norway into Danish territory. From there it was a short hop to Elfleda of Bernica and before I could click on another little green leaf in ancestry.com, my DNA was spread out over all the early kings of England, Ireland, Scotland and Scandinavia. Hilda of the Vandals carried me to Goths, Ostergoths, Rome, Constantinople. Even the Iceni Queen Boudicea who managed to kill 70,000 Romans appears in my direct line once I got back that far. Exciting stuff. I spent hours climbing up into my family's Yggdrasil — the giant Ash tree that holds our world together, according to Scandinavian myth. One branch of my family goes all the way back to Fornjtotur, King of Kvenland (Finland), who was born about 160 C.E. Legend has it that he's the king in the Finnish Epic, *The Kalevala*, a collection of old poetry telling of Finland's origins beginning with creation and a broken egg. Similar to the Celts' cauldron of plenty, the Sampo, a magic mill, grinds everything into being and like Yggdrassil, holds it all together. *The Kalevala* inspires art and beauty portrayed by Sibelius, for example. It wasn't written down until the 1800s when Elias Lönnrot collected the oral folktales. *The Kalevala*, which documents a northern stream of consciousness, one which eventually grounded the Hansa League into a forceful world economy, is extremely rich. As in the Arthurian grail story, one section relates how it is only possible to help the seriously wounded if you can recall the sacred origins of the world and can recite its whole history — from memory. I take it to mean we can be healed only by remembering Sophia and how she created *everything*.

According to Phil Zuckerman, who wrote *Society Without God*, only 20% of Swedes believe in God (as taught by the Lutherans), yet they still practice secular traditions with religious trappings. Advent, for instance, is a sacred national candle-filled season. Even though most people don't attend church, many children still get baptized and confirmed. Sophia has engrained herself there and you can see it in their culture. They *truly* care for the earth. And for one another. For instance, Sweden made hitting or spanking children illegal since 1979. It has the lowest infant mortality rate in the world. Sweden and Denmark's gap between the rich and poor is the smallest of all industrialized nations. "Wealth" is a communal condition. I'm glad my son calls Sweden his second home.

Thousands of family twigs later, I learn that even Norway's "saintly" Olaf was one of "mine." Olaf really wanted to marry Ingegerd, the older daughter of Olaf Erickson III (most men seemed to be named either Olaf or Haaken), the Swedish king whom he had defeated in battle. No love lost there. Thanks to a later dice game, Ingegerd's father and "my" Olaf eventually became friends. Well, they tolerated each other because they had a common enemy: Canute the Danish king. Canute later killed "my" thirty-five year old Olaf, so he had reason to be on guard. Ingegerd's father told Olaf that he couldn't marry her because she was betrothed to Jaroslav, a smart young man destined to go places in Russia. But he could have his beautiful younger daughter, Astrid. So the Swede-Olaf became my Norwegian-Olaf's father in law.

Olaf and Astrid soon had a daughter, Ulfild. After many battles with Canute, Olaf decided to go visit Ingegerd and Jaroslav in Russia. (Are you thinking what I'm thinking?) He took Magnus with him, his "illegitimate" son whose mother was not Astrid, but rather Olaf's beautiful slave woman, Alfhild. The DNA gets a little murky at this point, but I don't really care. They're all my "peeps." Off they went, both realizing that Magnus would one day be king of Norway after Olaf was gone.

Jaroslav wasn't called "The Wise and Just" for nothing. After his father Vladimir died, he ruled Kiev as well as Novgorod (the new city) justly and well. In fact, he introduced the first codes of law into eastern Russia. The text of one of those Novgorod chronicles was rediscovered and published in 1767. Among many other things, it established feudal law, abolished blood crimes, clarified inheritances, and outlined financial retributions for various crimes. It was called *Russkaya Pravda*, "Russian Truth." Clearly, Sophia was speaking justice through Jaroslav, but I believe it was Ingegerd who heard Sophia's voice most clearly. And her mother Astrid-Ingegerd before her. And *her* mother Sophia of the Obotrites, before her. Yes, *Sophia!* Ingegerd's family came from the Obotrite tribe — Slavic people who clustered all around northern Germany and into Sweden. What later became Lubeck was once a major Obotrite center. The Obotrites hated the Germans and, by association, they took issue with Christianity. That is, until St. Cyril, with his brother Methodius, 9th century Thessaloniki Greeks, carried Sophia — along with many Christian icons — up to the Obotrites. When Cyril was a child, he had a vision of Sophia, a beautiful woman, he said. The royal family most likely welcomed Cyril and his new alphabet. It's also likely that Ingegerd and Jaroslav had a copy of the first Slavic Cyrillic Bible on one of their palace shelves. Birch bark letters and early Finnish writing turn up as people continue to sift through Novgorod's rich cultural layers.

It's no coincidence that the first two major churches in Russia bearing Sophia's name are in Novgorod and Kiev — Ingegerd's balliwick. When Olaf and his son Magnus (later called "King Magnus the Good" of Norway) rowed down the Valkhov River and finally reached Novgorod, they no doubt worshipped in Sophia's oak Cathedral of Holy Wisdom. It was an earlier version of St. Sophia's Cathedral which now has a large cross on the main dome with *a dove flying from it.*

I have been collecting prints of Novgorod icons for years, never sure why. (Sophia's smiling.) I'm guessing Olaf and Magnus saw some of the originals of my copies. Using exquisite line and color, these icons portray the triumph of justice and goodness over evil and many show the face of a woman who obviously loves her son. When icons became old or broken, they were buried in the earth with all the respect one would give a real person. (Now they fetch big money in antique stores.) My physician friend, Michael, who spent much of his later career in the Ukraine establishing family practice clinics, tells of the dark time when Stalin turned the cathedrals into swimming pools and hay barns. People hid all the icons away. After the wall fell and communism no longer dictated how and where they worshipped, people dug them up. Icons appeared again in all the churches within days.

Olaf seriously considered giving up his warrior lifestyle and staying in Novgorod to "follow God's righteous judgments," as Snorri Sturlson puts it. Then he had a vivid dream. A man, whom he thought was the old king Olaf Trygvason in shining clothing, stood by his bed. The misty king said, "Go back to your kingdom and rule over it with the strength God has given you."

Ingegerd recognized the change in Olaf after that dream, and encouraged him to help people in need. Once she sent a young boy who had a boil on his neck to Olaf who simply touched him and the boil disappeared. Soon stories of Olaf's miraculous healings followed him everywhere. After Christmas, in 1008, he took 200 of his men and they got back into their ships and rowed back across Lake Ilmen heading back to Norway. He left Magnus under Ingegerd's and Jaroslav's excellent care.

Novgorod was never conquered by the Mongols. Those fierce "others" rode their little horses within a hundred kilometers of the city and then mysteriously turned back. Historians explain it this way: they didn't want to get bogged down in the swamps surrounding the city. I suspect Sophia and her protective icons had something to do with it.

Olaf returned to Norway and ruled from 1015 to 1030 and built a castle in Nidaros-Trondheim. He's buried in the cathedral. It's a little unclear whether it was his devotion to Christ, his love of gold or his itching battle-scars that motivated him to win over all the other upland kings of Norway, but he did — and then he went on to Christianize Iceland, the Orkneys, Greenland and the Faroe Islands.

Ingegerd raised her family and foster sons, including Magnus, all future rulers of Europe. Then she took monastic vows in Kiev, adopting the name "St. Anna." She's buried there, in St. Sophia's church in Kiev, if you ever care to visit.

Russia got its name from Rus, a province in Sweden. Jaroslav's great-great-grandfather, Prince Rurik, was invited by the Slavic people around 860 C.E. to come to Russia and carry out all legal and law-enforcement functions. He founded a dynasty whose descendents would rule the Russian lands for over seven and a half centuries.

SOPHIA'S MYSTICAL DANCERS:
MOTHER RUSSIA'S SOPHIOLOGISTS: VLADIMIR SOLOVYEV (1853-1900); PAVEL FLORENSKY (1882-1937); SERGIE BULGAKOV (1871-1944); AND VALENTIN TOMBERG (1900-1973)

For centuries Sophia seeped into Mother Russia's black soil like welcome rain. But it wasn't until the end of the 19th century that philosopher Vladimir Soloviev began to seriously write about his Sophia-experiences and inspired others to do the same. When he was nine, he was worshipping at a Russian Orthodox Pentecost service when Sophia appeared as a lady of "unearthly beauty." He saw her again when he was twenty. This time, he was in London in the Reading Room of the British Museum, reading all the books he could find on Sophia: the Old Testament, the Gnostics, Jacob Boehme, Gichtel, Swedenborg, Oeinger, Schelling. Sophia told him to close up the books and go to Egypt. He left for Cairo immediately. One night as he was attending an evening affair, she appeared and said, "Go out into the desert." So he did, still dressed in his evening black coat and tie. Some Bedouin nearly captured him, but dressed as he was, they thought he was the devil and let him go. While in the desert, he experienced a blissful, radiant vision of his "eternal friend" that never left him. "Today my Queen appeared to me in azure," he said. He was passionate about her!

Solovyov claimed Sophia had three parts: a higher part — the divine part; a lower earthly part; and a middle part that creates all of space, time and causality. He wrote: *"If the Soul of the World were to stop unifying everything through Herself, all created beings would lose their common relationship, the union of the cosmos would fall apart into a multiplicity of individual elements, and the organism of the world would transform itself into a mechanical mass of atoms."* Solovyov, like many mystics before him, was a synthesizer. He sought to combine Hebrew traditions, the Christ-dimension of God and the marriage of God and humanity, together with the physical, archetypal and spiritual worlds.

His Sophia-poetry inspired Pavel Florenski, a Russian Orthodox priest and mathematician who saw no contradiction between science and religion. Florenski once consulted with the Communists about the electrification of the Soviet Union. They respected and protected him — that is, until he became friends with someone Stalin executed: Nikolai Bucharin, who had worked with Lenin as an economist, but later opposed Stalin's industrial plans. Further-more, Stalin hated priests. So, he sent Florenski to a concentra-tion camp on the Solovetskiye Islands, and after December 1937, Florenski was never heard from again.

Florenski had mystical experiences that convinced him of Sophia's involvement with nature. And he tried very hard to get her back into her rightful place as the "bride" within the Christian trinity. She's the plan of creation, he wrote. He devoted one chapter to Sophia in *The Pillars and Foundations of Truth*, in which he synthe-sized Russian culture and spiritual thought. People said Florenski was a genius. They called him Russia's Leonardo da Vinci.

Florenski saw Sophia as the "Grand Root" of everything cre-ated. "She is one with God and many in creation." He identified her with Mary, but with a mysterious grandeur all her own. He identified three types of Sophia icons: the Novgorod icon shows her as an angel-figure with wings seated under Christ with angels above; in other icons she is portrayed as the Church or Body of Christ similar to how she appears in some of Hildegard's vision-ary art — she sits up above and all the people gather around and below; and a third icon type shows her as the Mother of God as she is shown in the famous Kiev icon of Mary cradling her son.

Another major Russian Sophiologist, Sergei Bulgakov, studied economics and symbology which he felt was a truer path to God than theology. He was Florenski's friend. Bulgakov was a theolo-gian and religion philosopher who was expelled from Russia and subsequently taught in Paris. While traveling the steppes of Rus-sia, he had a profound awakening which convinced him that na-ture is truly alive. He said, "The strong scent of grass was gilded by the rays of a glorious sunset. Far in the distance, I saw the blue outlines of the Caucasus.... I drank in the light and air of the steppes ... my soul was stirred.... The first day of creation shown before my eyes. Everything was clear, everything was at peace and full of ringing joy.…. There is no life and no death, only one eternal and unmovable now."

Around the time of WWI he spent a lot of time thinking about the tension between God and the world. He was committed to social welfare, and Sophia's wisdom became his path to penetrate the world's hidden meanings — to affirm creation's goodness and Sophia's connections to nature as the beginning of everything. It is Sophia, he decided, that gives everything, including the economic process, meaning. It is she who raises the world from chaos to cosmos. From his *Filosofia Khoziaistva*: "She shines in the world as primordial purity … in the loveliness of a child and in the gorgeous enchantment of a swaying flower, in the beauty of the starry sky and a flaming sunrise."

Valentin Tomberg, the most recent Russian Sophia-mystic was born in 1900 and took Florenski's thinking a bit further. Robert Powell, in *The Sophia Teachings*, points out that it was Tomberg who influenced Rudolph Steiner's thinking regarding how Sophia was incarnated into Mary at Pentecost. He proposes a Divine Feminine trinity in which the Divine Mother is found in the center of the earth: the Divine Daughter, or wisdom of the cosmos, embraces the Sun and the Moon and all the stars. Between them is what Tomberg calls the Holy Soul — creator of community and our ongoing evolution. Echoing the more familiar "Our Father" prayer, Tomberg introduced this "Our Mother" prayer during World War II:

> Our Mother, thou who art in the darkness of the underworld,
> May the holiness of thy name shine anew in our remembering.
> May the breath of thy awakening kingdom warm the hearts
>   of all who wander homeless.
> May the resurrection of thy will renew eternal faith even
>   unto the depths of physical substance.
> Receive this day the living memory of thee from human hearts,
> Who implore thee to forgive the sin of forgetting thee.

And who are ready to fight against temptation which has led
thee to existence in darkness,
That through the deed of the Son the immeasurable pain of
the Father be stilled,
By the liberation of all beings from the tragedy of thy with-
drawal.
For thine is the homeland and the boundless wisdom, and
the all-merciful grace,
For all and everything in the Circle of All.
Amen.

ONCE UPON A TIME:
The Little Prince

Once upon a time I flew my plane to the Sahara Desert. When I
landed — sort of by accident — I heard an odd little voice say,
"If you please, draw me a sheep!" Luckily I'm also an artist, so I
did. "And a box to keep him in."

The little person who requested the sheep and box asked a great
many questions. He was dressed in a long coat with stars on his
shoulders and had a sword in his hand, obviously a little prince
who had come from another planet, or maybe an asteroid about
the size of a house. Baobab trees grow there in great numbers he
told me. They'd take over if he didn't pull them up regularly. He
loves looking at sunsets. "I see them on my home planet up to
forty-four times a day."

He was worried about his sheep eating his one and only very
precious flower. "If the sheep eats it, the stars will be darkened."

So I told him, "Don't worry. I'll draw a muzzle for your sheep."

Before the Little Prince got to this desert, he'd met a yellow African snake who spoke in riddles. Next, he climbed a mountain and visited a rose garden. One day he met a fox. "Nobody up until then would be my friend," he told me. The Little Prince had explained to the fox that he was looking for people and the fox said, "Why? They have guns. But they also have chickens. Are you looking for chickens?" The fox said he couldn't play with the Little Prince because he, the fox, wasn't tamed: "Tamed, an act too often neglected. It means to establish ties." The fox explained that it's a very long process. "You must wait very patiently and say nothing because words are a source of misunderstanding. You should come at the same time every day — one must observe the proper rites. One only understands the things that one tames," the fox told him.

The Little Prince went back to visit the roses and told them that they were like his fox before he tamed him. Beautiful but empty. He told them about his one rose back home and how he loved and cared for it.

When he said goodbye to the fox, the fox told him a very simple secret: "It is only with the heart that one can see rightly; what is essential is invisible to the eye."

By this time, I was getting very thirsty and suggested to the Little Prince that we try to find some water. "What makes the desert beautiful," said the Little Prince, "is that somewhere it hides a well." He went on to explain that the beauty of everything — the desert, the stars — is something that is invisible. He found a well and soon it was time for the Little Prince to go home and because my plane was fixed, so did I.

But before we parted, he said, "I shall be living in one of those stars." I looked up. "And you will always be my friend," he said. "How will you get home?" I asked. The little prince laughed and explained that he couldn't take his body back with him; it was too heavy. Just then a flash of yellow told me that the snake had come back. The little prince fell into the sand without a sound. And disappeared. Ever after when I look at the stars and think of the little prince, I laugh.

Antoine de Saint-Exupéry wrote fairy tales for his daughter and illustrated them in the most wonderful ways. He once told Anne Morrow Lindbergh, "The writer, like the bee, gathers honey from whatever circumstances he happens to be in."

Sophia offers us opportunities and ideas at every turn. Just as the desert is beautiful because it has hidden wells, so does she. She patiently waits for us to be thirsty enough to notice her. The fox embodies her — all patience and wisdom. The fox reminds us that we tame each other by establishing ties. The story reminds us that we are, indeed, responsible for each other. Relationship is the key to everything! Sophia speaks through the Little Prince in explaining how everything is tied to everything else. And death is something to laugh at. Nothing, including death, holds power over us. We just laugh on our way to rejoin the stars.

SOPHIA IN THE SHACK

Anyone who has read William Paul Young's book, *The Shack*, the 2007 publishing phenomenon that has now sold well over three million copies, is introduced to a God who is a Black woman/mother/father called Papa, Jesus, the carpenter, and Sarayu, a free spirit who created everything. She loves fractals so she put them everywhere. She tells Mackenzie, the hero of the story who has tragically lost his daughter, that he has to give up his idea of good and evil and learn to trust in her inherent goodness. I, as you know by now, would consider this the Sophia personality. However, Young chooses to make Sophia yet another character, but part of the other three. Yet, instead of a quadrinity, God is still a trinity. A mystery.

The author paints this picture of Sophia: an extraordinarily beautiful, tall, olive-skinned woman with chiseled Hispanic features. She is the personification of Papa's wisdom and part of the mystery surrounding Sarayu. This radiant Sophia appears to Mack in a cave as a judge who tells him he must be his own judge. She showed him his dead daughter, now filled with joy.

I believe so many people pick up this book because they yearn to find healing for some atrocious life story of their own, as the author himself experienced. For many, it's the first time they have thought of God as being female — well, actually three women and a man, but all of them are "together." My friend Joe gave me a copy and wrote inside: "I hope it will be a source of inspiration and strength." It has been. We all long to be forgiven and loved, and we like to read about how it might happen. We all seek justice. Mackenzie learns that Sophia continuously repairs the past and forges forgiveness. It happens inside our "heart shacks."

Young describes Sophia as sitting straight and regal. She is breathtakingly stunning. "She *is* beauty," Mack thought. "Everything that sensuality strives to be but falls painfully short." Echoing Sergei Bulgakov, he describes her eyes like "portals into the vastness of the starry night sky reflecting some unknown light source within her."

ENNEAGRAM NUMBER 7

"Sevens" like to plan and perform. They can be rather idealistic and may tend to live more in the future than in the now, but their positive attitude enables them to create beautiful things. Number Sevens can be impatient but they are usually very joyful and can find giftedness in everything. They are kind, celebrate life and see the whole world as beautiful. They love to play and are filled with hope.

HER GIFT OF KINDNESS

When I think about the Norwegian kin I knew firsthand, the word "kindness" sums them up. They treated others with the respect they expected. Scandinavians didn't effuse praise, but when they wanted to say something positive about someone, a phrase they often used was, "So and so has a kindly nature."

"Umilinya Mother of God," c. 1500 Tempera on Wood, 19 cm x 23 cm

Nothing, however, represents kindness like the iconic face of Mary with her child. As a young woman she accepted her mothering role. Kindness does not chafe. Kindness radiates an aura of contentment toward the world — everything and everyone in it.

Five hundred years before Mary rocked her baby in Nazareth, Chinese philosophers were calling themselves the *Ju* — the kindly, the yielding. Although the Chinese may not have seen the connection, I find "Ju" very close to the Latin "Jus" — laws. Kindness demands fairness. Lao Tse and others sought to balance the more aggressive male powers with a strong blending of yin and yang, male and female. Confucius taught kindness and repaying evil with justice.

JUSTICE: HER CLARION CALL

I wonder what Confucius meant when he said, "Repay evil with justice?" Fair trials? Adequate legal representation? Uncorrupt judges?

Tarot decks always have a "Justice" card. It's a crowned woman sitting on a throne with scales in one hand and a raised sword in the other to guard against injustice. We have a "Department of Justice" and a blindfolded "Lady Justice" stands holding her scale. In Egypt, they called her Ma'at, brandishing her scales and a feather. She weighs our souls after death to determine whether or not we were just — her name, after all, means *justice, truth, order*. She sets out our tasks for us during life and is there, not to judge, but to welcome us after our final breath. A feather on the breath of God. Gentle as a rose; calm as the flicker of a candle.

Trying to get a better handle on what *justice* really means, I turned to the classic book Bellah and his friends wrote back in 1985: *Habits of the Heart*. They talk about three kinds of justice. "We need to reach common understandings about distributive justice — an appropriate sharing of economic resources — which must in turn be based on conceptions of a substantively just society. Unfortunately, our available moral traditions do not give us nearly as many resources for thinking about distributive justice as about procedural justice, and even fewer for thinking about substantive justice."

Substantive justice. Surely that's what Hildegard of Bingen was talking about nine hundred years ago. If she were here today, she'd probably say, "Look, you guys! You still haven't gotten it!" Just as the old prophet Amos preached, "Let justice roll over you," Hildegard challenged people to wake up and see how justice and harmony permeate our universe. In the face of injustice, she said, creation is not silent. It is our responsibility, as living sparks of God, to protect and renew the earth and treat each other and all beings fairly. Then "with justice for all" will no longer be a hollow phrase.

Caring for a rose, giving someone a drink of water — small actions *do* make a difference. One by one. It's always how things are accomplished. Perhaps even saving the planet!

The Crow-Crone in me sees so many things out of whack and unjust right now that it's hard to know what to focus on next. It would be ever so much easier to just lean back, eat a piece of that mountain-high meringue lemon pie John loves to bake, shut my eyes and deny bad stuff is happening.

But we're mired in a war some have labeled "The War of Flying Body Parts." Or perhaps a better description is "The War of Flying Spiritual Parts." Every war damages souls along with bodies. But because of the deceptive way this one got started, our sickness seeps ever so much deeper, until a spiritual gangrene takes over. Maybe we're suffering from PTSSD: post-traumatic soul-stress disorder. Our young men and women who return from war and seek healing can rarely find it, mainly because so few remember how to point the way. Families who once may have provided some respite, have often splintered. Churches that once offered hope, are too often empty. Or, have become so large seekers get lost. Communities that once held and supported people have mostly drifted off to wander cement box stores and fast food joints on the impersonal fringes of our towns. Those of us who watch the bombings and the atrocities, see not only children being blown apart, but men and women debased, raped, tortured and slaughtered. And if we look closely, we see our own ruptured souls splattered across the screen. Can you hear Sophia's tears splashing?

It's as if we have erased the words *Goodness* and *Hope* from the chalky blackboards of our hearts. When I look around, I see *materialism*, scrawled with a capital M. Buy this. Throw away that. You "need" more and more and more. As a result we demand more oil; therefore, we need more wars. We think we may run out of food and water. And if we think wars over oil are bad, imagine what wars over water are going to be like. We are immersed in rampant divisiveness. We seem to have forgotten how to cooperate, and instead, we flounder in swamps of stinginess and gullies of greed.

Sophia reminds us of *other ways* to be. But she doesn't pull any punches. She may be playful, but she also offers an overflowing platter of odd-meats we've come to call our *Inconvenient Truths*. Earth needs to throw off some poisons. And those poisons go deeper than just mercury in our water and carbon in our air. They extend to hate-radio and titillating trash-talk, to bullying and backbiting — to anything that demeans, divides and distresses.

It's not convenient to contemplate how to reverse, or at least stabilize, climate change. It's not convenient to figure out ways to clean up our airwaves or to vacuum out our hearts. It's hard for us to acknowledge, for instance, how many websites carry child pornography. And that nearly all of them originate in the United States. How did we get this way? We don't like to admit we're wrong and we dislike any kind of change. Some people call for a "return to" certain values; they cling to past ideas frozen in what may seem like an ice sculptured "better time." But clinging only breeds more fear and fundamentalism of all stripes. If we're alive, we won't clutch; we'll welcome change. As long as we live, our thoughts, our moods, our actions can make a difference — for good or ill. By our very presence, we influence the cosmos.

My friend, Otto Scharmer, who wrote *Theory U*, returned not long ago from Brazil and wrote in a blog: "Brazil has been much better and faster in coming out of the global economic crisis of the past two years. Why did Brazil manage so much better? Instead of giving the billions to bankers, they gave it to the poor, to the most marginalized. They invested it in education for all. They invested in better infrastructures for entrepreneurs and small business. And they regulated the banking sector." He said he was very impressed to see how much they had accomplished in only about ten years. "They've reduced the social divide, and are eradicating hunger and responding to HIV/AIDS in a manner that is a role model for all countries."

So many injustices ... but the good news is, there are so many of us to attend to them. *All* things are redeemable; we're all on a changing, Sophia-spiraling path, and it's very symbiotic. Paul Hawken calls it a movement without a name. *Blessed Unrest*. His research shows there are possibly two million organizations now working toward ecological sustainability and social justice. It's what the poet Gary Snyder calls the great underground. It's the river beneath the river.

A large appendix appears at the end of Hawken's book with definitions and vocabulary too lengthy to repeat here, but it's worth absorbing on your own time. You will find thoughts on Human Rights and Social Justice, Climate Justice, Disability Equality, Distributive and Economic Justice, Environmental Justice, Ethnic Equality, Gay Rights and Equality, Human Rights and Civil Liberties, Human Rights Education, Human Trafficking and Slavery, Social Justice Education and much, much more. Let Justice Roll!

I am reminded of what St. Basil the Great who lived in the 4th century wrote:

> The bread which you do not use
> is the bread of the hungry.
> The garment hanging in your wardrobe
> is the garment of one who is naked.
> The shoes that you do not wear
> are the shoes of one who is barefoot.
> The money you keep locked away
> is the money of the poor.
> The acts of charity you do not perform
> are so many injustices you commit.

Hawken ends his insightful book with a two-bus analogy. We're beginning to see how important the environmental bus is and people already on that bus think the social justice people need to get on board. Our house is literally burning but "the only way we are going to put out the fire is to get on the social justice bus and heal our wounds, because in the end, there is only one bus."

The Hagia Sophia in Istanbul, Turkey

SOPHIA'S SPECIAL GEO-SPOT:
HAGIA SOPHIA, ISTANBUL, TURKEY

It's called Hagia (Haya/Holy) Sophia — Ayasofya — Holy Wisdom. Meryemana. She proudly stands in Istanbul's Sultan Ahmet Square declaring Motherpeace. Her house has only half of the windows it had before the original 180 foot dome collapsed in 558 C.E. and even if one wag compared it to a rundown Victorian Railroad station, it's still a magical spot. Forty chandeliers once hung suspended from the "heavenly" ceiling. When Justinian saw it for the first time, he said, displaying a bit of temple-envy, "Glory be to God! O, Solomon, I have vanquished you."

Sophia lingers there in the corners and on the revived, but flaking mosaics. But, as in life, you have to really look for her. Check the relief on the Imperial Door, for example, that opens to the nave. If you look carefully, you'll see her there in the form of a dove poised over the Gospel of St. John.

Hagia Sophia church has had three incarnations. From 350 C.E. to 1453 C.E., she was a Christian cathedral, built in only six

A 9th century mosaic on the high wall of the apse in Hagia Sophia depicting Mary holding young Jesus

years by 10,000 workers. In 1453, Sultan Mehmet II took down her bells and added four minarets; it remained a mosque until 1935. The marble "gate to heaven" or *mihrap* — prayer niche — still points the way to Mecca. Because Mecca is southeast of the Hagia Sophia, it stands rather obliquely, sort of tilted, off to one side. Then, thanks to Atatürk, it was opened as a museum with many of its famous plastered-over mosaics again displayed for all to see.

When you enter, you're immediately drawn to the famous Madonna and Child fresco high up on the wall at the gate of the vestibule. Sitting on jeweled pillows, Mary seems to say, "Welcome to my house." Her beautiful kohled eyes mirror those of her son who sits so straight in her lap — her cathedra. He extends one sandaled foot. Off to Mary's left, the archangel Michael holds a scepter and a globe. Gabriel once guarded her right, but invasions and earthquakes have long since erased him. Tesserae once formed exquisite mosaics all over the walls and the ceiling — 150 million gold cubes, according to the guidebook. Most have been plundered.

You may wish to pause near one of the mammoth marble urns once dug up in a Pergamum peasant's field. It was most likely a wine vat which the Moslems later turned into a purification jar for water. Wine to water — a Cana wedding story in reverse. If you listen closely, you might overhear my guided tour: "This marble column goes way back to Justinian the Great who had a headache one day and leaned against it only to discover his headache was gone. This column will not only heal you, but also make your wish come true. But only if you place your thumb in the hole worn there over the ages, like this. You must turn your hand completely around without it leaving the hole." The group moved on. I wandered over to try it. "I want to write about this" was my wish.

A large worn circle of marble on the floor forms the "omphalmos" — the center where emperors were once crowned. I tried to imagine what it must have been like to worship here when thousands of candles illuminated fresh sparkling mosaics. Nathan, our younger son, whispered, "The air in here feels like water." It's one of many places where you can actually breathe her blue cosmic ether.

FROM SOPHIA'S NOTEBOOK

One day your breathing will carry you far beyond these inferior breezes and exhale you into a place of your own making. You'll create it and it will be. See it and it will be so. Call it forth and it will rise, shimmering, and you will laugh at the ease of it all. You will know your origin and your ending and you will dance dressed only in your own amazement.

I will wrap you in webbing so fine you will think for a moment it is spider-weaves, not tapestry for eternity. I will stitch you to me with needles of gold and threads of silkened light. You will be held fast by the sheer desire to be knotted and bound and blessed.

chapter eight

SHE SINGS US INTO SERVICE

Crop Circle: West Kennett, Avebury, July 30, 2004

· ·

"There is a candle in your heart, ready to be kindled. There is a voice in your soul, ready to be filled. You feel it, don't you?"

~ Rumi

MOUNTAIN JOURNAL ENTRY

Over night, Frost created giant etch-a-sketches on every window. Branches boast manicures of ice. Beautiful as they are, those vulnerable bending branches will crack and one day I'll drag them to a new burial ground as I clear more paths this spring — woodland-maps for me and the deer.

The Swedish word for candle is "living light." I blow mine out and relax into the drumming of my heart, thinking about what "the world soul" means. Behind closed lids I see glaciers groaning and calving at super speeds and melting ice poised to raise ocean levels, and I think, "What have we done to you, Mother?" I see raging fires and unprecedented floods and ask, "What are our options, now?" We can't call back the "dogs" or leash the dragons. If the temperature of our water rises even one more degree, we're in trouble. The past no longer holds possibility — only the now. Trees grow in rings around the memory of rain. We grow tomorrows around the moist circles of now. Snows run off her mountains; I hear her voice on the wind.

The Mikmaq people don't even have a word for "nature." Everything is *mintu* — harmony. Their ecosystem is held basket-tight in a seven-layered living lodge reaching under the earth and up to the highest heavens. Let's adopt their language, if only so we can speak hope.

HEARTBEAT QUESTIONS

If we were alchemists, capable of concocting a different planet, what would it look like?
How might we invest in a harmonious future?
Do our hearts sing in service to others?
What needs to be healed?
Who will be served by my actions?

MINDING OUR MOTHER

From space, Edgar Mitchell reported that earth looks like a sparkling blue and white jewel in a thick sea of black mystery. We've all seen the photos. Early Greeks viewed earth as a leather ball stitched in twelve equal sections — a dodecahedron swinging from a web of light. We're six and a half billion people — fast approaching seven billion — dancing on her surface. She'll have to tighten her equatorial belt a few notches.

The world, according to most creation legends, was formed by song or words flowing out of silence. Modern physics now confirms this; our worlds, they say, were born out of vibrations and fluctuations. When the Haida people speak, their language still emulates creation. Pacific coastal voices carry words built from the sounds of waves and birds.

Terry Tempest Williams, who wrote *Finding Beauty in a Broken World*, wrote of this kinship: "Our kinship with Earth must be maintained; otherwise we will find ourselves trapped in the center of our own paved-over souls with no way out." Her book documents, among other things, her love of mosaics and it describes how she helped create a beautiful glass-chip memorial to the people killed in Rwanda. T.S. Eliot's lines from "The Wasteland" inspired her title: *"The cosmos works by harmony of tensions, like the lyre and the bow; And so it was I entered the broken world, turning shadow into transient beauty...."*

After the genocide in 1994, 70% of the Rwandan population were women with children to support. Some of the women are now busy transforming their lives through art and trading. Their baskets turn shadow into transient beauty. The works of art are as lovely to behold, like their own proud artisan faces. You'll find many of these strong women and their traditional handicrafts at *www.trading4treasures.com.*

Hildegard cautioned us against injuring the earth. "All of creation God gives to humankind to use. But if this privilege is misused," she warned, "God's justice permits creation to punish humanity." We lived here for 30,000 years without upsetting our planet's balance, and then, 200 years ago, we began burning coal, gas and oil, and by 2007, our planet started to exhibit signs of carbon overdose. By 2008 there was little doubt. There are so many of us now, that our precious plants and animals disappear before our very eyes. We eat about seven trillion pounds of food a year. "As species vanish," Thom Hartmann says in *Threshold,* "the web of life becomes less rich.... It's like losing organs from your body. The salmon goes, a kidney is gone. Whales vanish, a lung is gone." Ninety percent of the big fish we had, when I was a kid, no longer swim the oceans. Shamefully, our largest crop now is turf grass for lawns and golf courses. Frank Lloyd Wright dreamed of Americans all living on acre plots with gardens for cooperative farming. I like to think his dream could still come true.

Like giant bear claws, cold, deep Finger Lakes scratch down across the map of central New York. Numerous historical plaques detail the lives of residents and visitors in these green valleys as they lived here over the past four or five hundred years. The first people moved their longhouse villages every twenty years to allow re-growth. Aided by the birds, Sky Woman fell to earth and landed on the back of a turtle. Then five nations, people of the Seneca, Cayuga, Onondaga, Oneida and Mohawk nations, joined to become one. They were loyal to the Great Law of Peace and called themselves the *Haudenosaunee* — the Iroquois People of the Longhouse. Women not only made the final decisions on important tribal matters — including who the tribal chiefs would be — they also controlled their birthrates with herbs, usually having a child every seven years. They were appalled at how the pioneer white women were constantly pregnant. As a result, there was never a shortage of food or healing herbs. Now twenty-six million people in America alone are "food insecure." That means they go to bed every night hungry.

To restore our honor, we need to remember. To pay attention. To honor. We can honor our food by figuring out where it comes from and how much it *really* costs. We can determine if it grew naturally or was raised in a factory. If it grew nearby or had to be flown to us. We can read labels and assess what chemicals we are ingesting. We can become good cooks. To honor plants, we can water and weed them. To honor animals we can talk to them and share their hurts and protect their lives. To honor people, we can smile at them, hug them, show them we value what each of them brings to today's "longhouses."

There are no longer any quick fixes. We may very soon have caused so much destruction, there'll be no *fixing* at all. But therein lies a tiny kernel of hope. Andrew Harvey reminds us that we are not asked to "fix" our existing system "but to radically transform it so we no longer, by our choices, threaten our lives and the lives of millions of species. And we can only do this by radically transforming ourselves." His book, *The Hope: A Guide to Sacred Activism*, also states, "The greatest darkness constellates the most powerful answering light; the greatest threat constellates the most impassioned energy of creativity." Refreshing words.

Harvey's one of our living lights. So is Bill McKibben who calls for changing politicians, not just light bulbs. We can also light candles and repeat the Eastern Orthodox prayer: "Mother, save me, protect me, heal me, illumine me, light up with your Eternal Light the dangers around me and in me, and give me the wisdom and faith I need."

She will. But we need to stop being eggplants. Sister Carol Coston says eggplants are heavy feeders and draw nutrients from the soil. "We'd go far toward sustaining a healthy web of life and creating alternative economic systems if, instead of being global eggplants, we acted more like earthworms ... conscious of giving back to the earth as much or more than we took from it."

A fawn can stand within ten minutes of birth. What's even more amazing, it gives off no scent at all until it's about four days old and can run from predators. Sophia provides. She will continue to provide.

Ravens not only have language, but regional dialects as well. Some live to be well over fifty years old. They see a lot from their air-borne vantage. They watch us devastate the land and denude our trees. They see the earth slip. They wonder why we rip minerals, pump oil, blow toxins. They notice water rising and rushing where there wasn't water before.

Sophia's earthy raven-dark wisdom leads us deep now, deep enough to see her roots, to sense the layers of rock and lava all the way down to her crystalline core. The time has come to balance her "moon wisdom" with our "sun-knowing." Daniel Goleman's book, *Ecological Intelligence*, underscores what most of us already know, but are still living — what Henrik Ibsen called "the vital lie." That's the story we tell ourselves because the truth is too painful. Climate change is bad and there are no band-aids. Government can't and won't fix it. Everything is all too linked for any easy "solutions." This is how Goleman ends his book: "We don't have to fix our planet, but rather our relationship to it ... the earth doesn't need healing. We do."

Over the years, to heal ourselves, we've used dried weasel hearts, crocodile blood, leeches, turtle fat, scalpels, herbal teas, meditation, prayer, dance, psychotherapy, antibiotics, scalpels, drugs. You name it, we've tried it. Well, maybe we haven't tried all of it yet. One Swiss pharmacology professor estimates Africa alone has 200,000 plants no one has yet examined for their medicinal properties. But we'd better hurry, since we're destroying our forests that hold these natural remedies — at an alarming rate. The Hebrew word, *tikkun*, means to heal, to mend what has been broken. Illness and wellness are just two concepts on the opposite ends of the high wire we humans walk. Health isn't static any more than illness is. Healing can happen even if the patient isn't "cured." Health is an attitude toward the entire "lifeline" we share — even our attitude toward death.

Sophia is god-in-action through our hands, our feet, our voices. But sometimes it takes a bit of encouragement from someone else to prompt us into action. That was true, even for Jesus. Jesus and his mother were invited to a big wedding party in Cana. She spotted a need. "Son, they're running out of wine!" It was she who encouraged him to turn those 120 gallons of water into wine — not the cheap box variety, either, but extraordinarily fine wine. It's Sophia who encourages us to do crazy and impossible things. She makes us dizzy with her fruity wisdom.

"Taliban" means "students of Islam" and, in 1996, they carried their Korans and Kalashnikovs through the Khyber Pass into Afghanistan. As a result, girls and women could no longer attend school. How unfortunate, because when girls learn to read, they teach their mothers, and soon whole families and communities are strengthened.

ENNEAGRAM NUMBER 8

Eights have lots of energy and can be very generous and protective. They like directness and often strongly believe people need to take care of themselves — take responsibility. Integrity is one of their core values. Eights like to be appreciated and to be fully informed. They make effective managers and serve in very large ways, but can lean toward the command and control model if they're not careful. They sometimes view life as a battle and can forget to live in the here and now. They also tend to hide their emotions.

WHOM DOES THIS SERVE?

Ancient grail-quests propelled armored knights around Europe looking for an honorable way to live. Through the tenth and eleventh centuries, stories followed their hoofprints. Some secret *something* was connected back to Christ, or maybe even all the way back to Solomon. What is this grail? People retold Wolfram von Eschenbach's story and Chrétien de Troyes' version. They debated whether the grail was a cup Jesus offered his disciples during their last supper. Or the spear that put him out of his misery on the cross. Or a plate, or a dish that Joseph of Arimathea brought to England on his tin trade route after he put his crucified friend in the grave. Or maybe the grail was a magic stone, or a book ... one that Jesus may have written himself.

One grail-book story involves a French monk in 717 C.E. who was given a tiny book, no larger than his hand. It began with Christ's crucifixion and the first line read: "Here Commences the Reading Concerning the Holy Grail." The book was stolen. He searched and searched, paying special attention to crossroads where the legendary Hermes' gifts often appear. *Graal* in Old Norse means the food people put out on a stone near a crossroad for wanderers. Likewise, grail stories feed our souls.

Who has "the graal book" now? Who is being fed? Some say the troubadours kept it safe. Other claimed that task fell to Percival or other Knights of the Round Table, or the Cathars, the Templar Knights, or the Masons. Or descendents of Mary Magdalene. We continue to search for Da Vinci codes and grail stories keep popping up. All the grail stories have this in common: no one comes to the grail alone, and it can be discovered only by those who are pure, simple and good.

"Whom does this serve?" is a principle grail question, and one that has niggled at me for years. Whenever I ask it, the answer comes: *Your brother or your sister who is in need — the one right in front of you.* But I've had some less than desirable experiences following that dictum. I learn later that people might not need or value what I'm offering them, and may actually be put off by my gift. So I now realize I must carefully determine what it is *they truly need* ... not *what* I *think they need.* Sometimes it may be that all I need to do is just listen. Or offer a hug or a smile. Or a genuine conversation. Sometimes it is money, but not always. Buddha encouraged us to follow this simple triple truth: "A generous heart, kind speech, and a life of service and compassion are the things that renew humanity."

My family physician recently attended a conference on "Spirituality in Medicine." She wrote me this email:

"People cannot believe I spent five days last week learning about medicine and spirituality ... like, what's there to talk about??

"I had two very ironic episodes on the trip home. One was not pleasant, but was a reminder of where I am. Then, the antidote. I met the "Buddha" in the parking lot at the Manchester airport. The shuttle driver asked me where I had been, and feeling edgy and complete and like taking a risk, I told him I was a doctor who had just been studying spirituality and how to bring it more to my work. 'Ahh,' he said, 'so often we fall in love with technology and forget about the soul.' Surprised out of my mind at his response and his affect, I said, 'Ummmm, yes, and (sigh) now that I have fed at the trough, I need to get back to work.'

'No,' said he, 'now that you have fed at the trough, you need to return ... to serve.'

"I guess I need to hang out in more parking lots."

I guess we all do.

Frances Perkins was born in Maine in 1880 and spent her early career working in jobs aimed at protecting poor young women. Like Jonna, my doctor, she was another Sophia-woman who managed to graciously and expertly balance marriage, family and profession. The New York City Shirtwaist Triangle Fire of 1913 killed 146 women and young girls who were locked into overcrowded upstairs rooms with dusty fabric, leaking oil from sewing machines, and men smoking nearby. That propelled Frances Perkins into fights for safer standards and factory inspections. She learned to "play the old boys' game" and when Franklin Roosevelt asked her, she became our first female Secretary of Labor. It was Frances who negotiated with labor unions and maneuvered through the murky waters of political party machines. It was Frances who masterminded Social Security, the Fair Labor Standards Act, mandatory fire protection for workers, public works, unemployment insurance, and Workers' Compensation. Like the taxi driver, Frances knew "you are fed and then you serve others." Frances' work embodied her Christian understanding: *The power of government should be used to protect individuals from abuse by corporate and industrial powers.*

BIRDSONGS AND ALCHEMY

A mourning dove perched on the wire right outside my open office window the very moment I began writing this paragraph. She was so close I watched her blink. She cooed and cooed and I cooed back in total amazement. I noticed that her beak never opened. Instead, her muffled call came from deep inside as she puffed out her upper chest and throat. Her song hummed out of her like those deep double notes from the throats of chanting Tibetan monks.

Rachel Carson began her 1962 classic, *Silent Spring*, by imagining a town in the heart of America where birds no longer sang. Feeding stations were empty. "The few birds seen anywhere were moribund; they trembled violently and could not fly. It was a spring without voices." She predicted a large-scale catastrophe if we continued to use harmful pesticides. While some, like DDT, have been banned, others have taken their place. Now we're producing pesticides at a rate more than 13,000 times faster than we did when Carson wrote about the birds disappearing. Even the EPA considers a third of all insecticides, well over half of all the herbicides, and nearly all the fungicides, to be extremely carcinogenic.

I regret to admit that I shot and killed a baby sparrow once. It was too little to fly and my boy cousins foisted their Daisy rifle on me and dared me. While I continued to shoot their cap guns, I never again aimed a BB gun. Sometimes that little bird's fluttering wings still haunt me at night.

In Vermont, we have a law against shooting songbirds. A local farmer, attempting to keep his strawberries from being eaten up, shot eight cedar waxwings and then left their little bodies lying among the rows of red berries as a warning to their feathered cousins, he explained. He was fined $300 a bird. What's the real value of a songbird? In Cyprus, Malta and Italy songbirds are trapped on lime strings and sold to restaurants. Jonathan Franzen wrote about "Emptying the Skies" in the *New Yorker* (July 2010) and the photos of little poached birds sickened me. Apparently, serving up songbirds is a returning "culinary art." Migratory birds were an important seasonal source of protein in the countryside, and older Cypriots today remember being told by their mothers to go out to the garden and "catch some dinner." Now it's a nostalgic — and expensive — treat. *Treat?*

I've read that the "secret" language of birds helps us to link up meanings in our brains we didn't know we knew: Atum-Ad-am-Atom. Babel-babble. Mother-Mater-Matter. Melchizedek, according some esoteric sources, could speak it. And Thoth, who was part-serpent, part-bird, and part-man. The Maya believe Quetzalcoatl, their serpent-bird, came to earth from the blood of a goddess, and acts as a guide to other realms.

Some say the language of birds — an alchemical language — can still be heard in parts of Provençal. The Koran calls the language of birds the source of Solomon's wisdom. It's the language of poets. Adam and Eve spoke this "green language" as the alchemists called it. And later, Solomon supposedly embedded secrets of the secret bird language into the sacred geometry of his temple. Gothic cathedrals, such as the one at Chartres, somehow imitated it. I stood in Chartres once, and I listened, intently. All I heard was "*Go home and research this building. The music will come.*"

On the surface, alchemy is the science of turning lead into gold, but it's really about transforming energy. And learning the language of birds. By tasting the dragon's blood, the Wagnerian Siegfried learns the language of the birds. My friend, Anne, a pipe-carrying "medicine woman" and an spiritual-alchemist in her own right, says we can learn to listen to hear the sounds before they become words.

Egypt's alchemical seed-puffs blew across the Mediterranean to Greece and over to Israel, where they became part of the Kabbalah, but they never really "took" in Rome. However, people in Arabia recognized their worth and, as a result, alchemical secrets eventually landed in Europe where even Jonathan Swift once wrote about the *Language of the Birds*. Fulcanelli (the pseudonym of a late 19th century master alchemist who wrote about the mysteries of the great cathedrals) said: "What unsuspected marvels we should find if we knew how to dissect words, to strip them of their barks and liberate the Spirit, the divine light, which is within." He believed Jesus taught this secret language of birds to his disciples. His stories had surface meaning and layers of Sophia truths that those without the ears to hear, missed. Symbols carry bird language. Consider the ankh, for instance.

*An
Egyptian
ankh*

This cross with a loop-like handle was usually depicted in sun-gold. It's the Egyptian symbol of life. If it was painted, the oval at the top, the feminine part, was red; the lower, more phallic portion, was white. Together, they create an emblem of sexual union. The cross itself has a vertical, penetrating line — male, and a horizontal, all-embracing line — female. Or the vertical, earth, can be seen as paired with the horizontal, heaven. People portrayed in Egyptian art often held ankhs out in front of them like tuning forks. Who knows — perhaps they helped to sense vibrations. One way to view an ankh is to see a head above a woman's outstretched arms. Or as a hand mirror. Or a woman (Isis) with a knotted shawl for carrying a baby. It's also the symbol for the planet Venus. Alchemy is rich in symbolic meanings, and the bird language of the ankh, like the grail, may never be de-mystified and fully explained.

Alchemical things hide out, like Sophia, in plain sight. Alchemical birds are usually the white dove, black raven and iridescent peacock. Renaissance alchemists referred to three stages of alchemy as: the black phase, where you sacrifice some *prima materia* to the flames; the white phase, where the milky white liquid rises out of the prima material; and the *rubiens* stage, where, if they were lucky, and the glass retort had not yet exploded, iridescent colors would begin to swirl together.

Victor Hugo created Quasimodo, the raw stone that he said creates the Great Work. In his day, alchemists actually met every Saturday in the courtyard of Notre Dame in Paris to discuss the *Spiritus Mundi* — the spirit [Sophia] that drives the world. She is the innate image-making and image-perceiving capacity in each of us which simply cannot be suppressed or controlled. Or totally understood.

As we become aware of how our energy swirls around, we can better understand what particle physicists have been telling us for years: our attention, our attitudes, our expectations can affect outcomes. What you focus on changes things. Sufi teacher Llewellyn Vaughan-Lee says, "We need to become more aware that our attitudes, which are polluting and violating the earth, can disrupt the balance of life. This is not just primitive superstition, but an understanding of the way energy flows in the physical world."

Isn't that exactly what shamans and energy workers do? Sew up tears in our world's fabric? Heal the rifts in our psyches? Mend frayed bodies? If we were all to become "planetary shamans" we'd each hold the knowledge of how to heal ourselves *and* our precious planet. We'd "climb up the sacred pole-tree" to somewhere over the rainbow where bluebirds fly, to the beyond behind the beyonds, to places only the birds know. We'd bring back needed knowledge of how to tend our earth-garden. We'd all whistle and chant. And the old stones would sing back to us.

Her Gentling

In Biblio-speak, "gentleness" is usually teamed up with "meekness" and "self-control." It may be easiest to notice how Sophia "gentles" us, in retrospect. After the fact. Like the fox who gently waits for the Little Prince. My old ancestors quietly hung around until I found them in my tree. Joel's clavichord music gentled the Stockholm dialogue circle. Seeds are gentle reminders that we can't tug a plant into blossoming. We can only be patient and wait for the wonders to appear.

Writers of scriptures say Sophia is "more beautiful than the sun. Surpassing every constellation ... gently ordering all things." Gently ordering. What a beautiful phrase. She's like any woman getting some new throw pillows and putting the dishes away. Arranging flowers. Straightening the towels. She puts things to order. Even those things that seem terribly unjust right now. I think that's how she'd want us to approach our lives. Gently.

Some gentle Italian students recently started a "hug" campaign. They go to busy shopping areas and hold up signs: *Free*

Hugs. People are skeptical until they see how it works — just hugs. And smiles. Soon everyone wants one.

"Amma," born in Kerala, India in 1953, and named Sudhamani, is known as the "hugging saint." She's built like those Mother figurines found throughout prehistoric Europe — short, compact, wide-hipped. But unlike them, she has a face and it's usually smiling. Her embraces offer tearful people physical contact. She preaches on how to solve global suffering as she laughs and chants and gives hug after hug after hug. Her hospital and university in southern India has, among many other things, built 6,200 homes for victims of the 2004 tsunami. Amma's gentle actions speak loudly to a world in desperate need of hugs.

The other day I read a new definition of sin which I believe Amma would also like: *Today I failed to have fun X number of times.*

Having fun and feeding people — a gentle winning combination. We know how. After all, women invented agriculture, if we can believe what we see recorded on clay tablets found in Mesopotamia (Iraq). A female is shown in early carvings teaching her people how to farm. Little knives have been found at ancient sites, such as Çatal Hüyük in Turkey. Male archeologists, operating from their comfortable mental models, assumed these little knives from 6400-5600 B.C.E. were instruments used in sacrifice. It turns out they were used to harvest grain. Isis was called The Lady of Bread. Growing plants and raising livestock demands nurturing — not controlling. And women are good at it. But then Yaweh came along in Genesis 4:2-5 and said: "Agriculture? Not so much. Give me meat!" Fields and women were despised. Allah tells his people in the Koran that women are like fields, so seed them as you intend — any way you choose.

But there is hope. Ecofeminists and others believe in grassroots movements. They gently affirm the sacredness of nature. Epitomized by the Chipo Movement in northern India, or by Julia Butterfly, the woman who lived for 738 days surrounded by chain saws high up in a California redwood tree — "tree huggers" are derided. But it is precisely in hugging one another — and trees and animals and plants of all kinds — that we'll recover a sense of the divine in the world around us. Charlene Spretnak says of Sophia: "All forms of beings are One, continually renewed in cyclic rhythms of birth, maturation and death. That is the meaning of her triple-aspect.... She expresses the dynamic rather than static model of the universe. She is immanent in our lives and the world.... All beings are *part of Her*, not distant creations." We can't hug what our arms can't reach. Partnering, stewarding, caring and nurturing will gently lead us to embrace what's up close and personal.

The Paradox of Serving and Being Served

The paradox of the grail is this: only by giving it away, can we keep it. Only by serving can we be served.

"Paradox-speak" is like "double-speak." We say things like: time is everything; time is nothing. Life ends; life goes on. I am connected to everyone on this planet; I am completely alone. *Para* means both "beside" and "beyond; *dox* means "opinion." We are of the opinion that things are always right next to us and at the same time, far beyond us. G.K. Chesterton said that paradox is a truth standing on its head, waving its legs. Sophia is a paradigm-shifting paradox player who waves at us all the time.

Paradox knows every side of a story. Take the paradox of those beautiful natural-colored Aran sweaters. Knotted into each intricate stitch is a woolen tale. Originally, each family on these islands off the west coast of Ireland used a signature stitch — a combination of yarn overs-and-unders that identified members of their family. Fishermen always wore them and if they were so unfortunate as to fall into the water, their sweaters, like a knit-purl morse code, identified their bodies as they washed ashore. Swimming to shore in the cold Irish seas would be impossible anyway, so the sweater also served as a heavy wet anchor, mercifully speeding their death. Sweaters warm and comfort; sweaters drown and shroud.

Anyone familiar with the I Ching knows that the Chinese recognize paradox in every living thing. We can't control paradox — only embrace it. Thomas Merton said that we travel toward our destiny, like Jonah, in the belly of paradox. And even if we don't actually embrace all sides of any story, we should recognize that they can still be true.

Remember the old tale of Pandora? What if Pandora's box wasn't actually a *box*. In fact, "box" may have been mistranslated from "jar." What if it were a jar for honey (remember, when Egyptians died, they fell into the "honey pot"), or wine, or even cremated ashes? What if it were a recognizable symbol for life *and* death? Sophia loves paradox-symbols. Rather than Pandora-Eve's curiosity releasing all sorts of bad things into the world, what if she opened her womb-honey jar to birth not only hope, which lies at the bottom of the Greek story's mythical "box," but also all creative possibilities? When "jar" became "box," Sophia, and all women, were *boxed*. Words get mistranslated all the time. Here's another one. Adam supposedly said, on the way out of Eden, that he left *hawwah* — mother of all living things. In Aramaic, *hiwya* means serpent. Her wisdom. And notice how close *hiwya* is to *Hiawatha*, the one who, with Peacemaker, brought knowledge and peace from Sky Woman to the Iroquois Nations.

Paradox is a close sister of irony. But irony usually and humorously pretends not to know something (not always — if it bites too much it's satire). Paradox, on the other hand, really does know it all. Paradox knows all about our food issues, for instance. Paradox knows that about 1.1 billion of us are overweight and obese and another 1.1 billion are seriously underfed and malnourished. You see? That goes deeper than simple irony. Or this paradox: we pretend to care about our home planet earth, yet we gut her at every opportunity.

Paradoxical, isn't it, that our lust for gold, our drive to find something we can hold on to that will last and provide security, is the very thing that is now polluting the Amazon. Illegal gold mining sends huge amounts of deadly mercury into the river's Peruvian headwaters and rips open and destroys hundreds of acres of the most precious land on our planet. The result: Our lust for gold makes our entire planet less secure.

Or this paradox: In an effort to disperse the oil in Gulf waters, British Petroleum used chemicals that did a great job of breaking up and hiding the oil molecules, but by doing so, sent them into the air. Now acid rain falls along the gulf shores and people find these chemicals showing up in their swimming pools and it's killing their trees.

More paradoxes: Our president accepts a medal of peace while he must oversee two wars that drip blood. Or, everything we hate in others also lives within ourselves.

The word *irony* comes from the Greek *eiron*, meaning to dissemble or to hide under false appearance. We've become very adroit dissemblers. I find it ironic that that word is so close to Irene, which in Greek means *peace*.

EMPATHY NEURONS

Ironically, it was Irene Sendler, a *Polish Catholic* social worker, who wound up saving *Jewish* children during World War II. She posed as a "plumbing-sewer" specialist, and day after day, she smuggled babies and children out of the Warsaw ghetto in her tool box. She knew it would only be a matter of time until they would all die, so she did what she could. Her dog, trained to bark viciously as they passed through checkpoints, prevented the guards from checking under the wraps.

Irena was eventually caught. The Nazis broke both her legs and arms and beat her severely, but she survived. Irena kept a record of the children's names in a jar, which she buried under a tree in her backyard. It wasn't until it was safe to dig it up again that she actually counted the names. Twenty-five hundred! Her story is told in the play, "Life in a Jar" and in a 2009 movie, "The Courageous Heart of Irene Sendler."

After the war, Irene tried to locate the families of "her" children in an heroic effort to reunite their families. Sadly, most had been gassed. She continued to place many of the children in foster families or with adoptive parents. Irena died at age 98 — with her empathy neurons still intact.

Since about 1995, evolutionary biologists and neurocognitive researchers have been chasing down empathy neurons — those little bits of our brains that allow us to feel and experience another's situation as if it were our own. Our empathy neurons were kicked into high gear by all the images and sounds from Haiti after the earthquakes, and from the tsunami in Indonesia a few years before. Many of us heard the NPR reporter, for instance, whose tear-filled voice brought us a vivid account of one little Haitian girl shaking and dying before his eyes because there was no medical care for her. Or those sun-burned faces after Katrina begging for food and water.

When people hear these stories they are quick to open their wallets. They text their credit card companies. I find myself wondering what might have happened seventy years ago if we had been able to send tweets and videos. We may have heard firsthand from Irena Sendler and her dog.

An avid C.S. Lewis reader, I was surprised to discover one I hadn't read before: *The Weight of Glory*. It appealed to me because I was, obviously, feeling glory's weight. It's an awesome resurrection-filled responsibility to "go and live." One morning I skipped to the last page and read Lewis' morning prayer: "Grant me to make an unflawed beginning today, for I have done nothing yet."

Mother Teresa often said, the more we have, the less we can give. And here's another paradox: Mary Poppins-type nannies can fly and be grounded at the same time.

ONCE UPON A TIME:
Mary Poppins — Sophia-Magic

I never explain. Nor do I give references. When I fly through the window at Number 17 Cherry-Tree Lane, I know the Banks family will not only need me, but are expecting me. All of them: Jane, the oldest. Michael next. Then John and Barbara, the twins. Katie Nanna had left and they need a new Nanny, so I ride the East Wind and land, hat in one hand and my ever-present bag in the other. They stand there, taking in my skinny presence: shiny black hair, large feet, blue eyes. I am their new gravity-defying Nanny, who can slide *up* the banister.

Out of my magic "cauldron-bag" I unwind my muffler and unpack, among other things, a large cake of Sunlight Soap. And a bottle with the label: "One Teaspoon to Be Taken at Bedtime." Each of my children goes to bed with a different taste in their mouth. To one, it tastes like strawberry ice and to another Lime-Juice Cordial. The little twins think it's milk.

The children want me to stay forever — "I'll stay until the wind changes," I tell them. And indeed, I will.

I take the children up Ludgate Hill near St. Paul's cathedral, which was built by a man with a bird's name. Bird Woman's "sparrers" fly around her head three times as she calls out: "Feed the birds, tuppence a bag." Jane and Michael know they are doves. I tell them how Bird Woman can speak bird language and when the birds get sleepy she spreads out her skirts as a mother hen spreads out her wings and the birds go creep, creep, creeping underneath. And as soon as the last one is safe, she settles down over them making little brooding noises, and they sleep there until morning.

"And it's all quite true, isn't it?" Michael asks, and of course I say, "No." Because it isn't, yet it is.

The author of Mary Poppins was a curious Australian named Pamela L. Travers. She used to gaze at stars with her father, who like Mr. Banks in the Mary Poppins tales, was a banker. He died when she was seven. P.L. was born on the cusp of a new century and died in 1996. Like her Mary Poppins, she was bigger than life and defied gravity in her own way. She sang and danced, studied the Enneagram and spent much time with Gurdjieff's "The Fourth Way." She met Yeats and T.S. Elliot, was introduced to theosophical thought in 1925, and spent some time with Krishnamurti. *Mary Poppins* was published in 1934, followed by eight more of her tales. According to her biographer, Valerie Lawson, P.L. hated the Disney movie version.

Travers was a part of the art scene in Santa Fe and Taos in the 1940s; she dabbled in clay and collected chickens. Her mother used to say to her, "Don't sit that way! You look like a hen," to which P.L. would respond: "That's what I'm doing." She loved hatching things; she was the founder and editorial director of *Parabola* magazine — "Where spiritual traditions meet" — the little magazine that still brings Sophia's wisdom to my own mailbox. To study is to question — to look at all sides of things, she believed, and her favorite question, which may also be Sophia's, was *Why?* She acted, taught, studied Sufism and knew Rumi inside and out. Once she gave an ostrich egg to the dean at St. John Cathedral in New York to hang over the altar as Greek Orthodox churches often do, to remind people of our inner re-birthing. She believed: "Myth is not merely a story but a reality lived."

Sophia's Mystical Dancer:
Emanuel Swedenborg (1688-1774)

The Swedenborgian Church says, "All religion has to do with life and the life of religion is to do good." That sums up the founder's credo. Arthur Conan Doyle called Emanuel Swedenborg the "mountain peak of mentality ... a great religious reformer and clairvoyant medium, as little understood by his own followers as ever the Christ has been." Furthermore, "in order to fully understand Swedenborg one would need to have a Swedenborg brain and that is not met with once in a century." Swedenborg not only inspired the Theosophical Society, he also influenced Steiner, Blake, Emerson, Yeats, and many other poets.

This brilliant Stockholm scientist, an assessor in the Royal College of Mines where he helped develop Sweden's mining industry, was also a philosopher. He headed a noble family, which enabled him to sit in the Swedish parliament. He wrote the first Swedish textbooks on algebra and calculus, he played the organ and spoke nine languages. He correctly identified brain and gland functions; he even formulated an atomic theory of matter. Researching anything from horticulture to geology to astronomy made him happy.

When he turned fifty-six, Christ appeared in a dream and commissioned him to disclose the inner, spiritual meaning of the Bible. No small task! So this man of reason spent his remaining twenty-eight years struggling to write about what he had seen and learned. It was hard to find the right words in mere mortal language, doubly difficult since he was encumbered by the strict teachings of his father who was the pietistic Lutheran bishop of Skara.

Lars Bergquist wrote a book on Swedenborg's 150 dreams called *Swedenborg's Dream Diary*. He said, Swedenborg's dreams were "stratified, ambiguous and phantasmagoric." He experienced "holy shivers." While Swedenborg never called her Sophia, he described how he "fell" into "Spirit" and associated her with water — a common symbol for wisdom. Sometimes he saw her as multiple "damsels of wisdom" or as a woman in black. Swedenborg felt he was a "work" with work to do, and thanks to her care and efforts, he was prepared for it. Like Hildegard, he called her *sapientia* (Sophia-Wisdom) — knowledge found through God. His dreams led him to conclude that only grace can save us. Swedenborg gravitated towards Moravian tenets (the Moravians believed they were the "true" Lutherans), one of which is that love must be complemented by deeds of love. He believed the world is a laboratory to refine the soul. And all religious systems have their place — not just Christianity.

For those of us who take past lives seriously, it's interesting to note that Rudolf Steiner claimed that the founder of the Jesuits, Loyola of Ignatius, reincarnated as Swedenborg.

"Spirit" taught and prepared him to concentrate and regulate his breathing. In fact, he said, he could hold his breath for almost an hour. He was told he would be given access to the entire spirit world and was one of the first to describe various spirit planes. His *Dream Journal* documents how his unworthiness and sinful nature surfaces again and again, but finally, he comes to the conclusion that love, whether it originates inside the body or from outside the body, is all directed by God. Good and evil struggle for our souls. Spirits and angels can both be duplicitous, he notes.

While there are a plurality of worlds and the human race is not from one earth only, Swedenborg said the entire heavens are one. He talked to St. Paul and other spirits. Once, while in Gothenberg, 300 miles from Stockholm, he saw a raging fire in Stockholm — a vivid psychic experience that turned out to be true, according to Kant, who later investigated it.

He witnessed people dying and entering a period of post-death self-discovery in which, he said, the social masks worn on Earth dissolve away and the true self is revealed. Each person then shapes his or her own eternity to correspond with their real inner nature. Some people become irrational, driven by fear and greed, and they enter into what Swedenborg called Hell. As he describes it, it's a condition which parallels the suffering we experience on Earth when we allow ourselves to be driven by blind greed or our own egos. There are no devils in hell to inflict punishments because, in the hellish spiritual state, each person acts out their own malice by tormenting others. Heaven, however, is a joyous condition and a state of expanded awareness. As a result, we perceive more and more of the grand plan of creation. The heaven which Swedenborg experienced, corresponds to deeds, not creeds. Therefore, persons from many cultures and religions form the societies of heaven — not just the Lutherans!

In one June 1744 dream, which I interpret as a Sophia image, he saw in a large cage a little bird, which had been concealed for a long time; but it still lived, had food and drink, and went in and out of the cage.

He ends his diary with a description of divine fireworks, similar to Hildegard's visions, that engulf him in a shower of sparks.

SOPHIA'S SPECIAL GEO-SPOT: MOUNTSÉGUR

Pope Innocent the Third, anything but innocent, smelled "heresy" wafting out of southern France, so in 1208 C.E., he sent in the troops. One troubadour song went like this: "Not a buzzard, nor a vulture but can smell our carrion as can these priests who hunt us down to kill us." The pope's men, along with Simon de Montfort with his catapults and war machines, destroyed castles and burned people at the stake. Rumors pointed to remnants of the templar knights sequestered deep in the mountains ... all governed by a heretic *woman!* Grail cups, vials of bloods ... all potential revenue-producing relics might be had for the cost of a one-sided battle. Not to mention the value of the land. History is *always* about following the money, and heretics included any poor person who refused to, or could not, pay their tithes — for that matter, anyone who opposed any ecclesiastical law. Whole neighborhoods were turned into garbage pits if even one "heretic" lived there.

The Cathars, who called themselves "Good Christians," were forced to wear large yellow stars. They clung to four main beliefs: love your enemies; help your neighbors; keep the peace; and refrain from violence. But they also had "strange" habits — they ate no meat or anything from an animal, including milk, cheese and eggs. They fasted on bread and water three times a week and practiced healing and the "laying on of hands." They believed in reincarnation and said the Lord's Prayer many times a day. Much too mystical! And the dove was their special symbol. When the soldiers moved in, they were forced to give up their lucrative wool and weaving shops and hide in caves, only to be found by the king's dogs. Then the entrances were sealed.

In one battle at a place called St. Cyprien's Bridge, some women sneaked down while de Montfort went to mass, stole his catapult, and managed to drag it back up the hill. After church, stones began raining down. A large one landed on Simon's skull and he died near St. Stephen, where he had just been shriven. His son Amalric then led the battles of this unholy war of Christians fighting against Christians.

But, on another level, the wars against "heretics" were the male hierarchy battling against a female force they couldn't control. After all, the Albigensian/Cathar Christians even allowed women to be priests and administer the sacraments! Everyone could read the Bible, not just the "church-sanctioned." In fact, these "heretics" attached the book of St. John to their belts and carried it around with them.

What would happen if this free religion spread? It could carry the whole region from the Alps to the Pyrenees, away from Rome, that's what. Furthermore, the Cathars and Jews controlled the salt and leather trade, eastern spices and African gold. Both had to go!

Over 5,000 men, women and children were killed just because the church labeled them heretics. One ex-Cistercian monk named Fulk led one of the crusades against the Albigenses, another name for the Cathars living near Albi in Languedoc. He told his soldiers, 'Kill them all! God will recognize his own!"

A beautiful rich widow named Esclarmonde de Foix was a person of special interest. After her family had grown, she decided to devote her life to Christ. Since she lived in Languedoc, below the Loire River, Gothic law still prevailed. There, women equaled men in property rights. Her lands extended way down to the Avtège River valley on one side of Mt. Foix, and all the way up to Montségur to the east. Foix is actually one of Montségur's three peaks.

Esclarmonde's castle grew up over much of an ancient original structure at Mountségur. Treacherous mountain passes still enclose dozens of deep lakes, and rushing rivers and caves twist under the earth, some as deep as thirteen miles. Paths wind down, down into the mountain's heart. It is said that on summer solstice, when sunbeams strike a certain place on the castle wall, an eight-pointed star shoots off into the mountains.

Her castle door was huge — six feet by ten feet. Deep inside was a chapel dedicated to Mary. Esclarmonde had a large library including books on alchemy. Many thought she protected the "grail." Some believed it was a book that contained Solomon's secret wisdom. It's one of the reasons, years after the Cathars were eliminated, that Hitler found this mystical area of such great interest, thanks to Otto Rahn who was sent off to southern France to search for the Holy Grail.

The pope's army blocked all mountain passes so the people still hiding underground at Mountségur starved. In 1244, several hundred men, women, and children were herded into a pen and burned alive at what people called the "Field of Fire." After the final siege ended, entrances to all the underground grottos were sealed. The castle was dismantled and no one was allowed to speak of the "Field of Fire." Dominicans forbade anyone to even mention the name Cathar, which means *The Friends of God*.

Just before the Cathar stronghold fell, a single Cathar figure wearing white armor appeared high on her castle wall. And then it disappeared. All the fortress's great treasures were, according to the tales, smuggled out before the castle fell. People still speculate on where it all went.

The day the king's men eventually reached the peak of Mountségur, some shepherds said they saw a white dove escape and fly over a chasm of granite in the mountain's flank.

SOPHIA'S GRAIL MAIDENS

Besides Esclarmonde, Mary Magdelene also finds her way back into our lives, thanks to such authors as Jean-Yves LeLoup, with *The Gospel of Mary Magdalene*, and Kathleen McGowan, with her truth stranger-than-fiction Magdalene-line novels, Dan Brown and many others. By paying closer attention to words and translations, we now learn that the Hebrew word *Zonah*, which Mary Magdelene was called, means both prophetess and prostitute. She may have been a wealthy priestess in Asherah's temple in Magdala. She may have been Jesus' lover. She may even have carried his child. What we do know is that women have been called prostitutes for a long, long time, whether they served men for money or not. Perhaps women can now be called "grail maidens" instead. The ones called to heal the world.

In *The Return of the Feminine and the World Soul*, Llewellyn Vaughan-Lee says, "Men can't heal the world. They don't know how to heal the world. It's women who have to do this healing. But first they have to learn to forgive the masculine for what it has done, because no healing can be done without forgiveness."

Women have every right to be angry. But women's anger can take on a volcanic and destructive stance if it's not channeled into healing. At a talk once, someone asked what the role of men was in all this and Vaughan-Lee responded: Your role is to protect women as they do their healing work.

I call on men to protect women as they ask for comparable wages. Protect women as they seek academic roles similar to men's. Protect women and children. Period. Honor our needs and our differences, as we pledge to honor yours.

Men are usually more in tune with systems and imagining what three-dimensional objects look like; they can usually read maps better than women — as my husband can attest — and men better assess technical abstracts as well as how moving objects move. Larry Summers got in big trouble at Harvard, though, by referring to research that suggested that women and men have differing competencies in math and science. *The Science on Women and Science* suggests, however, that women, like Irene Sendler, *do* have much more interest in empathy. Girls, on average, show more interest in sharing, turn-taking, and responding to others' distress. They can infer, even at age three, what others are thinking or intending and are more sensitive to facial expressions. Women seem to value relationships; men value power, politics and competition. Psychopathic and conduct disorders are far more common among males, and male-on-male homicide is thirty to forty times more frequent than female-on-female homicide. And, as history has shown, males are quicker to establish hierarchies and, therefore, can write the histories.

And histories tell us *men* were the scientists and the religious leaders. But remember, when science peaked in Europe, women had roughly four choices: get married; enter a convent; work as a maid or become a prostitute. Imagine how different things might have turned out if the lucrative dowries came with the men and women vied over whom to marry. Or if boys were sent to be locked behind stone walls only to learn embroidery, not the classics. Galileo's illegitimate daughter, Virginia, according to historical sources, "mirrored his own brilliance, industry, sensibility and virtue — she had an exquisite mind." But what happened to her? She couldn't be profitably married off, so she was sent to a convent. Her brother studied law at a university.

Today women earn over half the bachelor's degrees and 59% of master's degrees and more PhDs than men in humanities, social science, education and life sciences. But only about a quarter of the tenured positions in math are held by women and far fewer in the sciences. Many women still face hostile climates in academia as well as in corporate life. They also opt out of overly competitive environments where hidden sexism is oppressive.

Change comes slowly, but the Grail Maidens are coming out of hiding. Men are, according to *The Atlantic*, July-August 2010 issue, projected to dominate in just two of the fifteen job categories projected to grow: janitor and computer engineer. Women will dominate in all the rest. The old "command and control" model is morphing into something performance shows is more workable and therefore more profitable. Something "more Grail-Maiden like." Not as fast as in cultures that value boys over girls, but Sophia is making her presence felt more than ever before. Men such as Craig Barnes, the attorney who wrote *In Search of the Lost Feminine*, are helping. Here's a man who, as young trial lawyer, spent five years preparing a wage case on behalf of Denver's nurses and the trial judge ruled after deliberating only ten minutes *against* the nurses — 95% of whom were women. That ruling guaranteed that even graduate nurses would be paid less than tree trimmers. Along with most people, the judge had based his assumptions on the old stories the Greeks started telling and the ones we continue to tell: women are weaker than men because they don't support physical combat, violence, or wars; women are less capable than men; women can be debased and abused; women aren't fit to lead.

Not true! How long will it take to restore equality? In spite of the Equal Pay Act Congress passed in 1963, wages are certainly still far from equal. Comparing like jobs, the wage gap for people of mixed races or blacks, compared to whites, is disturbingly evident. It can be, according to 2000 studies, about $7.00 an hour lower for people of mixed race. While most of us chafe at the high CEO salaries, the time has come for female American CEOs to make up the 30% lower wages compared to their male counterparts. It's time Walmart's female managers (who at the time of this writing are only one in three) stop making $16,400 less than their comparable male counterparts. It's time women, in general, stop earning on average $30,000 a year less than the men in similar positions.

Furthermore, it's time Bible readers turn their attention to the verses showing Christ-Sophia's unconditional grace and love, rather than wallowing around in the verses filled with fear and anger, judgment and insularity. Then we can *all* sing again.

FROM SOPHIA'S NOTEBOOK

You can fly because you are grounded. It's a paradox — like Quetzelcoatl, the feathered serpent. Bound to the earth, but free to fly to the stars. Thoughts do create, and you are limited only by your willingness to imagine. You create your cages and prisons; you can unlock the door and fly as freely as you choose.

We don't fix things with super-glue. Returning to the "old" is not the only way to go, but old can support the new. Seeing people all lined up like little penguins on the wing of that USAir plane in the Hudson River taught you not to panic. Rely on the systems you have in place. Use what is offered to you. And above all, deal with the present. Practice on the little things for the larger things coming.

I throw out impossible paths and you wearily trudge along; I throw out ungainly nets for your toes to hook onto and you swing a bit, thinking, 'This is fun!" but you are reluctant to climb in abandoned gaiety. I send you visions and dreams and you sometimes write them down, you sometimes remember them. Often they are like milk-weed puffs before the wind — scattered but never lost, blown but not abandoned. You seize the edges and welcome the fringes, but you have yet to capture the center and hold the essence. Hug the core. I wait for you. I rejoice in your willingness to try and I will hold you and keep you. I will hold my chalice steady even as you now sip. I am yours to taste and devour. I am yours to hear until you collapse with the sound. I am yours to see, once your eyes can better stand the light. I am yours to touch and dissolve in my closeness. You sniff, now, but one day you will float in the heady perfume of my being.

chapter nine

SHE BINDS US TOGETHER

Crop Circle: Cherill, Wiltshire, July 17, 1999

. . . .

"God has arranged all things in the world in consideration of everything else. Everything that is in the heavens, on the earth and under the earth is penetrated with connectedness, is penetrated with relatedness."

~ Hildegard of Bingen

MOUNTAIN JOURNAL ENTRY

Surrounded by the quiet violet night, I feel morning coming. All life seems suspended in a web of fibers so fine I cannot count all the connections. Knots. Nexus points. Each an opening to something more.

Spring comes to Vermont's vert-green mountains in the space of a few hours. One March evening you go to bed, vaguely aware that some time during the late afternoon, all the bare brown branches migrated to magenta. Overnight, leaf buds spit new colors into the mauve-grey dawn skies. Through some miracle of light, the insides of trees turn translucent pink. The next thing you know, soft yellow-greens dribble down from the tips of the poplars. Spring greens flow across the quiet underpaintings of ocher and sienna to create a watercolor wash. Our neighbors hang buckets from their maple trees and after a long winter, my veins, too, pulse with sweet blood-sap. There's a Vermont saying, based on boiling sap, that describes how things always work out: *It'll sugar off*. Little peeper frogs send throaty calls across the valley and crickets vibrate the air. Like them, I'm greening up.

I write:

Sophia

She is the blood and the bleeding

the seed and the seeding

the sow and the mare

the step and the stair

the All and the One.

Sophia

She is the cloud and the shining

the pine and the pining

the beach and the tide

the narrow, the wide

the awe and the fun.

Sophia

She is the wave and the waving

the shares and the sharing

the thrust and the lance

the step and the dance

the moon and the sun.

Sophia

She is the wax and the bee

the root and the tree

the you in the me.

Sophia

HEARTBEAT QUESTIONS

How does my wisdom reflect Her Wisdom?

Am I alone in the universe?

How do I sense all things connected? Have I noticed any synchronicities?

As I prepare to complete this "Sophia Journey," do I view myself, my family, the earth, the universe, any differently?

HER MAGICAL MILKY WAY

The universe isn't a straight line. Just check out the Milky Way some dark night if you have any doubts. Scientists who can juggle numbers, think it all began around twenty billion years ago. "The universe exists as sleeping darkness, unknowable, unknown.... She stirs, dispelling darkness. She who is subtle and full of desire, imperceptible and everywhere now and eternal, who contains all created beings, wakes...." That's how Monica Sjöö and Barbara Mor begin their story of spiral feminine movement in the cosmos in *The Cosmic Mother*.

Like the ancient Athenians, I seek to learn more about the elegant order embedded in the *Kosmos* — the World without End. That word also means everything that is physical, emotional, mental and spiritual. A "patterned whole." Physicists continue to join my quest in trying to figure out what makes this universe-pattern work. And what part each of us plays in it.

On my office wall, to the left of my computer, thanks to *National Geographic*, hangs a map of the Milky Way. The Swedes call it the Winter Street Leading to Heaven. The Kalahari call it the Backbone of the Night. Its nebulae, molecular clouds and galactic bulges help me put things into perspective. Over there's *Omega Centauri*. And there, a freckled arm named *Carina*. And in the center, a swirling comma of light spills out in ever-increasing circles. The Geographic footnote says of the center: "*The million-plus stars packed into a globular cluster such as Omega Centauri are senior citizens of the Milky Way. Unlike human retirees, however, every star in the cluster is about the same age, billions of years older than our 4.6 billion-year-old sun. Peering between dust clouds towards the central bulge of the Milky Way, the Hubble Space Telescope focused on a rare, clear region in the Sagittarius star cloud. These Sagittarius stars formed at different times; most are older than the sun. They sparkle like an assortment of gems on a jeweler's velvet pad.*"

Star maps show many more than the seven sister stars within Pleiadies' cloudy constellation nestled deep within Taurus — perhaps 300 or more. Most people with good vision can see, with the naked eye, from seven to nine celestial star-doves in this Sophia-cote. They're more visible if you squint and focus a bit to either side of the fuzzy Pleiadian star-cloud. Using peripheral vision brings clarity to most things.

Sister Gail Worcelo at the Green Mountain monastery says, "The galaxy in which I pray is 100,000 light years wide. A single light year is equal to six trillion miles. Our nearest neighbor, the Andromeda Galaxy, is 2.3 million light years away. Vastness."

Vast, indeed. Three-fourths of the way down my vast Milky Way map, at about "5:30," if you're looking at this view of the cosmic-clock head-on, you'll see our *Orion Arm*. On its wrist, like a little ID bracelet, the mapmakers have hung a sign with a pointer: "*We are here.*" Not "I," not "you," but "*we.*" All together, we sing our complex cadences across the heavens. Under the sign, three more arms swirl out into hallowed space. Like the vertebrae of our marble-rimmed meadow labyrinth, this close-up view of my Milky Way anchors everything I know. I hang, together with everything and everyone else, suspended and tightly wrapped in Sophia's milky stars. And what better symbolizes Our Mother than "breast milk." Latte. It's interesting to note that El Shaddai means "God of the Mountain" but *shad* is the Hebrew word for breast. Since *ai* is an old feminine ending, *El Shaddai* means "the Breasted One." Lo and behold! A *mighty God* with breasts is mentioned no fewer than forty-eight times in the Bible.

The Jungian author, Marie-Louise Von Franz, reminds us in *The Feminine in Fairy Tales*: "The star map is a beautiful mixture of order and disorder, there are regular and irregular events, like meteors. Behind the word *constellation* there is a whole mystery; one knows, more or less what one means by it, but it points to a mystery."

In 1888, Vincent Van Gogh wrote to his brother Theo, not to ask for money this time, but to write about his plans to paint the stars. "I must also have a starry night with cypresses...." Such a sky symbolized for him God's beneficent and eternal surveillance of the universe — and that we are one. The cypresses symbolized death, a concept he lived with most of the time.

He wrote to Theo again from Arles in August of 1888, two years before he took his own life: "In a painter's life, death is not perhaps the hardest thing there is. For my own part, I declare I know nothing whatever about it, but to look at the stars always makes me dream, as simply as I dream over the black dots of a map representing towns and villages. If we take a train to get to Tarascon or Rouen, we take death to reach a star. One thing undoubtedly true in this reasoning is this, that while we are alive we cannot get to a star any more than when we are dead we can take the train." After repeated stays in mental hospitals, poor Vincent finally decided to take the "death train" to the stars. His beloved brother died six months later.

In 1953, when Dag Hammarsjöld was the Secretary General of the United Nations, he arranged to have a six and a half ton block of polished iron ore brought from a Swedish mine to New York. One hot summer day, I stood by this "stone of light," in the Meditation Room just to the right of the entrance's reception desk, and marveled at its size and its cool surface. I felt pulled into its magnetic mystery and co-mingled with the "stars" deep within. I wondered what this stone offers to a building that many feel is home to all earth's families. Surely the stars connect us. Surely we can understand what it means to be neighbors. Good neighbors.

When Hammarsjöld's plane crashed near the Rhodesian border in 1961, the world lost a brilliant peacemaker. His posthumously published journal, *Markings*, was my first introduction to serious journaling, as well as to spiritual thinkers like Meister Eckhart and Rumi. This Swedish giant not only brought stars to the UN — he brought wisdom. He quickened our hearts by such thoughts as: "God does not die on the day when we cease to believe in a personal deity, but we die on the day when our lives cease to be illuminated by the steady reflection, renewed daily, of a wonder, the source of which is beyond all reason." "To love life and men as God loves them — for the sake of their infinite possibilities." "Somebody placed the shuttle in your hand: somebody who had already arranged the threads." "We act in faith and miracles occur." He reminded me that I was not the oil or the air — merely the point of combustion, like the stars embedded in his black rock. It's a great relief not to have to carry the oil or move the air, but just simply be there.

I'm not sure why I fixate on Van Gogh and Hammarsjöld's deaths being linked to the stars. But deep down I know they were — and I know my own death will be as well. Sophia spirals among the constellations, floats on flash-points of sunlight, and radiates among us.

Sometimes I picture the cosmos like the Jacob's Ladder Lillian asked us to paint for her brother Edward. There's movement in the cosmos albeit more spiraling than linear. Things come; things go. Big things like stars and black holes. But the patterns hold because she's bracing the ladder for us. The ladder, the sky — it's all "her."

The irregular aspects of nature and the universe have puzzled scientists for a long time. Then, in the 70s, some far-sighted mathematicians and their friends began to find order in disorder and computers began to help them speak in a new language of fractals and bifurcations. A brilliant French contemporary of Einstein's — mathematician and philosopher Henri Poincaré — wrote about how the universe isn't a machine with replaceable parts, but a system that can take erratic turns. Turbulent even. His work was rediscovered by Fritjof Capra who began explaining to us non-physicists how living systems don't respond to control, only to disturbances. You can kick a stone and pretty much figure out what's going to happen. If you kick a dog — or another country — you're never sure. He set out in *The Tao of Physics* to show harmony between Eastern wisdom and Western science. Physics, he envisioned, could be a path with a heart, a path to spiritual knowledge.

In his classic, *Turning Point*, Capra begins with a message from the I Ching — that ancient synchronistic Chinese oracle-philosophic system, in which we hear Sophia's voice: "After a time of heavy decay comes the turning point. The powerful light that has been banished returns. There is movement, but it is not brought about by force.... The movement is natural, arising spontaneously. For this reason the transformation of the old becomes easy. The old is discarded and the new is introduced. Both measures accord with the time; therefore, no harm results."

Capra's brother, Bernt, used *Turning Point* as the basis for his movie, *Mind Walk*, set at Mt. St. Michel — Michael's mount off the coast of Brittany. Three present-day pilgrims meet there by "chance" to discuss the interconnectedness of the universe. One says of the mount, "This place is watching you." Indeed, Sophia-Michael watches.

Mont St. Michel or Saint Michael's Mount off the Normandy coast of France

What jump-started this cauldron that holds 100 billion galaxies, each with hundreds of millions of star-suns, each with so many planets circling around them, and the possibilities of so much other life? How would Sophia want us to approach all this potential? I tend to think she'd prefer the Novrogod School of icon painters' philosophy which was: don't focus on the "good" or the "evil." Focus just on forces that must be in correct relationship with one another, and in harmony with the universe.

When Stephen Hawking's tremulous voice started to echo far beyond the Cambridge campus, we took notice. A lot of people bought *A Brief History of Time*, but like me, I'm guessing, they didn't read it all. Then came a "briefer" history, and now, *The Grand Design*. He thinks the eventual goal of science is to find one single theory that unites the whole universe. In *The Grand Design* he discusses the "M Theory: multiuniverses all "happening" together, overlapping theories for one grand unified field. This is exactly what Maharishi, who died in 2008 at age ninety-one, spoke of. A grand unifying field. So it seems Capra's dream of uniting eastern philosophy with western science has come true. I notice, however, that Hawking doesn't talk about the "S Theory" (and I don't mean the string-theory which he does cover.) I mean *Sophia-universes* which run on unconditional love. Maybe that possibility isn't challenging enough for physicists.

Recently Hawking has assumed a "The sky is falling. Run tell Turkey-Lurkey" stance regarding our future. If we don't figure out how to get off this planet in the next 200 years, he says, we won't be able to. These words and other end-times prophesies are enough to make you stash beans and rice in the basement and hope you have a hand-operated can opener.

Furthermore, Hawking now believes we *will* be contacted by space beings and he told *The New York Times* in 2010 that we should be very careful how we deal with those "others" who are surely coming here to mine our goodies. They might treat us with the respect we treat ants. Maybe. Maybe not. Making contact, he cautions, will be very risky. But I believe we free-willed humans risk contact with "good" and "evil" every day of our lives. But if we are truly one, then what do we have to fear? There may be some beings not yet convinced of this love, and they could be trouble, but Christ-Sophia's unconditional love carries the cosmos as surely as it carries everything on earth.

Concepts of *Love* or *The Cosmos,* and certainly Sophia, are too big for us to get our puny minds around. But there is order in what we perceive to be disorder. Calmness within chaos. In his *Consolation of Philosophy,* Boethius said, "What room can there be for random events since God keeps all things in order." One author who wrote about seeing this order is Jostein Gaarder, a Norwegian novelist. It's more than appropriate to mention one of his books here since it's called *Sophie's World.* It all starts with two questions posed to fifteen-year-old Sophie Amundson: *Who are you?* And, *Where did the world come from?* Sophie's father leads her on a merry cosmic chase. He explains that when we gaze at a star in the Milky Way, which is 50,000 light years away, we are looking back 50,000 years into time. Dizzying stuff. Furthermore, he tells her that the universe has no fixed geography because it's still happening. Galaxies continue to fly through the universe at colossal speeds. "All stars and all planets belong to the same family.... We are a spark from the great fire that was ignited many billions of years ago."

If that seems unduly chaotic, there's a reason. John Gribbin put it this way in *Deep Simplicity,* "Chaos begets complexity and complexity begets life. Without chaos, we would not be here."

We hear fiery music all around. Goethe once wrote about Beethoven's Fifth Symphony: "If all the musicians in the world played this piece simultaneously, the planet would go off its axis." What magic!

THE MAGI

I've always connected the Magi, who found Mary and Jesus in a backwater town half way around the world, with magic. Caspar, Melchoir, Balthazar, or whatever their names were, set out on a most unreasonable trek. Magic always goes beyond reason. Jacob Boehme said, "Magic is the best theology, for in it true faith is both grounded and discovered." It takes a great deal of faith to pack up your camel saddle bags and head out across hot deserts simply to find a baby and deliver some presents.

A legend from the Book of Seth tells of a race in the Far East. They gathered twelve of their most learned and called them the Magi; when one died, another was chosen. They were gentle, silent people. Every year they climbed a mountain and meditated for three days, waiting for a star to appear. Finally it did. They followed it for two years until they reached a special mother and child. Other accounts says it took them closer to six years. Ann Catherine Emmerich, a visionary German nun, said they arrived on the evening of December 26, 6 B.C.E. when there was a conjunction of Mercury and Saturn. Emmerich was born in 1774, had many visions as a child, and then, at twenty-eight she began "seeing" many details of Christ's life. Clemens Brentano, a novelist and poet, visited her while she was very ill in 1818 and offered to record her visions. (She'd been told "the pilgrim" would come to help preserve her revelations.) They worked together until she died in 1824; she lived on only water and the Eucharist for a decade prior to her death.

Robert Powell's *Chronicle of the Living Christ* captures Emmerich's life and her visions. I was particularly struck by her description of Jesus raising Lazarus. He put his right hand on his head and breathed on him seven times, infusing him with the gifts of the Holy Spirit. Sophia is present throughout Emmerich's tales.

Magi: The Quest for a Secret Tradition, written by Adrian Gilbert, tells of two histories of the world that run parallel. One is visible; the other hidden. The ancients encoded, as we have noted, hidden Sophia knowledge into temples and pyramids, in songs and dances. Even into Tarot cards. Pythagoras was initiated by the Magi and studied astronomy and geometry in Babylon. When he was fifty-six, he returned to Samos and spent the rest of his life teaching these bits of ancient Zoroastrian wisdom and Hermetic teachings. As above, so below.

Some scientists say our universe is likely 13.7 billion years old. It's hard to compute numbers that large. For instance, we have spent, to date, a *trillion* dollars on two recent wars. A trillion dollars of military-related expenditures ... about $750 billion for Iraq and close to $338 billion in Afghanistan. Ten billion a month! Line up the money we've spent and it dwarfs the age of our universe. What sort of world might we have created with such resources? Try to imagine how many homes and businesses we could have equipped with solar energy. Or how many children we could have fed. A Danish activist spray-painted a message onto the sidewalk outside Obama's Copenhagen hotel: "Change the politics, save the climate." *Change our hearts,* could be Sophia's spray-painted message. *Change our hearts, save the universe!*

A Chartres-type labyrinth

Labyrinths:
Her Circling Paths

"By following an invisible thread we connect to the Source, to the Sacred. We can't see it, and yet some deep part of us knows it is there. This innate awareness gives us solace and peace during stormy times."
~ Lauren Artress, *Walking a Sacred Path*

When you take your first step onto a labyrinth, you wonder if you'll get lost, and then the path shows the way, so you stop worrying. By moving through perplexing passageways and turning at what seem like odd moments, we all eventually get to the center. It's a life metaphor.

When we feel ready, we retrace our steps, as if other dimensions — other worlds — wind us back to where we started. Nothing lays out paths quite the way a labyrinth does. Unlike a meander or a maze, it resembles a Celtic knot — easily followed; one way in and one way out. Walking it can become body prayer. The labyrinth, then, is a prayer circle, a spiritual practice that teaches us that all paths are to her center.

Moving into a labyrinth is a graceful walk toward a mini-death. We give up control and step out onto a mystical road, not sure what sorts of massive minotaur we'll encounter. It's good to hold an important question in mind. Perhaps any of the old Sphinx questions will do: "Who are you? Where do you come from? Where are you going?"

Reaching the center may offer an enlightening moment. Or not. Labyrinths aren't programmable. Some people experience a re-entry into the birth canal. A trip around the convolutions of the brain. Or a ride inside a potter's wheel where you feel as if your impurities are being thrown off by all the turnings. Perhaps a bit like dizzying dervish dancing.

Walking back out again frees us to contemplate how the insights we may have received can be manifested in the "real" world. Lauren Artress, author of *Walking a Sacred Path*, reminds us that the pathway to heaven isn't vertical — nor is it straight. But it is welcoming and expansive.

"Cretan" labyrinths have seven paths to the center; "Chartres" has eleven. In some esoteric traditions, eleven is the number that stands for knowledge. Walking a labyrinth helps us know who we are. Whether we consciously intend it or not, we become Gnostics — *knowing* ones. It's not a magic formula. It's not a pill to speed up enlightenment. But it is a powerful possibility.

No one knows how labyrinths work, but most people who have access to one call it a spiritual tool. It shows us Sophia's hidden liminal places — those edgy spots where we are torn loose from our binding, confining egos. She walks with us from our linear peripheries to our circular center. And the center is like a pole star around which the heavens spin in a whirlpool of energy.

Some theologians warn against syncretism — the fusion of beliefs or practices. I embrace it. The labyrinth embodies *all* practices and no practices. It's universal. Like Sophia. I'm fascinated that the word *syncretism* also comes from Crete. It originally meant the unity of all Cretan cities. It's an odd word that belittles and denigrates — an "illogical path" or an attempt to fuse things together without reason or critical examination. But if the word truly means unity, then it's a word we can, without apology, embrace. Most of us have no problem using its cousin, *synchronicity*, a word that does suggest an illogical coming together.

Early labyrinths smacked of *her* walkways and were, as a result, condemned by early church fathers. Still, labyrinths sneaked into churches all over Europe. Some still appear on walls and people "walk" them with their fingers in a solitary meditative practice before entering the worship space. Most, like the one at Chartres, appear on floors. The story of Ariadne's/Sophia's thread can be told many ways.

Like Moses, Ariadne's father, King Minos, received direct instructions from God. So begins this complicated labyrinth story layered with deceptions. In one of his more manipulative moments, Minos begged to be made king, over his brothers, and prayed to be sent a sign: "Send a white bull from the sea to show me I am to be king and in return, I promise to sacrifice it." Sure enough, one day a white bull swam up from the sea. Minos took one look and said, "Oh, this bull's too special. I'll sacrifice another plainer one from my herd. God will never know."

But Neptune/Poseidon did know and that started a raucous round of bovine deceptions.

A labyrinth is a pathway of paradoxes. Barbara Hand Clow calls it "experiential geometry." It leads the walker away from herself to inner truths, where she can discover who she really is. Here's another paradox: the labyrinth is a "truth-teller," but, at least according to the Greeks' soap opera version, it was founded on deception and lies.

Minos married the sun princess, Pasiphae. Daedelous, the royal family's master architect, made Pasiphae a wooden heifer costume to deceive her husband. Deep in a cave near Knossos, she mated with the heavenly bull and later gave birth to a bull-man, the Minotaur. Ariadne deceived her father by thwarting his plan to sacrifice Athens' prince Theseus to her half-brother, the Minotaur. Theseus volunteered to be one of fourteen youths sent, as they were forced to do every nine years, to feed the Cretan beast. Ariadne fell in love with him the moment he jumped off the boat and gave him a spear and a ball of golden string to guide him back out of the dark labyrinth. Safely out, Theseus then made up some "cock and bull story" about loving her, so she agreed to go with him. But then he dropped her off on an island — pregnant — and sailed home. But not without even more deception. Before he left Greece, his father told him to raise a white sail so upon his return, he'd know he was safe. But Theseus "forgot" and sailed into harbor with a black sail billowing. His grieving father leaped off the harbor cliffs to his death, leaving the throne to ... well, Theseus of course.

Labyrinths have long been Sophia's walkways. The first paths may have been formed by following the steps of a goddess crane dance. Some Basque traditions still practice the geranos' spiral steps. The labyrinth we built in our meadow replicates the stone labyrinth which was strategically placed so worshippers had to walk over it to reach the altar. Like ours, it's slightly less than 42 feet in diameter. Different laws apply when you walk the labyrinth. It's a place people have, for centuries, danced the Round Dance, following the "pretend" road to Jerusalem. It was called a poor person's pilgrimage; you could visit Chartres if you couldn't afford to go all the way to the actual Holy Land.

You enter, moving to the left, and before you know it, you're caught up in *holy time*. The spirals remind us that the world doesn't line up in neat rows. The sage in *Hanta Yo*, Wanagi, says: "*Recognize the spiral path upon which you move level to next high level, a spiritual path upon which you evolve toward the wholeness of the one. You live on one earth, one earth with many planes. The same invariables — the absolutes — extend onto each plane, but you encounter more spiritual infusion at each level.*"

Instead of a Minotaur at the center, our Vermont labyrinth has flowers. And thyme. And a bench. Our young neighbor boy who helped us construct it was the first to walk (rather run) it. "Karen, this is a-mazing!" When he got to the center, he realized it had some sort of special meaning. "Oh I get it. God is here, but you don't have to stay." Very wise for an eight-year-old. Standing too long on hallowed ground might singe your toes. One of my Sophia-friends said she felt very heavy as she walked to the center, and then extraordinarily light as she returned.

Jean Gebser, a Swiss professor of Comparative Studies and Applied Psychology, said that if the cave (also a Sophia symbol) represents security, peace and the absence of danger, then the labyrinth expresses seeking, movement and danger. Again, Sophia is the both/and.

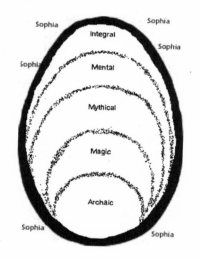

A redrawing of the Gebser "egg"

In *The Ever-Present Origin*, Gebser outlines all the labyrinthine structures we have created for ourselves as humans. He calls these stages the mutations of consciousness. Although he doesn't call her Sophia, he says the Mother force forms our *Archaic Structure*, our origins. She is our creatrix, the egg of our inception. But in my cosmology, she is everything that is the egg and everything around the egg. Building over that archaic beginning becomes what Gebser calls *the magic structure*. Humans and nature now began to interact — cave paintings, statues (the earliest ones, all of a female figure) and petroglyphs abounded. Over that earlier time period, we built our *Mythical Structure*. We began telling stories about how we "free ourselves" from nature, how we talk, how we write, how we travel around. We moved the Great Mother, to matter, meter, music. Then about 1500 C.E., we developed our *Mental Structure*. (I apologize to the people in China and India who will find this to be a very European-centric timetable.) This is when the rational phase of our development kicked in. Finally, we reach the *Integral Structure*. That's us. Now. This is Sophia coming home and she's bringing with her an integral wholeness we have not experienced before. She brings a transparency and a consciousness of spirit we were too asleep to realize before. An openness. A completeness. *A presence.*

Gebser's final chapter is called "Concretion of the Spiritual." We live on a star among stars, he says. Because the spiritual "is not bound to the vital, experiential, conceptual or reflective — a new possibility for perceptual consciousness of the spiritual for the whole of mankind one day had to shine forth." We approach that time.

In French, the labyrinth is called *La Lieue* — "The Place." Three hundred and twenty yards of twists and turns. The *labrys* — axe shapes or crescent moon shapes — form the turn-around places. As we follow "Ariadne's Thread" through our life-labyrinths, we begin to realize that *Someone* has already laid out our path. *Someone* encourages us to take those first steps onto a most amazing journey. Hildegard wrote about that "Someone" in 1170: "*I, the highest fiery power, have kindled every spark of life and I emit nothing that is deadly. I decide on all reality. With my lofty wings I fly above the globe. With wisdom I have rightly put the universe in order. I, the fiery life of divine essence, am aflame with the beauty of the meadows. I gleam in the waters. I burn in the sun, moon and stars. With every breeze, as with invisible life that contains everything, I awaken everything to life.*"

The first labyrinth may have been constructed in Egypt. It had twelve courts and 3000 chambers, half of which were underground, and was filled with "sacred" crocodiles. You wouldn't have wanted to take a wrong turn!

Like planets circling a central sun, labyrinth paths take us out and back again. Jewish theologians call the labyrinth sacred instruction. It's a simile for Torah. The 113 blue-black marble lunar stones around Chartres' labyrinth create Sophia's Moon calendar. Each of the four quadrants has 28 cusps. That way everyone could figure out when Easter was. Worshipers used to walk to the center of the labyrinth and back out again before going up to the altar for communion. Some still do at Chartres, if it's not covered with folding chairs. On the afternoon of Easter Day, 13th century people danced, holding hands, through the labyrinth as they tossed a large yellow ball symbolizing the sun. They sang, in triple-rhythm drumbeats, hymns to Mary aka Ariadne, aka Sophia.

Cicero's cosmos is embedded in this amazing design. Earth is in the center. All the planets are represented and the three outer pathways represent the World Soul — Sophia encircling it all. The six petals in the center were thought to be: plants; minerals; animals; humans; angels; and Our Lady and Her Son. Or the six days of creation. A labyrinth is a hologram of wholeness. All things reside in Sophia; Sophia resides in all things.

That fated September morning when 9/11 images of falling towers, smoke and ashen faces crossed our TV screen, I felt the Minotaur's breath hot on my shoulders. When I could not bear watching another film loop look of towers falling, I turned off the TV and headed to our labyrinth. My body ached. My head hurt. The trees around the labyrinth were already tinged with subtle September yellows and a few streaks of orange; the late morning sky was a clear blue, but when I looked up, all I could see was grey. Blinking, I imagined those killer planes flying overhead and crashing into *me* — again and again. I crossed my arms tightly across my upper chest and stepped inside the circle.

Fear is a powerful force. It can wreck our immune systems, leaving us more vulnerable to infections and, of course, cancer. Science has finally come around to admitting that Sophia-like activities — meditation, yoga, laughter, play, and labyrinth walking — can act as an antidote to fear and anxiety. Ariadne's thread leads us back.

Like many others that day in September, I thought, "This could be a threshold point for us — it could offer us a new way of facing threats. A new way of "being" within "one world." But when other women, such as Barbara Kingsolver, Susan Sontag, Naomi Klein, and Oprah, publicly expressed similar thoughts, they were quickly ridiculed. Shut down. Shut out. After all, we *had* to be a warrior nation. Anyone not subscribing to that was in league with Bin Laden. Co-terrorists. Bring on the cowboys. Bring on the Super Heroes. Bring on the Marlboro Men. Everyone knew we had to retaliate and beat those war drums. Everyone knew we had to protect ourselves. One Rocky Mountain news columnist summed it up this way: "Bands of brothers don't need girls." Everyone knew it then, but now most are not so convinced that war is the answer. To anything! On September 11th, Ariadne was discarded once again on the shore as the black-sailed warrior ship pulled out. Sophia's voice was again stifled.

But not for long. Rather than repeating, "How could they do this to us? Oh, poor us!" Sophia, on the other hand, encourages us to ask, "What have we now learned?" "What is the true meaning of power?" "What will it take to turn hate into love? Injury to pardon?"

Whom are we to serve?

The labyrinth at Chartres originally had a bronze trinity in the center: Aridane, Theseus and the Minotaur. It was removed and turned into cannon fodder during the French Revolution; now the center is simply paved with stone. The circumference measures 666 feet — an unusual number, known by many as a sacred goddess number; others call it the mark of the beast. Still others claim it's our human number — signifying our continual balancing of good and evil. The morning of September 11th was a pivotal 666 moment. We had a choice.

In walking the labyrinth, at some point, we inevitably return to our beginning. Even far-sighted mortals, as Tolkien told it, can get a glimmer of the Deathless Land. "And those that sailed furthest set but a girdle about the Earth and returned weary at last to the place of their beginning; and they said: 'All roads are now bent.'"

Like a giant spring, a labyrinth can at any moment release its coiled power, power like none of us have ever experienced before. Sophia's power. She challenges us to follow the serpentine path to the center, where we find, not the scary minotaur, but our silent selves.

A WEB OF SYNCHRONICITIES

Every now and then, we catch her messages hiding in synchronicities, those events in life, as Carl Jung explained it, that bunch up together even though one doesn't cause the other. You think of someone and just then they call you. You look for a particular book in the library and it practically falls off the shelf into your arms. You wake up with a tune in your head, and later, there it is on the radio. You hear a new word and before the day is out you've heard it several more times. These are spontaneous, unplanned events, but the meanings are linked in a wonderful way that convinces us that these weren't just random occurrences, but rather, clues to the fact we're part of something much larger than ourselves. If we weren't all suspended from the same Mother-spider web, they wouldn't occur. We live within a magical holographic field that doesn't move from A to B to C, but rather, crisscrosses and spirals. We're part of her system of acausal orderliness. Creation unfolds and we participate in the unfolding. The unconscious "knows things," and often reveals these things in dreams. The Great Mother's energy, somehow, connects all our archetypes to each other. Our physical and psychic living spaces overlap like exact designs under tracing paper. We hold the drawing pen and make of these Divinely Chaotic templates whatever we wish to make of them.

One kinetic copper and stainless steel sculpture by Utah artist Lyman Whittaker is called "Double Spinner." It catches the breeze and moves together but separately and usually in opposing directions. The two moving parts are connected at the center, but move independently like the Greek definitions of *kairos* and *chronos* time. *Chronos* time is measured by clocks and calendars. It's external order. *Kairos*, on the other hand, is "time out of time" — it's not measurable. It's the time lovers know, the time we experience when we "let go" and enter another dimension. The time of being fully present when we make art, music or conversation. That's where we experience our inner "isness." Where these two join, synchronicity happens. It's where chance meetings occur. It's the air hole through which Sophia breathes. An eternal union of matter and mind, of psyche and spirit.

The author of *Watership Down* wrote another book I value: *The Unbroken Web*. In it, Richard Adams says the earth has a spinning soap bubble around it. All our thoughts, all our human experiences, down to the aroma escaping from my kitchen at this very moment, gets trapped by the soap bubble. A story-teller can reach up and grab part of it, use the information found there, and then release it so it snaps back again and continues on in rotation until someone else wants to "pull it down." The web spins continually around us so that every point gets positioned over every other point on earth at some time. This accounts for how the same stories, the same ideas, often show up in different places at the same time, and among different people who haven't communicated with each other. Centuries from now, all our thoughts and stories and ideas will still be swirling around inside the bubble. Who knows who will grab them and pull them down. And for what purpose.

HEARTHS AND MOTHERBOARDS

During one of Vermont's coldest snaps, the software "motherboard" in our furnace malfunctioned. It's the device bolted onto our propane furnace that heats our water and keeps our house warm. So, we burned wood. Our Hearthstone stove is the only hearth we have, and as we settled in around it, nestled inside our snow-globe with a crackling fire, we were hypnotized by coals glowing bright red-orange. It almost erased my concerns about how much a new motherboard might cost. Instead, I remembered Hestia and Bridget, and all the ancient females keeping all hearths and anchoring people's lives to the center of earth's fires.

We are all Vestal Virgins — keepers of "her flame." Each of us is a miniature "Motherboard" in some fashion. We may not "smoor" peat fires each night, as Irish women did, banking the coals for tomorrow, with this Gaelic blessing, but we can remember that whatever we have to do the next day, we can blow life into it.

The sacred Three
To save,
To shield,
To surround
The hearth,
The house,
The household,
This eve,
This night,
Oh! this eve,
This night,
And every night,
Each single night.
Amen.

No matter what fears we face during the day, we can invite The Sacred Three to protect us through the night.

Old hearths offered a sitting place, a story-telling place, a place where people gathered to share food and drink. The hearth was where heaven and earth met in Old Ireland, and once a year, one's fire was extinguished completely. Then, from the big community Beltane fire at Tara, center of all Irish life, it was relit.

The furnace guy came. While it's not as much fun to sit around a basement furnace to tell stories and tip a few, I keep telling myself the functioning Motherboard IS down there. Making us tea. Making sure we're safe. Keeping us warm.

Sophia's Mystical Dancer:
Rudolf Steiner (1861-1925)

Steiner, a child of an Austrian gamekeeper, was born in 1861 and later studied in Vienna. As a young man, he met a mystical herb-gatherer, Felix Koguzki, who taught him the "language" of plants, about healing, about seeking, and about his purpose here on earth. "You have several tasks to accomplish during this lifetime," Felix said, "One is to show people how, together, we must reverse the plunge of western thought and culture into materialism. And you must show people how *real* the spiritual world is. Explain birth, death and rebirth." Though Steiner grew up believing that we each choose what we do and our mission is not predetermined, he followed this mystic's advice.

At thirty-six, Steiner moved to Berlin to become an editor, most notably of Goethe's writings. He had his first "experience" of Christ at forty. After that, he developed three ways of what he called "living thinking" — higher seeing, higher hearing and intuitive penetration. Uncommonly prolific, he wrote 3,000 books in German — only 200 or so have been translated into English at this point. He gave over 6,000 lectures outlining spiritual wisdom — Anthropo**sophy** — a path of scientific spiritual knowledge.

Tall and thin, his brown eyes sparkled with a glint of gold. Every photo shows his jet black hair. He often slept only a couple of hours at night, and, at times, he gave up to five and six lectures a day. Avid readers call him a genius in at least twelve fields, including architecture, education, medicine, bio-dynamic farming, esoteric Christianity, and, of course, cosmology. The world, he said, is a cosmic thought, and its meaning can dawn only in our souls.

Steiner developed his main body of work between 1900 and 1925. He died in 1925, a feared enemy of the emerging Nazi state. Many artists and musicians have been influenced by Steiner's teachings, including Kandinsky, Mondrian, Joseph Beuys, Claude Debussy, Carl Orff, Zoltan Kodaly, and Emile Jaques-Dalcroze.

Steiner often said: "*I believe* will be replaced by *I believe what I know*." Knowledge is nothing if it doesn't lead to divine Sophia knowledge. His "golden rule" advised that for every step taken toward the pursuit of "higher knowledge," you need to take three steps toward perfecting your own character.

We live in very long cycles. The first he called "Old Saturn, Old Sun, Old Moon." During these very long periods, humans were suspended in a deep dream-state. Waking consciousness was not possible until the fourth cycle we are now in, called appropriately enough, "Earth." After this long cycle is completed, we head to the future "Jupiter" cycle, a great turning point in human civilization when communities will be founded on spirit, not blood or genetics, and people will be more psychically advanced. All earthly beings will have the potential to be filled with love. Sophia, it appears, will be very evident. It will be followed by "her" Venus era. And way off in the future comes what he called the "Vulcan" cycle filled with universal consciousness. And possibly by "unstoppable" super intelligent human-machines like gigantic spiders. Each cycle seeds and prepares people for the next one. That's why what we do *today* is so very, very important.

For over three thousand years, Isis was well known in Egypt and the Mediterranean, even as far east as India. Isis and Osiris were considered brother-sister, bride-groom. Steiner said that Sophia is the new Isis dispersed throughout creation and Isis and Osiris are now Sophia and Christ. Isis, Mary/Sophia — the black Virgin — now works in daylight.

William Blake, strongly influenced by Jacob Boehme, captured this feminine concept in *The Marriage of Heaven and Hell* when he said, "The Eternal female groan'd! It was heard over all the Earth."

We live, Steiner taught, in "sheathed" bodies, like those colorful Russian Matreuska dolls. Starting with the smallest "doll," our outer physical body, he tells us, is connected to the mineral world. Then comes the etheric body, the one that sort of loosens up when we are around seven years old — about the time we get our permanent teeth. It lives and thrives as plants do, and is called the "life body" because it's connected to all our organs, muscles, bones and nerves. Without it, the physical body would decay. The etheric body is set into motion through meditation and the activation of our chakras, or energy spots, found within the physical body. In certain dim lighting, you can see a "light-sheath" around people's heads like luminous halos — the kind of golden circles painted by early artists around "holy" people's heads. Dreams are an art-piece of the etheric world; it is the etheric body that remembers all these things. Even from one lifetime to the next. Next comes our astral body.

Given how little sleep Steiner got, it's ironic that he believed sleep to be very important to our health … that's when parts of us go "off" to explore. The astral body, which shows up at about age fourteen, and the next, fourth body — the ego body — become very active while we sleep. Like a couple of teenagers, they tip-toe out through the tops of our heads on their nightly dates. And, like responsible teens, they always return before we wake. They're connected to us by golden Ariadne threads. When we are about to wake up, they return from the labyrinthine night to rejoin our physical and etheric bodies that have remained in bed the whole time. Steiner says they enter through our fingers and limbs. I think those involuntary jerks we sometimes have at night are connected to their comings and goings. When we wake up, it's good to integrate them gently. That's why it's not a healthy idea to wake up to a shattering alarm-clock or loud radio. Be still a bit and remember your dreams.

When we are fully awake, the astral body interpenetrates our etheric and physical bodies to keep us orderly. It's our Great Organizer. It brings Sophia's cosmic laws right deep down inside us. When we dream, we are actually outside both our physical and etheric bodies, and it's our astral and ego bodies that "do" our dreaming. When we wake up, they bring ideas back to us, but we might not recognize them for a couple of days. In a playful twist, as our physical bodies age, our ether bodies grow younger. Oscar Wilde whimsically put it this way: "The soul is born old, but grows young. That is the comedy of life.

The body is born young and grows old. That is life's tragedy." Steiner has also explained that for women, the etheric body is male; for men, the etheric body is female. What this means, of course, is that Jesus' physical body was male, but his etheric body was female. Small wonder, then, that Julian of Norwich and others who could sense his etheric body called him female. What's more, our etheric bodies are not just confined to our own physical body. Sophia sets into play a wonderful interchange between *everyone's* etheric bodies.

Before a human baby clothes itself in a physical body, its etheric body gathers up, from Sophia's surrounding cosmos, everything it will need on earth. Because babies sleep considerably more than adults, they are more open to Sophia's influences than we adults.

The astral body, which contains animal feelings, carries disease along with all our pleasures, desires and passions. If you crave alcohol or caffeine, for instance, blame your astral body. It also carries all our memories. It stamps pictures into the etheric body at night, and then the etheric body gives us our "dream" pictures and elaborates on them during the day. Like the etheric halo, the astral body can also be seen under certain conditions; it's egg-shape swirls around the body in colorful rays and flashes of little aurora borealis twisting together. The astral body, with its whirling wheels, like lotus centers, has two parts: one is given to us at birth, and another part is created by the "I" of who we are — our larger self. This is the "biggest doll" of your set — the part of you beyond this earth life. We can call it anything we like ... our "ego," the "soul-me," "super I." "Higher Self."

Our astral body increases in size depending on how ready we are to accept Sophia's influences. Creativity, and every good artistic impulse, strengthens our astral bodies. Sophia's wisdom can be more easily accessed in our clever astral bodies. That is, for instance, where all mathematics is stored as well as everything that still remains to be discovered. After the physical body dies, the etheric body lingers for about three days. At this point, the astral body takes on a rounder, more mobile shape, and stays intact for awhile. Then, it too "dies." Steiner says it usually takes about one third the length of one's earth life before it completely disappears. The "I" part of us, however, never dies.

Anyone wishing to learn more about Steiner's "cosmic take" on things can readily find his books, or visit what is the most complete website of his books, lectures and articles at the Rudolf Steiner Archive (*www.rsarchive.org*). There, you will find much more than this little Sophia-tale can begin to tell.

ENNEAGRAM NUMBER 9

Number Nines are magicians in that they can usually see all points of view and strive to maintain inner stability. As a result, they shun conflict and strive for equanimity in relationships. Nines can be overbearing in their desire to help people understand *everything*. They wonder why others don't operate as they do. They create nurturing rapport and foster deep levels of intimacy. But they have to remember what it is that *they* need. They are prone to addressing life through symbols rather than the real thing. They can be forgetful and are usually "really on" or "really off." They can be stubborn and are easily bored. They often forget the past and their "nows" can be blurred and unclear. Nines live by the nine words that Neale Donale Walsch says in *The New Revelation* that could heal the world: "I can understand how you could feel that way."

HER GIFT OF LOVE
Underlying every aspect of Sophia is her unconditional love. We need do nothing — *nothing* — and she will still welcome us "home."

Just as we are. By her example, she teaches us how to love each other. There are many ways to express love. In fact, if you speak Sanskrit, you'd know ninety-six words for love. How many can you count? Think of the different feelings that come up when you "see" that particular love object. Love for your partner, love for your parents, love for your siblings, love for your pets, love for your neighbor, love for your good friends, love for your mentor, love for your colleagues, love for your spiritual advisor, love for your house, love for your ... well, you get the idea. Don't overlook ways to name your love for Sophia, your "big" mother, sister, friend. The Greeks call this one *agape*.

Love. That's Sophia power! When time stops and we recognize *kairos* time spinning around us, our problems are reduced. We can see how things balance and fit together. We can see how symbols help us form a gigantic database of consciousness — and we know we have the correct updated software to access them. I believe that's one of the reasons J.K. Rowling's books, rife with symbols — unicorns, dragons, phoenixes, snakes, lions — appeal so universally to people, young and old, wherever they live. Symbols and ideas, like powerful mentors, are deeply shared.

"Kissing swallows" from a portion of the Spring Fresco, 1500 B.C.E., from the ruins of Akrotiri on the island of Thera/Santorini.

SOPHIA'S SPECIAL GEO-SPOT: CRETE/KNOSSOS

"Out there in the wine dark sea there is a rich and lovely island called Crete, washed by waves on every side, densely populated with ninety cities ... one of the ninety cities is a great town called Knossos and there for nine years King Minos ruled and enjoyed the friendship of Almighty Zeus."

~ Homer

In the ancient Mediterranean, people danced like cranes and gracefully moved through labyrinth designs that venerated the Great Mother. Then around 1500 B.C.E., due to earthquakes and volcanic explosions, invading nations, wars and evolving trade-changing economies, all that disappeared. Sophia had to hide. The "gods" took over. Men ruled.

It's natural for orphans to search for their birth mothers. Crete means "strong or ruling goddess." I believe that's why places like Crete, and more particularly, the palaces of Knossos and Phaestos that honored and held scared female presence at its center, draw so many tourists — including, one autumn, my husband and me. We learned about Arthur Evans who excavated these ruins around 1900 and named these beautiful brown-eyed artistic people "Minoans" after the legendary king Minos. We don't know what they called themselves because we haven't cracked their language yet, but we marvel at their creations: frescoes overflowing with brilliant reds, yellow lilies and poppies, dolphins, green monkeys, kissing swallows. Trees. Bees. Snakes. Cycles of life. And at the center of it all are women — the feminine principle writ large. Living here was not only beautiful, but easy. Running water. Sewers. Clever storage devices. We saw no moats or walls that kept people out. In fact, "commoners" lived right next to the ritual spaces.

Why did this place speak so profoundly to my heart? I didn't have answers for that until I read Craig Barnes book, *In Search of the Lost Feminine*. He outlines five values of this "Minoan" culture that are expressly at odds with patriarchy.

1. The images indicate honor was paid to life-forms that died or disappear and are reborn. Death is not portrayed as evil, but rather a way to imagine our human immortality.
2. Time is seen as cyclical — in seasons. Their art was not fixed on progress or linear destinations. They enjoyed the "now."
3. The feminine principle is obviously honored. Images of women far outnumber images of men, who are shown bringing them gifts, never harming them.
4. Sexuality is celebrated and valued.
5. People experience ecstasy and joy as shown in paintings, carvings and figurines of acrobats leaping over bulls, dolphins playing, women dancing on mountain tops.

Nowhere in these artifacts and buildings is war glorified. No spears, no swords. No images of violence of any kind. There are images of the labrys, the double axes, but we have no evidence they were used violently rather than ritualistically. Nowhere is there evidence of kings or thrones. In the thousands of images, brutality to women is never pictured and certainly never celebrated.

Barnes is a lawyer and he brilliantly brings Father Zeus (and all father-gods) to court. "The evidence would show," he says, "that invaders rode into Greece and the Middle East on horses, with composite bows, and in lust for property accumulated from trade and piracy, frantic to hold the accumulation for their sons. The evidence would show that storytellers picked up their cause and immediately began to malign women and women's views of immortality, views that had long been held in Crete but that made the accumulation of male property impossible. The evidence would show that under the banner of the first completely patriarchal gods, Zeus and Jehovah, the conquerors raped and pillaged these people ...

the consequences for Western history have been to make war seem desirable at any cost ... to make the future seem grim because life is less important than the way one dies or the property one leaves behind to his sons."

Mary Renault, in her novel, *The Bull from the Sea*, wonderfully imagines that Minos is actually a leper who wears a bull mask to cover his disfiguration. Her Minos asks Theseus to mercifully kill him with the sacred double-edged axe. However we choose to interpret the man-bull story, it's clear from the remaining art in Crete today, that in honor of this early story, young men and women on Crete were trained to be bull-dancers — daring acrobats who leapt across bulls' deadly horns and risked their killer hooves. Spain's running of the bulls is still a risky, although rather watered-down, imitation of these earlier Cretan rituals.

Crete remains an island calling to the Sophia-hearted.

NOVALIS: A SOPHIA POET

The early people of Crete showed Goethe the way. In *Faust*, he puts these words into Sophia's mouth: "I flow this way and that. I am birth and the grave, an eternal ocean, a changeful weaving, a glowing life. And thus I work at the humming loom of time, and fashion the earth, God's living garment."

The 18th century poet, Novalis, who was influenced by Goethe once wrote: "In everyone dwells the heavenly mother in order to give birth to each child forever." He calls Sophia "Mother Queen of Every Country." "Matrix of the Universe." "The Source of Light."

Steiner was impressed by Novalis and indicates he was a preincarnation of Victor Hugo. Novalis' earlier lives, as also noted by Steiner, included Elijah and John the Baptist. This scientist and creative writer's real name was Frierich von Hardenberg. Most people thought this young German Romantic was simply a dreamer and didn't pay much attention to him. Many still don't. He studied philosophers such as Kant and Fichte and spent a great deal of effort trying to describe the "I" behind the "I" — that higher stage of ourselves. He decided it's the artist within us that will best reach a realm of spirit or magical truth. Each of us is part of a holy design — "personifying omnipotent points." He would have loved the pointillist painters. We're not Sophia, but we're Sophia-dots.

Most of Novalis' work is still only available in German, although Margaret Mahony Stoljar has done an admirable translation of his *Philosophical Writings*, which begins with this definition: "Philosophy cannot bake bread — but it can bring us God, freedom, and immortality."

His fiancée, *Sophia*, died at 15. Her name symbolized for him all love, womanhood and philosophy. He died when he was twenty-nine, believing "death is at once the end and the beginning — at once separation and closer union of the self." Spirit, he wrote, is perpetually improving itself, and we will understand the world when we understand ourselves.

All learning, he said, can be transformed in "magical chemistry, mechanics and physics ... in magical astronomy, grammar, philosophy and religion." Novalis would have loved Hogwarts. Especially Hermione.

ONCE UPON A TIME:
Harry Potter Series: Hermione Granger

There were other girls at Hogwarts, of course, but my best friends ever since our first train ride on the Hogwarts Express were Harry Potter and Ron Weasley — the 6th red-headed kid in their very large and crazy family to go to our school. Now and then I helped them with their homework since learning things has always been very easy for me. I learn all my course books by heart. And spells come easily to me because I know Latin. But I can't speak Parseltongue. Only Harry can do that.

Sometimes I can be bossy. And I just blurt things out. Like that time I told Ron that his spell on his rat, Scabbers, wasn't very good. It was true, but I suppose I didn't have to be so blunt about it. I probably seem threatening to boys who might already feel a bit insecure. Especially Ron. But once when Harry and Ron saved me from a troll, I knew they really did like me.

My name comes from the Egyptian Hermes who was responsible for an old document called *The Emerald Tablet* — it contained all sorts of symbols and knowledge. Well, for those who can understand it. So I like my name. Harry's mother's name was Lily. That's a flower all strong women like. He misses her. A lot. Harry's mother was a "Muggle-born" witch and his father was a "pure-blood" wizard. I'm a Muggle-born witch as well and some unkind people call me a "Mudblood." Names can hurt, but I know who I am. Unlike Muggles who are easily deceived, I can usually spot the truth.

I was so relieved when the three of us were chosen to live in Griffendor, the "Lion" house. Harry is very good at Quidditch. He's a Seeker — in so many ways. I'm usually the last person to break the rules, but sometimes rules need to be bent a little to help your friends. But I don't like it when little people, like the house elves, are taken advantage of. Or are the butt of jokes. It's wrong to make slaves cook and clean! Just wrong. Not once in *Hogwarts: A History*, which is over a thousand pages, are house elves even mentioned. We're oppressing a hundred slaves in just our school alone! It's simply not right.

Magic never bores me. It's exciting to live in a world where everything hasn't all been explained yet. Dumbledore's a very good wizard. He's forgiving and generous. He stood up for Hagrid, our friend. And he takes special care of Harry. Dumbledore, you may already know, means "bumblebee" and I think we can learn a lot from everything around us, like bees and trees, and even dragons and unicorns and hypogriffs. Harry's wand is made from the special holly tree. But Harry doesn't think he's better than anyone else. In fact, he doesn't even think he's good. But I know he is. So does Ron.

We've learned to survive trolls, snakes, spiders, grindylows, blast-ended skrewts and manticores. The Death Eaters and Dementors, and even Voldemort, couldn't kill us. I can name him now, thanks to Harry. Dumbledore said we should use proper names for things because fear of a name increases fear of the thing itself.

I was put to sleep a couple of times — like Sleeping Beauty and Snow White — although I never thought of myself as beautiful. My "prince" woke me, and in the end, I found true love, too. Life is so much better than even the most wonderful fairytale.

Rawling: A Sophia Sister

When the Harry Potter books were published, some "religious" people were afraid that Hermione and her friends would corrupt their children with heretical ideas of witchcraft and the occult, so they held "holy bonfires" to burn the books. They want children to follow *rules* (like Percy Weasley did). It shakes them to think there may be real power in these books. We always burn what we fear. But they forget how much "magic" flows everywhere — even through-out biblical pages: jars and jugs that never empty; water that parts; locusts that rain down; walls that fall down when trumpets are played; snakes that talk; bushes that burn but don't burn up; lions that don't harm people; magic writing on the walls; vats into wine; food for the masses from one little lunch; the sun that stops, cur-tains that tear by themselves; and dead people who don't stay dead.

Until we understand nature, even science is "wizardry." For good or ill. Remember how Madame Curie's lab glowed?

Adults and children continue to read about Harry Potter and watch the movies because fantasy sheds light on our hidden places and beams hope through our shadows. Children discover that they too have "magical powers." One twelve-year-old girl who was kidnapped in California figured out how to escape from the car when her captor went into a convenience store. She said later, "I remembered Harry Potter never gave up. I figured if he could do it, so could I." So, even without a magic wand, she managed to use a key on the ring the bad guy had left in the ignition and escaped.

From Hermione and the others, readers learn about real friendships and how people care for each other. They learn to accept the finality of death as part of life's cycle. They learn about justice and being willing to sacrifice for friends. But above all, they learn that love is stronger than evil.

Rawling studied the classics and French at Exeter. She reveres language. The Quidditch game, for example, comes from the Latin *quidditas* for "giveness." Harry is given much through his involvement with the game. She introduces resurrection themes. Her favorite painting, she once said, is Carravaggio's "Supper at Emmaus," where Christ reveals himself to the disciples. Food plays an important role in her stories, as do friends, like little Christs, who reveal themselves to each other. Harry's life parallels that of Jesus in many ways.

Rawling's first book was published as *Harry Potter and the Philosopher's Stone* in England, where they may be more in tune with alchemical language than in the U.S., where the title became the "Sorcerer's Stone." "A stone that makes gold and stops you from ever dying." That's what Voldemort wanted. Harry got the blood-red stone because he didn't want to use it. People seeking the "grail stone" for their own purposes, will never find it, the headmaster explained.

Rawling "got" the entire plot one day while riding on a train.

The Harry Potter books were the first children's books to make it onto the *New York Times* bestseller list since E.B. White's *Charlotte's Web*. Unlike Harry, Charlotte hasn't been condemned, but both characters embody love, forgiveness, magic, and sacrifice. Strength and courage coupled with gentleness and kindness is a winning combination — for books, as well as for life off the page.

Sophia's Mary-Pentecost story is filled with "magic" too. Flaming tongues of fire. Rushing winds. Parseltongue-language. The Harry Potter series and Pentecost reminds us that wisdom is embedded everywhere. Magic is afoot and wizard robes and peaky hats are given to anyone with an outstretched hand to receive them. The word "magus" means "One able to hold power." Can we? Are we up to it?

SOPHIA'S SOCIAL NETWORKING

One of my web-spinning Sophia-friends, Rebecca Norlander, pointed out to me that Arthur Koestler wrote in, *The Ghost in the Machine*, that within all living things — from cells to human beings to universes — there are two basic impulses: a self-assertive impulse designed to support independent survival, and an integrative impulse designed to connect independent units with others, thereby producing and revealing a new and emergent dimension of being.

Now I better understand the popularity behind the old TV show, "Friends." They were "emerging." No, seriously, they were. And so are we. But since it was difficult to get to the Cheers bar in Boston, people started to find each other online. Social networking looks like a giant spider's web, or Indra's web with nodes hooking people-diamonds. All attached and connected.

Facebook is larger than several major countries combined. One study discovered that happiness tends to be correlated to social networks. It makes sense. We live in a time of deep separateness, so connecting with anyone makes us feel more whole. But of course, the truth is, we're already all connected just as our planet is all connected. And when there are "dead zones" in our oceans, there are "dead zones" in our hearts.

Jon Stewart, my favorite news commentator, and one of the few with any substance, says: "The Internet is just a world passing around notes in a classroom." The Internet offers many paradoxes. It seems so personal, yet it's open to *everybody*. You think it's private, but cookies leave crumbs all over the net. It's a giant synapsing nervous system (sometimes more nervous than at other times) interchanging packets of information and stamping passports. I can stay at home, yet travel anywhere in seconds. The Internet was originally rooted in research and academia — a potlatch culture with give-away information. Many of us argue it should stay that way.

Is the Universe one vast net as the Buddhists claim? If so, she is, as Sri Ramakrishna said, "the Spider and the world is the Spider's web she has woven.... The spider brings the web out of herself and then lives in it." And now we learn we live not just within one universe, but a multi-verse with worm holes and trapdoors and cosmic tunnels.

Niels Bohr and Werner Heisenberg told us that the universe exists as an infinite number of overlapping possibilities. Our awareness simply locks them in. But it is non-judgmental love that acts as the catalyst. We aren't just impassive observers. We participate! We ask! We receive!

My Norse ancestors measured time by the eight tides — each three hours long. Roughly translated, the eight hours were called: midnight, dawn, morning, vaporlessness, noon, rest, evening, and shadow. They prayed by casting runes, thereby fitting themselves neatly into Midgard which is, as I understand Scandinavian myth, an ever-expanding universe capable of holding everything that is and is to come. Midgard Big-Banged us into one cosmic postal code, connecting us to everything. Prayers are the letters we stamp, or the emails we send off into the ether with one finger. They keep the earth safe.

Religious orders sprang up all over medieval Europe as monks and nuns assumed the first line of defense against demons by praying eight times a day, from Lauds to Matins. Muslims pray five times a day, facing Mecca, for the same reason. Disciplined prayers strengthen the links between our conscious minds and the ever-expanding cosmos.

Sophia continues to sing to us from the whale-bottomed ocean floor to our ever-expanding universe. She promises to be present in us, around us, over us, under us. As musician Jen Pumo sings in "moon": *all over the moon, all over the moon / you can see the shadow / you can see the future / a better way, gotta be a better way 'cause we can see the promise.*

We are connected through our feelings — not through mere words. Once our prayers are held deeply inside us, this magical universe we live in projects our thoughts everywhere.

Likewise, when we're afraid, when we harbor negative thoughts, we send them off everywhere too. Einstein said our universe is like looking at the tail of a lion. We don't see it all — but it's real and it's there. We are a part of something much larger than we can imagine. We encompass all the Enneagram numbers. All the astrological symbols. We live within nested realities, a fun house of mirrors, and she is our Mother-Mirror. We are her little mirrors as well as the faces projected back from the mirrors. And to make things even more complicated and chaotic, there may be more than one mirror. But I go to sleep at night — and sleep very well — knowing Sophia holds all the mirrors.

Sophia has now led us to the end of her "initiatory" journey of nine paths to healing and abundance. She's offered us many avenues, and taken us to places we may not have been before. Her journey is similar to what an alchemist once described: *This journey feels like an angel taking your arm and introducing you to star powers.* In fairytales, the heroine goes on a pathway to find *eros*, friends discover *philia*, and through it all, Sophia reminds us all of the unconditional love, *agape*, waiting for us at every turn.

Everything that lives is holy. Each of us, craftswoman and craftsman, help co-create her ongoing creation. But we no longer have the luxury of being by-standers. Because she is experience, connection, interconnection, and wholeness, so are we. Like the young child Jesus, who sits in Mary's lap in all those famous icons and frescoes, we can climb up into her welcoming lap and join him there. She's big and full-blooded enough to hold all of us spiritually anemic, love-starved, anorexic, undernourished, confused and lonely souls. She's as close to us as our breath. Sophia, our mother-sister-friend invites us to snuggle up, settle down and smile.

My story is always your story. You are my face. You are my hands. You are my heart. I stand ready and waiting to be of assistance. When people "wake up" they know I have always been there. From the very beginning. Time is your construct. When you are more ready to notice, then you sense me, feel me, for I am of experience. Mystical for many. Less ephemeral for most. I am the cushioning hen-like image Christ painted. The one who births and keeps on birthing. Who creates and keeps on creating. Who sings and keeps on singing and dancing. And playing.

You're resourceful, wonderfully committed and talented people, so you're going to get me "right." It's not so much about being effective, but being open. So relax. I'm here with a host of helpers — most of whom you can't see. Others of you see them, but in ways words are inadequate to describe. But you get the point, don't you? You're not in this alone. Trust that what unfolds next will be exactly the thing that needs to unfold next. You will be of service. You will be the best you can be — that's what will manifest.

Wisdom, as you are learning, is so much more than "knowing." Wise ones know when to be still. You have the wisdom to say "No!" The wisdom to balance. The wisdom to continue to create. The wisdom to spend time in solid friendships. The wisdom to help heal. The wisdom to bravely speak. The wisdom to just understand. The wisdom to go where others perhaps do not dare to go. The wisdom to confront abuse. The wisdom to not make things worse. The wisdom to realize what motivates people. The wisdom to know it's not always the same as what motivates you. The wisdom to know how to give. The wisdom to know how to receive. The wisdom to honor the energy in others. The wisdom to value what others contribute. The wisdom to keep stirring, to keep my cauldron bubbling.

Be willing to "see" and "hear" beyond what you have always seen and heard. Ask the powerful questions. Listen to what comes.

I have always been here. And I always will be.

ADDITIONAL RESOURCES

Beyond Business as Usual: Practical Lessons in Accessing New Dimensions
by Michael W. Munn, 1998, Butterworth-Heinemann.

Blessed Unrest by Paul Hawken, 2007, Penguin Group.

Broken by Addiction, Blessed by God: A Woman's Path to Sustained Recovery
by Penny Mary Hauser, 2010, Liguori Publications.

Business and the Feminine Principle: The Untapped Resource
by Carol R. Frenier, 1997, Butterworth-Heinemann.

Chakra Balancing by Anodea Judith, 2003, Sounds True.

Christ Power and the Earth Goddess: A Fifth Gospel by
Marko Pogacnik, 1999, Findhorn Press.

Coming to our Senses: Healing the World and Ourselves through Mindfulness
by Jon Kabat-Zinn, 2005, Hyperion.

Crop Circles: Signs, Wonders and Mysteries
by Steve and Karen Alexander, 2007, Chartwell Books.

Crop Circles: Signs, Wonders and Mysteries
by Steve and Karen Alexander, 2006, Chartwell Books.

Deep Play by Diane Ackerman, 1999, Random House.

Divine Sophia: The Wisdom Writings of Vladimir Solovyov
by Judith Deutsch Kornblatt, 2009, Cornell University Press.

Eve's Seed: Biology, the Sexes and the Course of History
by Robert S. McElvaine, 2001, McGraw Hill.

Goddesses and the Divine Feminine: A Western Religious History
by Rosemary Reuther, 2005, University of California Press.

Green Sisters: A Spiritual Ecology
by Sarah McFarland Taylor, 2007, Harvard University Press.

Habits of the Heart
by Robert Bellah, et al. 1985, University of Chicago Press.

Hunab Ku: 77 Sacred Symbols for Balancing Body and Spirit
by Karen Speerstra and Joel Speerstra, 2005, The Crossing Press.

Illuminations of Hildegard of Bingen
by Matthew Fox, 2002, Bear & Company.

In Search of the Lost Feminine: Decoding the Myths that Radically Reshaped Civilization by Craig S Barnes, 2006, Fulcrum Publishing.

Isis Mary Sophia: Her Mission and Ours
by Rudolf Steiner, 2003, Steiner Books.

Labyrinths: Ancient Myths and Modern Uses
by Sig Lonegren, 1996, Gothic Image Publications.

Lucy's Legacy: Sex and Intelligence in Human Evolution
by Alison Jolly, 1999, Harvard University Press.

Money and the Meaning of Life
by Jacob Needleman, 1991, Currency, Doubleday.

Nature Spirits & Elemental Beings: Working with the Intelligence in Nature
by Marko Pogacnik, 2009, Findhorn Press.

Peace Movements Worldwide [3 volumes]
by Marc Pilisuk and Michael Nagler, 2010, Praeger Publishers.

Pistis Sophia: A Coptic Text with Commentary
by J.J. Hurtak and Desiree Hurtak, 1999, The Academy for Future Science.

Return of the Goddess
by Edward Whitmont, 1982, Crossroad Publishing.

Sacred Geography: Geomancy, Co-Creating The Earth Cosmos
by Marko Pogacnik, 2007, Lindesfarne Books.

Sacred Geometry by Robert Lawlor, 1992, Thames and Hudson.

Secrets in the Fields: The Science and Mysticism of Crop Circles
by Freddy Silva, 2002, Hampton Roads.

Sophia: Aspects of the Divine Feminine
by Susanne Schaup, 1997, Nicholas-Hays, Inc.

Sophia: Goddess of Wisdom by Caitlin Matthews, 1991, Mandala.

Sophia: The Future of Feminist Spirituality
by Susan Cady, Marian Ronan and Hal Taussig, 1986,
Harper and Row San Francisco.

Sophia: The Wisdom of God by Sergei Bulgakov, 1993, Lindesfarne Press.

Sophia-Maria: A Holistic Vision of Creation
by Thomas Schipflinger, 1998, Samuel Weiser, Inc.

Sophie's World by Jostein Gaarder, Farrar, Straus and Giroux, Inc., 1996.

Squaring the Circle: Geometry in Art and Architecture
by Paul A. Calter, 2008, Key College Publishing, Springer.

Stone Age Soundtracks: The Acoustic Archaeology of Ancient Sites
by Paul Devereux, 2001, Vega.

The Divine Matrix: Bridging Time, Space, Miracles, and Belief
by Gregg Braden, 2007, Hay House.

The Dove in the Stone by Alice O. Howell, 1989, Quest Books.

The Emerald Tablet: Alchemy for Personal Transformation
by Dennis William Hauck, 1999, Arkana.

The Ever-Present Origin by Jean Gebser, 1985, Ohio University Press.

The Field by Lynne McTaggart, 2003, Quill, Harper Collins.

The Genesis and Geometry of the Labyrinth
by Patrick Conty, 2002, Inner Traditions.

The Gift by Lewis Hyde, 1979,1983, Vintage Books, Random House.

The Gnostic Gospels by Elaine Pagels, 1979, Random House.

The Goddess Guide by Brandi Auset, 2009, Llewellyn Publications.

The Goddess Re-Awakening by Shirley Nicholson, 1989, Quest Books.

The Hidden Intelligence: Innovation Through Intuition
by Sandra Weintraub, 1998, Butterworth-Heinemann.

The Hope: A Guide to Sacred Activism
by Andrew Harvey, 2009, Hay House.

The Language of the Goddess
by Marija Gimbutas, 1989, Harper San Francisco.

The Millionth Circle: How to Change Ourselves and the Word
by Jean Shinoda Bolen, 1999, Conari Press.

The Mist-Filled Path: Celtic Wisdom for Exiles, Wanderers and Seekers
by Frank MacEowen, 2003, New World Library.

The Most Holy Trinosophia and the New Revelations of the Divine Feminine
by Robert A. Powell, 2000, Anthroposophic Press.

The Return of the Feminine and the World Soul
by Llewellyn Vaughan-Lee, 2009, The Golden Sufi Center.

The Shaman Ayahuasca: Journeys to the Sacred Realms
by Don José Campos, 2011, Divine Arts.

The Skeptical Feminist: Discovering the Virgin, Mother & Crone
by Barbara Walker, 1987, Harper and Row.

The Sophia Teachings: The Emergence of The Divine Feminine in Our Time
by Robert Powell, 2001, Lindesfarne Books.

The Soul of Money: Reclaiming the Wealth of Our Inner Resources
by Lynne Twist, 2003, W.W. Norton.

The Web in the Sea: Jung, Sophia and the Geometry of the Soul
by Alice O. Howell, 1993, Quest Books.

Through the Labyrinth: Designs and Meanings over 5,000 Years
by Hermann Kern, 2000, Prestel.

Waking Up in Time: Finding Inner Peace in Times of Accelerating Change
by Peter Russell, 1998, Origin Press.

Walking a Sacred Path by Lauren Artress, 1995, Riverhead Books.

The Web in the Sea: Jung, Sophia and the Geometry of the Soul
by Alice O. Howell, 1993, Quest Books.

Wheels of Life by Anodea Judith, 1989, Llewellyn.

Wisdom's Feast: Sophia in Study and Celebration
by Susan Cady, Marian Ronana, Hal Taussig, 1986, Harper & Row.

Wishful Thinking: A Seeker's ABC by Frederick Buechner, 1993, Harper.

Woman Awake: A Celebration of Women's Wisdom
by Christina Feldman, 1989, Arkana.

INDEX

ABOUT THE AUTHOR

Teacher, writer, editor, publisher, KAREN SPEERSTRA, has twenty-seven years of publishing experience and now assists and coaches other writers through her company, Sophia-Serve (*www. sophiaserve.com*). She also works with and writes for several website initiatives, including *www.ourluminousground.com* and *www.powersofplace.com*.

She is the author of *Earthshapers*, a young adult historical fiction, and the following non-fiction books: *Hunab Ku: 77 Sacred Symbols for Balancing Body and Spirit*, co-authored with her son, Joel; *Divine Sparks: Collected Wisdom of the Heart*; *Our Day to End Poverty*, co-authored; *Questions Writers Ask: Wise, Whimsical, and Witty Answers from the Pros*; and *The Green Devotional: Active Prayers for a Healthy Planet*.

Karen Speerstra lives in central Vermont.

DIVINE
A R T S

ரॱॶ an imprint of MICHAEL WIESE PRODUCTIONS

DIVINE ARTS sprang to life fully formed as an intention to bring spiritual practice into daily living. Human beings are far more than the one-dimensional creatures perceived by most of humanity and held static in consensus reality. There is a deep and vast body of knowledge — both ancient and emerging — that informs and gives us the understanding, through direct experience, that we are magnificent creatures occupying many dimensions with untold powers and connectedness to all that is. Divine Arts books and films explore these realms, powers and teachings through inspiring, informative and empowering works by pioneers, artists and great teachers from all the wisdom traditions.

We invite your participation and look forward to learning how we may better serve you.

Onward and upward,

Michael Wiese
Publisher/Filmmaker

DivineArtsMedia.com

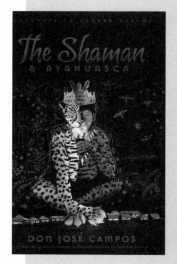

THE SHAMAN & AYAHUASCA
JOURNEYS TO SACRED REALMS

A FILM BY MICHAEL WIESE

WINNER
BEST DOCUMENTARY
FILM
ALBUQUERQUE
FILM FESTIVAL

As interest in ayahuasca grows, so does the question of how to explain this mysterious phenomenon to the uninitiated seeker.

"Filmmaker Michael Wiese's latest documentary, The Shaman and Ayahuasca: Journeys to Sacred Realms, meets this challenge with remarkable grace. Wiese and his companions — his wife, photographer Geraldine Overton, and their charismatic translator, Alberto Roman — go on a trip to the Amazon to meet internationally known shaman Don José Campos. Shot in various locations around Peru, the film explores the role of this powerful plant medicine in Amazonian culture through a series of vignettes and intimate interviews with Don José and several of his close associates. Each person brings a unique perspective to the emerging picture, weaving threads of indigenous wisdom, contemporary science, and existential philosophy into the complex tapestry of the ayahuasca experience. In mind-bending portraits of jaguar-skinned shamans enshrouded by seeing-eye vines, the spiritual alchemy between man and nature that takes place in the ayahuasca realms is magically revealed — a deeply introspective story of healing and discovery."

— Stephen Thomas, *RealitySandwich.com*

"This is a gem of a movie — contemplatively paced, beautifully photographed, and filled with insights into the practice of ayahuasca shamanism in the Upper Amazon. The interviews with shaman José Campos, visionary artist Pablo Amaringo — the last before his death — and phytochemist Julio Arce Hidalgo provide a solid grounding for the story of the filmmaker's own quest for healing and understanding. Poignant and moving, the film is enriched with an evocative soundtrack by Peruvian recording artist Artur Mena Salas."

— Steve Beyer, author, *Singing to the Plants*

DVD ALL REGIONS $24.95 · ORDER NUMBER: SHAMAN
ISBN: 9781932907834 · 72 MINUTES

SPIRITUALITY

THE MESSAGE
A GUIDE TO BEING HUMAN

LD THOMPSON

Soul: \'sol\
noun: the immaterial essence, animating principle,
or actuating cause of an individual life.

*"I have come to guide you, not to coddle you. The
first and greatest lesson that you are learning is
that you are free. You are free to choose. You can
choose to live a life that is prescribed by society, or
you can choose to break the form and know more
of yourself than is ordinarily known."*
— Solano

The more you listen to your Soul and act upon its values and urgings, the more
graceful and joyous your life becomes. With powerful recommendations on how
to achieve greater awareness of your Soul's curriculum, *The Message: A Guide
to Being Human* is an indispensable source of wisdom for seasoned spiritual
practitioners and new seekers alike.

*"Simple, profound, and moving! The author has been given a gift... a beautiful
way to distill the essence of life into an easy to read set of truths, with wonderful
examples along the way. Listen... for that's how it all starts."*
— Lee Carroll, author, the *Kryon* series; co-author, *The Indigo Children*

LD THOMPSON was born in Indiana and educated at Indiana University and
Alaska Pacific University. In his twenties, a profoundly mystical experience com-
menced his spiritual journey. As a result, he dedicated his life to deepening
the transformation that he experienced, and to integrating the knowledge and
wisdom he received. LD travels the world working with individuals, groups, and
corporations in the U.S., Australia, Japan, Germany, and England, as a teacher,
advisor, and counselor. LD currently balances his time between the California
desert and an island in the Pacific Northwest.

$16.95 · 256 PAGES · ORDER NUMBER: MSGHUMAN · ISBN: 9781611250008

24 HOURS | 1.800.833.5738 | WWW.DIVINEARTSMEDIA.COM